PATHS LESS TRAVELED

Tramping on Trails
(and Sometimes Not)
to Find New Hampshire's
Special Places

Gordon DuBois

DORRANCE
PUBLISHING CO
EST. 1920
PITTSBURGH, PENNSYLVANIA 15238

Dorrance Publishing Co
585 Alpha Drive
Suite 103
Pittsburgh, PA 15238
Visit our website at *www.dorrancebookstore.com*

ISBN: 978-1-6453-0677-1
eISBN: 978-1-6453-0667-2

To my wife Nancy for always supporting me in hiking my own paths less traveled.

*There is a road, no simple highway between the dawn
and the dark of night,
And if you go no one may follow, that path is
for your steps alone.*

Robert Hunter

It is remarkable how easily and insensibly we fall into a particular route, and make a beaten track for ourselves. How worn and dusty, then, must be the highways of the world, how deep the ruts of tradition and conformity! I did not wish to take a cabin passage, but rather to go before the mast and on the deck of the world, for there I could best see the moonlight amid the mountains.
  Henry David Thoreau, *Walden*

What a thing it is to sit absolutely alone,
In the forest, at night, cherished by this
wonderful, unintelligible,
perfectly innocent speech,
the most comforting speech in the world,
the talk that rain makes by itself all over the ridges,
and the talk of the watercourses everywhere in the hollows!
Nobody started it, nobody is going to stop it.
It will talk as long as it wants, this rain.
As long as it talks I am going to listen.
    Thomas Merton, *Earth Prayers From Around the World,*
    Edited by E. Roberts and E. Amidon

I'll walk where my own nature would be leading,
Where the wild wind blows on the mountainside.
    Emily Bronte

Mountains return to us the priceless capacity for wonder which can so insensibly be leached away by modern existence, and they urge us to apply that wonder to our own everyday lives.
    Robert Macfarlane, *Mountains of the Mind*

The feeling of solitude is vital to the enjoyment of the mountain experience. Most people go to the hills to get away from city crowds, to drink deep draughts of nature's cool wildness. Sitting alone on an alpine summit, with rolling forested ridges dropping away on all sides, no sign of man in any direction, is a unique and priceless aspect of wildness.
    Guy and Laura Waterman, *Wilderness Ethics,*
    Preserving the Spirit of Wildness

Table of Contents

Chapter 3 - Conservation Lands of the Lakes Region • 115

Chapter 4 - Leaving the Crowds Behind • 149

Chapter 5 - Whacky Bushwhacks • 203

Afterword • 251

Thanks • 273

References • 277

Introduction

Two roads diverged in a wood, and I-
I took the one less traveled by,
And that has made all the difference.

Robert Frost

When I was a young boy I spent many summers with my Aunt Bea and Uncle Harry at their home on Raquette Lake, in the Adirondack Mountains of New York State. I whiled away my days fishing in crystalline mountain streams and swimming in the lake. I picked raspberries with my cousin Mary, caught frogs among the lily pads, and camped out with my friend Bob, roasting hot dogs on an "Indian fire." He called it an Indian fire because Native People built small fires to cook on, not big roaring fires like the campers of today. However, the thing I loved the most was tramping through the woods. I would take off into the forest for hours on end, following old wood roads, hunter trails, and herd paths. These openings into the Adirondack woodland took me deep into what I thought was wilderness. I usually had no idea where a path would lead me. I was on an adventure to find out. It was an expedition to discover mysteries hidden in the darkened woodland. For some reason I was drawn to the unknown as well as the beauty of an undisturbed forest.

Sometimes the path took me to a mountain pond, a fast-running stream, an uninhabited hunter's camp, headwaters of a small river, a viewpoint on a ridge or just back to where I started. I would be gone for hours on extensive explorations. By some unknown instinct within me, I always was able to find my way back to their home. They believed I had an inborn compass to guide me.

Those same forces that led me on these exploratory missions as a child are still with me today. I'm driven to find the paths that will lead me to parts unknown: woods roads, abandoned railroad beds, herd paths that will take me to a desolate mountain summit, an abandoned logging village, a remote ridgeline vista, a stunning waterfall, or a patch of speckled trout lilies. I am drawn to those wild places that aren't trampled by the masses who flock to the popular mountain trails.

When driving through the passes and notches of New Hampshire to begin hiking a path less traveled, I pass trailheads that are crammed with cars and people. The trails are crowded with all sorts of folks wanting the unique experience that only nature can offer. But I wonder, can they find that special place when it's filled with the babble of conversation drowning out the call of the raven, squawking on cell phones, drowning out the solitude, trails trodden into eroded gullies, alpine vegetation trampled by roving feet? My antidote to this madness is to find those trails and paths that take me away from the crowds, to find the solitude that only nature can provide.

Wendell Berry from his poem *The Peace of Wild Things* describes it superbly:
I go and lie down where the wood drake
Rests in his beauty on the water, and the great heron feeds.
I come into the peace of wild things...I come into the presence of
        still water.
And I feel above me the day-blind stars
Waiting with their light. For a time
I rest in the grace of the world, and am free.

The idea for this book came about three years ago, when I was asked by a journalist at the *Laconia Daily Sun*, Laconia, NH, to write an outdoor column on hiking. At that time I didn't consider myself a writer, but my love for hiking and my desire to share that love with others spurred me on. I began writing a regular column in 2015 and have continued since. Many people throughout the Lakes Region of New Hampshire who regularly read my articles asked me to speak about my hiking experiences. The audiences were always enthusiastic and suggested I gather my columns into a book. I thought about it, but never seriously considered publishing my writings. Then I attended an Appalachian Mountain Club (AMC) workshop, *Writing From the Mountains,* led by Christine Woodside, Editor of *Appalachia,* the AMC's mountaineering journal. I was encouraged by Christine and others at the workshop as well as friends who I hike with to seriously consider writing this book, a compilation of my hiking columns published in *The Laconia Daily Sun,* Laconia, NH.

With the help of two close friends, Dick Widhu and Susan DiPietro, with whom I have spent many hours hiking paths less traveled, this book has become a reality. It was born out of the love I have for hiking, especially the obscure trails that are often overlooked. This is not your typical hiking guide, but accounts of hikes that I hope will inspire you to find your own path to follow or perhaps discover a path described in this book.

Most hiking destinations have a story to tell. Some in particular have unusual and fascinating tales and a few tell of significant aspects of New Hampshire's past. In fact they convey the unique character of the Granite State. Chapter One describes treks that take the reader on journeys into New Hampshire's past. Much of the state's rich history is found in the forests and mountains: the stone walls, abandoned lumbering camps, granite quarries, lost ski areas, forgotten railroad beds, logging tote roads, ghost towns and plane crash wreckage sites. All of these places have a story to tell that can lead to a better understanding of our cultural and economic past.

If you live in the Lakes Region of New Hampshire or spend your leisure time here, you will find in Chapter Two stories on treks that define living in the Lakes Region. Over the 40 years that I have lived here, I have come to fully appreciate all that the Lakes Region has to offer, including the plethora of hiking trails which characterize the quality of life that's unique to the Lakes Region.

Chapter Three takes you onto trails that will lead you to special places set aside for permanent protection by local, regional and state conservation organizations. The conservation movement was started by John Muir and others in the late 1800's. It continues today through the efforts and hard work of non-profit organizations like the Lakes Region Conservation Trust, the Society for the Protection of New Hampshire Forests, as well as well as town conservation commissions. These conserved lands are a testament to the commitment by ordinary citizens for the protection and stewardship of our natural resources.

If you are looking to hike where you won't find hordes of other trekkers, where you may find solitude and peace, Chapter Four will help you find that out-of-the-way place. Chapter Four takes you on trails where you can amble without listening to the chatter of others, find solitude and be at peace with your inner self. In *The Mountains of California,* John Muir states, *"Climb the mountains and get their good tidings. Nature's peace will flow into you as sunshine flows into trees. The winds will blow their own freshness into you, and the storms their energy, while cares will drop away from you like the leaves of autumn".*

Whether you're interested in hiking off-trail or just want to read about places that most people never encounter, Chapter Five will take you there. Bushwhacking is a unique experience that's not for everyone. As a matter of fact few people intentionally hike through blowdowns and thickets of hobblebush. Most people prefer marked trails. I prefer to hike off-trail. I have a greater chance of spotting wildlife, experiencing solitude, finding a remote pond or a mountain view. If you would like to vicariously experience bushwhacking, or attempt a bushwhack, then this chapter is for you.

The Afterword contains five essays that may be helpful when preparing for a hike. Whether it be a winter stroll in the woods, rambling with your dog, getting and staying fit, or hiking safely, these essays can be beneficial to you, as you walk your own path less traveled.

Chapter 1 - Hiking into History

*If you don't know history, then you don't know anything. You
are a leaf that doesn't know it is part of a tree.*

Michael Crichton

Introduction

On just about any hike in the woods we are tramping through
history: stones walls mark the boundaries of a settler's land; a
cellar hole their home; a pile of rocks is an indication of their efforts to clear the land for a pasture or garden, cemeteries mark
the final resting spot of an individual or family. We use abandoned railroad beds and obscure tote roads as trails. There are
numerous signs in the woods that tell us of life lived not so long
ago. These are signposts that can provide an understanding and
appreciation for the life led by our early settlers, as well as those
who made a living from tourism or those who carved out a living
from the rugged mountains of New Hampshire. Theodore Roosevelt said, *"The more you know about the past, the better prepared you are for the future."*

*Abandoned summit station and snack bar
Whittier Mountain Ski Resort*

5

A Blast from the Past

Many travelers driving on Rt. 16 in Ossipee, NH must wonder about the large stanchions sitting near the junction with Rt.25, in the McDonalds' parking lot. They probably ask themselves, "What are those towers used for?" Those towers are recollections of the past, when small ski areas dotted the New Hampshire landscape. The towering relics of a bygone era carried skiers to the summit house of the Mount Whittier Ski Area. Mount Whittier is actually a misnomer as the ski area sits on the side of Grant Peak and Mount Whittier lies farther to the west. It was common to find ski hills in most every community, sometimes several. In New Hampton, where I live, there was the New Hampton School ski area on Burleigh Mountain and Mail Box Hill on Old Bristol Road. Remnants of these areas can still be seen, including the tow houses that held the car engine that ran the lift. I remember an older resident of New Hampton who used to ski Mailbox Hill, telling the story of her scarf getting wrapped around the tow rope and being dragged up the hill, almost into the engine gears, before the tow was stopped. Do you have recollections of being hauled up a hill holding on desperately to the rope, as your gloves slipped on the ice covered rope?

From Colebrook Tow in Colebrook to Morris Hill in Hampstead, family and locally owned ski areas were the places where children learned to ski and families spent weekends enjoying winter fun together, without having to spend a lot of money. There were over 200 small and medium size ski areas that operated throughout the state. Locally, the Arlberg Inn ran a small operation in the 1950s. The Gilford Outing Club operated a rope tow on Rt. 11A near Gunstock from 1950 to 1992. In the 1930s Fred Weeks used to bring skiers from Boston to his dairy farm on Weeks Road to ski the west side of Mount Rowe. A few small ski areas still remain such as Mount Eustis in Littleton and the Red Hill Family Ski Area in Center Sandwich, but these are rare.

In the 1970s and early 80s I used to drive by the Mount Whittier Ski Area on my way to Maine. The parking lot on Route 16 was filled with cars and the tram was busy shuffling would-be skiers up the mountain to the summit station. Since Mount Whittier closed in 1985 the area has fallen into decay. Trails have become almost completely overgrown. Lifts have degraded to the point that they could never operate again. Despite all this, the gondola cable still remains, along with the towers, including one in the McDonald's parking lot. The owners tried to resurrect the area in the form of an amusement park, but could never seem to make a go of it. The towers are a reminder of times long past.

Wanting to explore the abandoned Mount Whittier Mountain Ski Area for many years I decided to head up to Ossipee on a clear cold January day, with my dog Reuben, and see what I could find of the once thriving ski resort. I was accompanied by Steve, Beth, Ken, and Karen who were also intrigued by the idea of visiting the defunct ski resort. We were not to be disappointed. We arrived at the parking lot off Route 25 near the junction of Route 16 and followed Newman Drew Road. Just past the Bear Camp Campgrounds we found the gondola towers crossing the road, climbing up the side of the mountain. We pulled off, put on our winter hiking packs and snowshoes, and headed up the lift line. The Mueller 4-person gondola was installed around 1963 and was one of the first of its kind to be built in this country. It was unique because it started at the parking lot on Rt.16 and picked up skiers at a mid-station. The area was started in 1949, and at its height operated rope tows, several T-bars, and the gondola lift on 80 acres of terrain.

After a short time climbing the lift line we spotted the gondola base station, now decrepit and falling into disrepair. However, the cables, gears, pulleys, and large geared wheels were still in place as well as the loading platform. It seemed as if the base station was waiting for a few repairs before being put back into business.

We left the decaying shell and continued climbing the steep incline, following the still existent cable and towers, to a sharp ice-covered rock ledge. Here we made our way into the woods to bushwhack up the side of the mountain.

After returning to the lift line we eyed the summit gondola station perched at the summit. Once we reached the top of the mountain we were stunned by the amazing views: the Sandwich Range, Mount Kearsarge, Ossipee Lake and the hills of Maine. I could understand why the gondola ran year-round, carrying summer tourists and winter skiers to the summit restaurant to experience these fantastic views. We found relics lying around the summit: signs, cables, lift machinery and even a rusted tank truck with an unknown purpose. The ski trails from the summit were obscured by nascent trees that had grown back since the area was closed. The forest was in the process of reclaiming what had been taken away over 60 years ago. Nature always has a way of filling a void.

After our explorations on the summit, Steve, Ken and Karen hiked off the mountain taking a tote road to the base, while Beth, Reuben and I descended by following a network of ski trails. We began a slow and tedious climb down the mountain, trying to find the once wide open, steep slopes. The slopes, which cascaded down the mountain, were covered with trees and bushes. We cautiously wove around stands of trees, shrubs and rock ledges, trying to find any semblance of a ski trail. We stumbled into an abandoned T-bar lift station, with cables and T-bars still in place. The steep terrain made footing tricky. As Beth and I lumbered our way along down the mountain I pondered on the closing of Mount Whittier. It was in an ideal location, right off a busy highway, great views from the summit and one of the first gondolas in the country. Why did it close? Several reasons: the steep and rocky terrain was not friendly to the beginner skier or family, snow making equipment was never installed and the lift equipment was not upgraded or modified, and liability insurance became a huge economic drain. Most importantly, the ski industry changed dramatically in the 1980s. The larger more attractive ski resorts were only a few hours drive farther north. People wanted, "more bang for their buck."

When we reached the base of the mountain we discovered the T-bar tow house, along with a map of the ski area and a few other relics. I looked up the mountain, toward the summit, and envisioned throngs of skiers racing down the slopes, the base lodge bustling with activity, skiers waiting in line to catch the next T-bar to pull them up the mountain, cars jammed into the parking lot, screams of children as they took their first spill on the beginner's hill. As I stood on the abandoned grounds of Mount Whittier, the utter silence was hypnotic. The stillness was briefly interrupted by a gentle breeze whistling through the empty, dilapidated buildings. Standing in this deserted lot I only saw the wreckage of a ski area that at one time thrived. Mount Whittier is among the many corpses of ski areas that used to flourish throughout New England. Now most of them are obscured by the forest that has overtaken their slopes and decomposed buildings. For more information about lost ski areas in New Hampshire go to (*nelsap.org/nh*).

Mystery of the Cog Car

The old cog railroad passenger car was sitting on Mount Oscar, just waiting for us, as storm clouds moved in bringing a cold rain and wind. Fran and I had just roamed around the summit cliff of Oscar, admiring the views to the east of Mount Hale and the Zealand Valley. It was now time for lunch, and what better way to enjoy ourselves than by sitting inside this relic of a famous Mount Washington Cog Railway. As we ate our lunch, with Reuben looking for a few tidbits, we wondered how the car got to the summit of Mount Oscar, also called the West Summit of Mount Rosebrook. When we got off the mountain we would

*Mount Washington Cog Railway car on summit of Mount Oscar,
Bretton Woods Ski Resort*

inquire at the Bretton Woods Ski Resort information center. Meanwhile, we could wonder, speculate and guess until the rain stopped and then make our way down the ski trails.

Fran, Reuben and I began our day driving to the Bretton Woods Ski Resort on Rt. 302. The ski area is laid out on the northeastern slopes of Mount Rosebrook (3,004 ft.) Mount Stickney (3,065 ft.) and Mount Oscar (2,748 ft.). The advantage of climbing these mountains, as opposed to many others which are bushwhacks, is that they can be climbed using the wide open ski slopes and maintenance roads of Bretton Woods Ski Resort. This was a day for revelry: no whacking through thick woods or underbrush, no cliffs to climb or swamps to cross. Just an easy climb to the top, and admiring the views as we hiked.

These three mountains, along with Mount Echo (3,084 ft.) are part of the Rosebrook Mountain Range. This obscure, small range, lies just north of Crawford Notch and is named for Capt. Eleazer Rosebrook, an early settler in the White Mountains. In 1790 his daughter Hannah married Abel Crawford, inn keeper and builder of the Crawford Path. In the late 1700s Rosebrook, along with Crawford offered accommodations to weary travelers walking along the path through Crawford Notch. However, after the construction of the Tenth New Hampshire Turnpike in 1806, Capt. Rosebrook expanded his operation to include a tavern and inn called the "Old Red Barn" which is considered by some as the first summer hotel in the White Mountains (*WhiteMountainHistory.org*).

When Fran drove into the parking lot we were greeted by a few employees of the resort who were gearing up for summer business. Bretton Woods came on the scene as a major ski destination in the 1970s. At this time I-93 was in the process of being completed. Soon ski enthusiasts would be able to quickly and easily reach the western White Mountains from cities in southern New England. In 1969 a group of investors named the Mount Washington Development Co. purchased the Mount Washington Hotel and 10,000 acres of adjacent land. By 1972 the owners began construction of the Bretton Woods Ski area. On December 29, 1973 the ski resort opened with 1,100 vertical foot ski area, two double chair lifts, a T-bar and 30 acres of snow making. With the hotel and ski area investment of over $100 million, ownership ran into financial troubles. By 1975, the company found itself in debt to the tune of $14 million. That, coupled with a depressed housing market, led to the ski resort closure. Subsequently, the ski area and the Mount Washington Hotel came under ownership of several other investments firms. In June, 2006 the hotel and ski resort, along with related properties were purchased by CNL Lifestyle Properties. In 2009 Omni Hotels and Resorts initiated a lease of both hotel and ski resort and in 2015 Omni purchased the entire property for $90.5 million.

Of course the Mount Washington Hotel and the surrounding area have their own unique and fascinating history. In the late 19th century, before the Mount Washington was built in 1902, there were three large hotels in the area: the Fabyan House, The White Mountain House, and the Mount Pleasant House. Also located along the Tenth New Hampshire Turnpike (what is now Rt. 302) were two or three sawmills, a charcoal kiln, a school, a settlement known as "Stovepipe City", a tavern, a store, a tree nursery, barns, a wye for turning trains, engine houses, two railroad stations, boarding houses for railroad employees, private homes, a toll house for the turnpike, and many other establishments associated with a small community in the north woods. Now the only vestiges of this early community are a few cellar holes and the Mount Washington Hotel, the granddaddy of the grand hotels in the White Mountains, built by Joseph Stickney, New Hampshire native and business tycoon who died shortly after its opening.

As Fran and I worked our way up a maintenance road the views began to reveal the Presidential Range, although the summits were enshrouded in clouds. We passed Chutters, a mountainside branch of the famous candy store in Littleton, which boasts the "longest candy counter of its kind anywhere", 112 ft. long. Here we found a replica of the store, but it was closed for the season, no candy today.

We continued our easy climb reaching the summit's high speed chair lift station. Directly behind the lift station we scrambled a few feet to the summit of Mount Rosebrook, with no views. After a quick glance around for any markers signifying the summit (we found none) we started down the ski trail, to find the path to Mount Oscar. Within a few 100 yards we found a well-marked trail leading us through a beautiful spruce and fir woodland to Mount Oscar. As we approached the summit we noticed the famous Cog Railway Car. We passed by it and hustled up the rocky top summit. We were stunned by the views. The ledges offered amazing vistas to the west and north. I ventured down the rock-strewn face, hoping to find signs of the rock climbers' route up the southwest cliff. There are over 19 defined routes which are accessible from Zealand Rd. I was hoping to find a climber ascending the cliffs, but the ropes were vacant. Reuben and I then began the climb back to the summit in search of Fran. The wind was picking up and I could see storm clouds moving in from the west. When I reached the Cog car I found Fran and we made it inside before the rain hit. We enjoyed a relaxing lunch in comfort, watched the rain fall and wondered how the car got here. I later found out that in the early 1990s the cog car was hoisted to the summit of Mount Oscar by helicopter. At that time the owners of the Mount Washington Cog Railway also owned Bretton Woods Ski Resort, as well as the Mount Washington Hotel (As told to me by an employee of the Mount Washington Cog Railway).

Following lunch we walked to the Oscar summit lift station and began our trek back to the parking lot. On the way down we passed beautiful patches of wildflowers, including spring beauties (*Claytonia virginica*), trout lilies (*erythronium americanum*) which are medicinal and edible, and lupine or lupinus. This lupine was most likely not wild lupine (*lupinus perennis*) which is native and considered rare and threatened in the New Hampshire, but the garden variety (*lupinus polyphyllus)* and probably escaped from gardens located close by. The Mount Washington Hotel, with its distinctive red roof, stood out in the distance. The clouds had lifted off the Presidential summits, offering us a spectacular view. We completed our hike of two mountains in four hours, taking our time and stopping for an extended lunch.

A trek to the summits of Oscar and Rosebrook would make a fine day hike for a family or those not wanting to hike the crowded paths out of Crawford Notch. The ski trails are gradual and open with many routes you can choose from. A map of the ski area is available online at (*brettonwoods.com/winter-sports/trail-maps*) or at the visitor center. The rewards of this short, easy hike are the views and a chance to have lunch in an old passenger car from the Cog Railway.

The Granite State's Granite

Derricks in quarry used for lifting granite blocks

In North Conway, New Hampshire, hidden behind big-box stores, convenience stores, a 3 lane highway and other trappings of modern day America, lies a hidden historical treasure: the abandoned town and granite quarries of Redstone. I traveled to the Conway area for many years, when I worked for the New Hampshire Department of Health and Human Services. I spent much of my time in the Redstone area and I always wondered, "Why it is called Redstone?" Most of the people I spoke to didn't't know either, except to say that there were some granite quarries in the area.

I contacted my friend Dick to see if he was interested in exploring the quarries. We met at my house and traveled up Rt.16 to North Conway. I knew we were in the area called Redstone, because the name of the store we passed was called Redstone Variety. We drove around the area and found some gravel roads and then finally located the granite markers indicating this area was the former town of Redstone, a town built around the Redstone Granite Quarries. In the early 1900s it was one of the largest quarries in the New England area.

We brought our mountain bikes and when noticing the biking trails we jumped on our bikes and headed down an old railroad bed. As we made our way along the trail we became overwhelmed with what we saw: giant lathes, steam compressors, gigantic cables, derricks, a three story carpenter shop, sheds, and tools for cutting granite, on and on. We had found an important piece of New Hampshire's past: the granite business that fed New Hampshire's economy for a hundred years and helped to give it the name, "The Granite State". Now this former town and quarry lie abandoned, left to nature to reclaim. I wondered, what is the history of this quarry and why is it not known by more people as a historic site?

When I returned home I did some research and found that the quarry was founded on the side of Rattlesnake Mountain in the late 1800s. In 1886, the North Jay Granite Company of Maine bought land on the mountain, which became known as the Redstone Quarry. A cutting yard was established at the base and a railroad spur connected to the nearby Maine Central Railroad line. The first stones shipped in 1888, were used for paving stones in New York City, and for building Union Station in Portland, Maine. The village of Redstone grew up around the quarries to house workers and their families. In its prime it provided all the amenities of town life: churches, a school (K-8), a poolroom, railroad station, a dance hall and stage, rooming house, post office, a company store and twenty houses for permanent employees.

The Redstone quarries continued to operate for the next 50 years, producing quality red and green granite blocks for buildings in Boston, New York, Washington, D.C., Denver and even Havana, Cuba. In addition the Hatch Memorial Shell in Boston, Grant's Tomb in New York, the National Archives building and the George Washington Memorial Masonic Temple in Washington are among many buildings built of Redstone granite. Locally, the Laconia Railroad Station was built of the red granite. Until the great depression of the 1930s the Redstone quarries flourished. With the downturn of the economy and the advent of lime and cement for building construction the quarries met their demise and eventually closed in 1948. The Nature Conservancy and the State of New Hampshire now own the entire property. More can be learned about the quarries and the village of Redstone at, (*redstonequarrynh.org*).

As Dick and I wove our way through and around the many old roads and paths that once carried hundreds of men to work in the quarries, we found a plethora of old equipment used to quarry the stone and shape it into building blocks, columns or paving stones. The most impressive sight was the green quarry, with two large wooden derricks still standing in the quarry pond, reminding us of the immense task of cutting and hauling blocks weighing more than several tons to the buildings used for cutting and shaping the blocks. From here we climbed to the top of the quarry and had spectacular views to the west, overlooking the Moat Mountains and the Three Sisters Summits.

After spending several hours exploring the quarry we headed out to find the network of mountain bike trails that begin at a parking area off the By-Pass Road. The trail system is extensive and includes trails of varying difficulty. Dick and I found a nice single-track, and after about a 3-mile ride we reached Bear Pond.

The Redstone quarries and the adjacent trail system for hiking or biking is ideal for any outdoor enthusiast, especially if one is interested in New Hampshire history. This is a perfect location for families to explore our past and marvel at the early twentieth century technology that drove our economy in the Granite State.

The Crash Site of a B-18

B-18 bomber

On January 15, 1942, a little over a month after Pearl Harbor, The Littleton Courier ran this headline:

"Two Killed, Five Injured in Bomber Crash on Mount Moosilauke. Last Night, Explosions Heard in Lincoln, North Woodstock. Two men were killed and five narrowly missed death when a bomber, described as a Douglass B-18 crashed on Mount Moosilauke, between North Woodstock and Warren last night. It was reported that the big plane was loaded with four bombs, three of which exploded to shake the countryside for miles around. Working feverishly all night a crew of more than 50 volunteer searchers, including experienced woodsmen rounded up by the Parker Young Company at Lincoln, U.S. Forest Service Rangers and

*members of the State Police, made this morning a dramatic res-
cue of five of the seven man crew and rushed them to the Lincoln
Hospital."*

The B-18 bomber crash site on Mount Waternomee, a sub-peak on
the east side of Mount Moosilauke is just one of several plane cata-
strophes in the White Mountains that I have learned about over
the past year. There are three other well publicized plane crashes
that have occurred in the White Mountains since 1950.

In 1968 a Northeast Airlines Fairchild Hiller FH–227C, with thir-
ty-nine passengers and a crew of three aboard; pilot, co-pilot, and
a stewardess, crashed into the north side of Moose Mountain on
its approach to the Lebanon airport in foggy conditions. Seven
people were fatally injured, while many more suffered severe injuries. The rescue effort was hampered by darkness, the remote
location of the crash site as well as rain and freezing temperatures.
On November 30, 1954 another Northeast Airlines flight struck
the southern slope of Mount Success on its approach to the Berlin
airport. The plane, a Douglas DC-3, had left the Laconia airport
with three passengers and four crew members on board. (Who
remembers regular commercial flights from Laconia?) The plane
was flying in snow squalls, with limited visibility, attempting to
make an instrument landing when it ran head long into the mountain. Everyone on board survived the crash, but two crew members
succumbed to injuries following the crash. The remaining survivors were not rescued until December 2nd due to weather conditions and the remoteness of the crash site.

Another noteworthy tragedy occurred on Feb. 21, 1959 when Drs.
Ralph Miller and Robert Quinn, Dartmouth Medical School pro-
fessors and doctors at Mary Hitchcock Hospital, died when their
single engine Piper Comanche went down in the Pemigewasset
Wilderness, northeast of Lincoln. They were on their way back to
Hanover after making medical calls, when their carburetor iced up

in severe winter weather. It wasn't until May 5th that the wreckage was spotted from the air, after a massive search involving hundreds of volunteers. The two men survived the crash, managed to build a fire to keep warm in the sub-freezing temperatures and even fashioned primitive snowshoes in an attempt to hike out of the wilderness in deep snow. However, they died of exposure about eight days after the crash. The crash site is now marked with a memorial erected by Dartmouth faculty, students and friends.

Intrigued by the story of the B-18 plane crash and the subsequent rescue efforts I planned a hike into the crash site on Mount Waternomee. The site can be accessed off Walker Brook Road, near the junction of Routes 118 and 112 in Woodstock. This unofficial but well-trodden path is fairly easy to follow, but offers a steep climb as you near the crash site. On this exploratory mission I was accompanied by hiking partners, Ken, Karen, Steve and our dogs Skipper and Reuben. As we progressed up the trail, about 2 miles, we began to spot large chunks of metal scattered about the forest floor. As we continued our investigation further into the crash site we encountered the remains of the wings and propeller engines, along with parts of the fuselage. In the midst of the wreckage we found a memorial marker which read, "Honoring the World War II U.S. Army Air Crew Who Crashed in a B-18 Bomber on Mount Waternomee in Woodstock, N.H., January 14, 1942". There is also a memorial plaque to Fletcher Craig who survived the crash and went on to fly a P-47 Thunderbolt in the European campaign. Throughout the area we found the remains of the bomber that was blown apart when the three, 300 - pound bombs exploded, ignited by leaking aviation fuel. As we sat contemplating the tragedy of the crash, we wondered about the circumstances surrounding the crash. How did it occur, why, who survived and how were they rescued?

These questions led me to the Mountain Wanderer Book Store in Lincoln to see if Steve Smith, the owner, could provide some answers. I was shown a small book entitled, *The Night the Bomber Crashed,* by Floyd W. Ramsey. This account of the crash provided all the answers. The B-18 was a small bomber that was quickly put into service with the outbreak of WW II. It was used primarily for reconnaissance. The plane took off from Westover Field in Massachusetts on an anti-submarine patrol, almost reaching the coast of Newfoundland. On the return flight the weather turned foul. Blinding snow and fierce winds drove the plane well off course.

1st Lt. Anthony Benvenuto, pilot, was unaware that the plane was flying almost 300 miles inland, believing he was over the ocean, when in fact he was headed toward the high peaks of the White Mountains. Compounding the problem was the fact the crew was trained to fly B-24's, a much larger bomber and subsequently they didn't have the necessary navigational skills to compute the drift factor caused by the storm off the New Jersey coast. When seeing lights on the ground the crew assumed they were over Providence, RI, when in fact they were eyeing the lights of Concord, NH. As the pilot dropped to 3,000 ft. to prevent ice build-up on the engines, with the crew finding the plane more difficult to handle and not even knowing their location, they crashed into the mountain.

The second part of this story is centered on the amazing rescue effort launched within a half hour after the plane disappeared into the wilderness. In the towns of Lincoln and Woodstock, residents heard the roar of the exploding bombs. They immediately began a search and rescue effort. Area citizens, Forest Service Rangers, NH Fish and Game personnel, even woodsmen from the Parker Young Company joined together to reach the site and rescue five crewmen who amazingly survived the crash. Sherman Adams, an employee of the Parker Young Company, later Governor of New Hampshire and Chief of Staff for President Dwight Eisenhower, was a leader in the rescue efforts. The survivors were brought down the mountain in a blinding snow storm and rushed to local hospitals. The bodies of the two crewmen killed in the crash were brought down the mountain by Army personnel who arrived at the scene the following day.

After spending time at the site and reflecting on the tragedy that occurred here, we began our trek back down the mountain. It was a sobering experience, knowing that two men had died at the crash site. The wreckage is a memorial to the victims of the crash who gave their lives in defense of their country. The U.S. Forest Service has posted a notice that pieces of the wreckage are not to be removed. It states, *"Under the authority of the Antiquities Act of 1906 the historical remnants in the vicinity of this notice are fragile and irreplaceable."* This isolated spot on the side of Mt Waternomee serves as a memorial not only to the men who died here, but to all service personnel who put their lives on the line every day.

This is a moderately difficult hike of 4 miles round trip, climbing steeply as you near the crash site. The trail is well marked and maintained. It would provide a wonderful opportunity to share the story of the B-18 with children. There is also an impressive waterfall just off the trail that can be accessed quite easily. It serves as a nice place to cool off on a hot day and contemplate the experience of visiting the B-18 crash site.

The Thriving Village of Livermore, When Timber Barons Ruled the North Country

The roar of Sawyer River accompanied us as we made our way along an abandoned road to the once flourishing village of Livermore. As we walked along I imagined the villagers heading to the Sawyer River Railroad Station in Crawford Notch. The once

Remains of the brick power house

busy road is now just an obscure pathway in the woods. In several areas the trail is hidden due to flooding and forest encroachment, and I could hear a stiff wind blowing through the naked trees overhanging the path. The sound of the wind gusting through the bare trees brought me back to the time when the train engines would sound their whistle as they hauled loads of lumber from the Livermore saw mill to the main line of the Portland and Ogdensburg Railroad.

Earlier that day I set out with several of my hiking partners to find and explore the ruins of Livermore Village. We met at the Sawyer River Road trailhead just a few miles west of Bartlett. After our hike along the abandoned Livermore Road, we arrived at the remains of the village. Now the fun began, exploring the crumbling foundations and trying to figure out what these hulking structures were. At first we noticed the stone foundation of the company store, office and post office. A safe was lying at the bottom of the foundation. It was here where workers probably lined up for their paychecks. Livermore was a company town.

We explored further and found the ruins of the steam-powered saw mill and power house, along with the school, two boarding houses, aqueduct pillars, and several cellar holes. The Village of Livermore has all but disappeared, except for the foundations and brickwork that now define the town. In its heyday it was home to over 200 inhabitants: loggers and woodsmen, mill workers, and railroad men along with their wives and children. However, by the mid-1930's Livermore was practically a ghost town, with only a few remaining inhabitants. The majestic spruce and fir trees that supported the community were cut and sold as millions of board feet of lumber, used to build the mill communities farther south. All that remains now are crumbling foundations. The forest and the Sawyer River are slowly reclaiming their terrain that was taken away in the early twentieth century when the timber barons ruled the north country of New Hampshire.

Several years ago I was fortunate to hike with Peter Crane, PhD. Peter oversees the Mount Washington Observatory Discovery Center's Gladys Brooks Memorial Library, which has a prized collection of books, maps, prints, photos, and other material relating to the Observatory, Mount Washington and the White Mountains. Peter has a wealth of information on the history of the White Mountains and wrote his doctoral dissertation on the history and folk life of Livermore Village. He was kind enough to send me a copy of his doctoral dissertation and I devoured it in one night of reading. It told about this tiny village carved out of the wilderness by the Saunders family and the people who lived there who called this community their home. At the turn of the nineteenth century there were many villages centered on the logging industry: Zealand, Carrigain, Thornton Gore, Johnson Village, Gale River Settlement, and Passaconaway. Most of these villages have been lost to time, their history forgotten and town folk long deceased. However, thanks to Bartlett Historical Society, Peter Crane and other historians such as C. Francis Belcher, and Bill Gove, the history, folk culture and stories of Livermore Village have been kept alive.

Having dug into this wealth of information about Livermore Village and the Sawyer River Railroad I found their history to be fascinating. Livermore was founded by the Saunders family. The Saunders made their money in the textile business, building and operating mills along the Merrimack River in Lawrence, MA. Later, they realized the potential of harvesting lumber from the extensive forests of Northern New Hampshire. In 1874 the Saunders Family founded the Grafton County Lumber Co. and thus began the Sawyer River Railroad and the village of Livermore. The first mill was built in 1875. This mill was destroyed by fire the same year it was built, but a second mill was put up shortly after.

Main street in Livermore. Workers' houses are to the left, and the Saunders house is at the top of the rise

From this point forward the town grew quickly and took on the identity of a typical New England village: babies were born, funerals occurred, holidays and birthdays were celebrated. The 1890 census speculates that the population of Livermore was 103 persons living in 18 separate dwellings. By 1920 the population rose to 200. Livermore was different than many other logging towns at the time. It was a family oriented community. Households were dominated by immediate and extended families. The school, serving up to 28 students, with two teachers, had an extensive collection of writing and arithmetic books as well as copies of classics including *Robinson Crusoe, The Song of Hiawatha, and Tom Brown's School Days.* The Saunders' family mansion overlooked the village and was an impressive structure. It was the pride of the community.

Livermore continued to prosper through the early part of the 1900s due to the extensive holdings of the Saunders family. The mill was cutting between 3,000,000 to 11,000,000 board feet annually. In addition the Saunders operation was using selective cutting, meaning the forest was managed for long term productivity, rather than short term profit. This practice was in sharp contrast to that of other timber barons, like J.E. Henry. *The White Mountain Echo,* a tourists-oriented regional newspaper, called Henry, *"Not a lumberman, but a wood-butcher, a mutilator of nature, a destroyer of the property of a thousand for the benefit of himself."* (Peter Crane, *Glimpses of Livermore: Life and Lore of an Abandoned White Mountains Woods Community,* unpublished dissertation 1993).

By the mid-1920s, with the oncoming Great Depression, the value of sawed lumber dropped substantially. That, combined with a massive flood on the Sawyer River, wiping out many sections of the railroad including several bridges, spelled the demise of the Grafton County Lumber Company, the Sawyer River Railroad and the township of Livermore. Eventually in 1936, under the Weeks Act, all the Saunders' forest holdings, including the village, were sold to the U.S. Forest Service, and became part of the White Mountain National Forest. A few residents remained as "hangers-on", not wanting to leave the village they loved. In 1944 the federal government auctioned off some of the equipment in the mill and boarding house. Finally in 1951 The NH State Legislature revoked the town's charter and Livermore disappeared into obscurity.

As we continued on our archeological quest we spent quite some time trying to figure out how the mill's sophisticated technology of the early twentieth century was used to saw timber. Fran pawed though the fallen and broken bricks of the powerhouse and found an inscription printed on the bricks, "ASCOT". Playing detective, Fran returned home and learned that the bricks were manufactured near Sherbrooke, Quebec and must have been transported by rail to construct the powerhouse. We also imagined what the community looked like in the bygone era when the timber industry dominated the North Country and this town bustled with activity. Fortunately we had an old map of the town along with several pictures of village buildings. Excitement ran through our small group of "want to be" archeologists as we continued to look through the ruins, trying to find artifacts.

Wandering through the remains of the village we found several foundations of homes, steel rails left behind when the Sawyer River Rail Road was abandoned and most of the rail was sold as scrap metal. We even discovered the cement school foundation complete with a 2-holer still intact. We scoured the area for other remnants of town life such as jars, dishes and tools. We found some shards of glass and pottery and a baker's warming oven used at the boarding house. Under the authority of the Antiquities Act of 1906 the historical remnants in the vicinity of Livermore Village are not to be removed. We left the glass and ceramic shards, bricks, pieces of the boiler and other fragments of the village where we found them.

We wrapped up our archeology/history hike by returning to the parking lot via the way we came, following the abandoned Livermore Village Road. We passed by the foundations of the Saunders' mansion and houses that had lined Railroad Row, the village main street. We passed the foundation of the boarding house that housed many woodsmen who worked in the woods, cutting down the giant spruce covering the mountain sides. The last memorabilia we found were parts of the boiler from the train engine that hauled logs and lumber up and down the rail line. The village of Livermore is no longer, but the past in still alive, found in the crumbling foundations of this once proud mill town. You can explore an important part of New Hampshire history by visiting this site and experiencing history when timber barons ruled the North Country.

The Lime Kilns of Black Mountain

I had heard of the lime kilns located in the town of Haverhill, NH, but I really didn't know what a lime kiln was or how it was used. I also heard from fellow hikers that these lime kilns are located near the Chippewa Trailhead that leads to the summit of Black Mountain. Therefore, why not climb a mountain and at the same time learn something about lime kilns.

Before I set out on my quest, I did some research on the lime kilns in Haverhill and discovered some amazing information. Mining limestone in New Hampshire was very rare. Limestone is a sedimentary rock, composed mostly of the skeletal fragments of marine organisms, such as coral and mollusks. It has been used for hundreds of years for building construction, sculptures, mortar, glass making, fertilizer, and even in toothpaste. The kilns in Haverhill were part of a very important industry the 19th century. The mined limestone was heated in the kilns, which are huge ovens, and turned into a powdered form, which was then packed into barrels and shipped throughout New England. The two

Lime kiln circa 1883

Haverhill kilns were built in 1838 and 1842 and operated profitably until 1888. The woodland surrounding the kilns provided the wood needed to fire the kilns at high temperatures.

With this knowledge in hand I set out, not only to see these structures, but also to climb Black Mountain, one of the most prominent peaks in western New Hampshire. Black Mountain (2,830 ft.) lies west of its much more dominant and well-known cousin, Mount Moosilauke (4,802 ft.). I chose to explore the lime kilns and climb Black Mountain from the Chippewa Trail which is accessed from Lime Kiln Rd in Benton. Lime Kiln Road leaves NH Rt. 25 about 5 miles west of Glencliff, NH.

With Reuben, my dog, along for another adventure with Gorbo (my AT Trail name) we found the trailhead about 3.5 miles from Rt. 25. There was limited parking, so I parked on the side of the road and began my adventure into a unique part of our state's history. Within a few minutes I reached the signed trail that led me to the first kiln, and then to the other much larger kiln, that is a massive structure of native stone. Located next to the kiln is an interpretive sign explaining the history of the kilns. I also discovered, further along the trail, the Civilian Conservation Corps camp that was built during the depression under the Roosevelt administration. A stone mason who worked at this camp rebuilt the kilns and they now stand as an historic treasure. The kilns are maintained by the Heritage Committee of the Town of Haverhill.

After spending a considerable amount of time exploring the area, I set out to begin my climb up Black Mountain. The path back to the Chippewa Trail led me an old logging road and subsequently to another old woods road that passed a rather large stone foundation. The trail then began to steeply ascend the mountain. After about a mile of climbing I came to ledges that offered views to the south and west, down into the Connecticut River Valley and into Vermont. The trail continued to climb sharply in sections, mostly over rock outcrops that offered outstanding views in all directions. I finally reached what I thought was the summit, but I noticed a higher crest of rock ahead and knew I needed to continue another quarter mile to my destination, the summit of Black Mountain. The rocky ledges at the summit provided spectacular vistas and I was captivated by the beauty that surronds the western summits of New Hampshire. As Reuben and I settled down to eat our lunch, we were entertained by two ravens gliding back and forth above us, riding the updrafts, and calling out in a language only they could understand. I have learned that ravens have a vocabulary of over 500 words. What could they be talking about?

As I was finishing my lunch, the solitude of the summit was broken by voices of oncoming hikers who were out to enjoy the summit just as I was doing. I decided to begin my trek down the mountain, choosing to bushwhack along the rocky crags toward another outcrop of cliffs. I rejoined the trail after an exhilarating decent that would lead me back to my truck. As I was headed down the mountain, there were several trekkers headed in the opposite direction. I had a chance to chat with a few and I learned that this mountain is one of the most well-liked climbs in the Upper Valley. Little did I know that this rather small mountain held such a popular following.

Not wanting to end my day, I decided to try and find the limestone quarries that provided the bulk of the limestone for the kilns. I followed several old roads from the base of the kilns, but I couldn't find the quarries. The day was getting late, so I began heading back to the parking lot. Reuben was hungry and I knew Nancy was waiting supper for us. In the back of my mind I have a suspicion that someday I will return to this wonderful historic site and attempt again to locate those limestone quarries. But until then, I'll remember this memorable day on Black Mountain.

Hiking Abandoned Route 3A and Old Hill Village

Nestled along the Pemigewasset River just north of Franklin lies Old Hill Village or the remains of the village that was moved to higher ground in 1940. Now the reborn town of Hill sits along Route 3A, the main artery between Franklin and Bristol. Someonedriving this road, passing through the town would only see a general store and a few homes. Through the trees one may spot the school, town offices, church and a few other homes set off the highway on Crescent Street. One would have little idea that this town is a planned community, created out of the U.S. Army Corps of Engineers' design to harness the river waters of the Pemigewasset River, by building a flood control dam in Franklin, thus flooding the original village.

I first learned of Old Hill Village about 30 years ago when a friend invited me to cross-country ski the old Route 3A. The abandoned road bisects the uninhibited village, and offers an ideal track for cross country skiing. It was a crisp cold evening in January when we parked at the gate of the old road. It led us down to the time-worn streets of the village. Snow blanketed the ground and the light of the full moon reflected off the fresh snow creating a sparkling light show as we skied along the almost perfectly flat roadway. It was a memorable evening and I have often returned to ski or walk the roads of Old Hill Village.

Stone Bridge on abandoned Route 3A in Old Hill Village

I decided to return by walking the road from Bristol. I drove to Bristol from my home in New Hampton, taking Route 104 and turning left onto Route 3A south. I drove about two miles until I came to Profile Falls Road. Turning left I headed down into the river valley, and drove into the parking lot adjacent to Profile Falls. A marked trail led me to the picturesque falls that are worth the trip just in themselves. As Reuben and I were starting out we noticed a musher's truck loaded with 12 sled dogs. They had come for the day to run the road from the parking lot to Old Hill Village and back again, a total of 12 miles. I stopped to chat with the dogs' owner and musher from South Berwick, Maine. She told me she came to this area because it's an ideal place for the dogs and her to train. She explained that it's used by many others in the sled dog community for training and she planned to return the following day. It was an amazing sight to watch her as she calmly hitched up her 12 Siberian Huskies and take off down the road. I think Reuben wanted to join them, but must have realized that a 12 mile run might be a little too much for him.

I began walking with Reuben along the road, which showed tracks of previous walkers and skiers. We passed along old stone walls, foundations, fields and dams that reminded me of an earlier time when this road was once lined with homes, farms, and businesses. Back then it was busy with traffic, but now it lies silent, with only the calls of chickadees and a few crows breaking the peace and quiet. When we reached Dyer Brook we crossed the bridge and found a side path that led into the woods. We walked along this trail which led us down along the river. The path turned out to be a loop trail that took us back to the road, ending at the abandoned farm site of C. Favor, one of the early settlers in the area. Reuben and I returned to the parking lot, walking a total of three miles which was a nice warm-up for the day. I then decided to drive to Hill and hike into Old Hill Village and once again explore the streets of the abandoned village.

Hill was first settled in 1765 and called New Chester, because the original proprietors were from Chester, NH. By the late 1700s several families began settling along the banks of the Pemigewasset River. The river provided a route for transportation and the river bottom land offered tillage for crops, and meadows for grazing livestock. In addition, Needleshop Brook dropped steeply to the river and the early settlers realized they could harness the power of falling water to run a sawmill and most likely a grist mill. It was an ideal location for a settlement in the wilds of New Hampshire during the post-colonial period. In 1836 the name of the town was changed to Hill in honor of Governor Isaac Hill, 1836-1839. He also served in the New Hampshire Senate and the U.S. Senate from 1831-1836. Many were opposed to the name change, perhaps because Hill was a staunch Jacksonian, and on the day following changed from New Chester to Hill, a letter was posted in town, *"Twixt Hill and Hell, there is but one letter, if Hill were to be called Hell, it would be much better."* (Hill Historical Society, *(hillhistoricalsociety.com/our-story.html)*) and the Hill Village Library).

Over the next 100 years Hill grew and prospered. Mills were erected on Needleshop Brook. Two churches, a library, town office, two schools, and a railroad station were built. Stores opened, families moved in and built homesteads. Even an orphanage, the Golden Rule Farm, was located in the center of town. In 1889 Hill fielded a baseball team. Main Street was graced with stately trees and family homes lined the thoroughfare. In many ways it was an idyllic small New Hampshire village, but it all changed in 1938. In that year villagers learned they would have to move to make way for a flood control reservoir. The U.S. Army Corp of Engineers developed plans to build a dam in Franklin, as part of a comprehensive strategy of flood risk management for the entire Merrimack River. The project began in November, 1939 and was completed by 1943. Perhaps there was increased impetus to construct the dam because of the Great Hurricane of 1938, when many towns along the river were flooded by torrential rains. All homes and other structures along the nine mile flood plain, from the proposed dam to Bristol, had to be destroyed or moved. As one might expect, Hill residents were upset with the idea that they had to move, not only their homes, but their entire community to higher ground. However, they gradually began to accept the idea and stubbornly started moving the entire village, including the cemetery, to its current location. By 1941 the new Village of Hill was relocated, including the school house and town hall. About 30 homes were built and occupied by this time.

I drove to Needleshop Brook Recreation Area which lies just above Old Hill Village off Route 3A. I parked the truck and followed an old road that led me along Needleshop Brook and the foundations of several mills that lined the water way. What was once a thriving community was now woods and fields. I walked along the abandoned road and found signs placed in locations where once stood the hotel, orphanage, town hall, store and homes. My imagination wandered back to the time when Hill was a close-knit community, villagers working, attending church, going to school and shopping alongside one another on this tree-lined street. Now the new village stands as a testament to the villagers' fortitude and courage to rebuild, not only their homes, but also their spirit of community. In the words of Hill resident Ed Amsden, *"When you consider what the new village cost in personal and town indebtedness you've got to admire these people for their willingness to do a lot of extra work and make a lot of sacrifices, all for an ideal. They wanted to stay together badly enough to do whatever they had to do as a price."* (Hill Historical Society, *(hillhistoricalsociety.com/our-story)* and the Hill Village Library).

After walking the road for a mile and exploring a few byways, Reuben and I returned to my truck. I know I'll be back to Old Hill Village and the vast trail system along the Pemigewasset flood plain.

If you would like to visit the area you can choose to start at Profile Falls in Bristol or Needleshop Brook Recreation Area in Hill. Either way you will be well rewarded, whether biking, skiing or walking. As an added prize you may encounter a dog sled team running the trails with you. It's a beautiful sight to behold.

Flat Mountain Pond and the Beebe River Railroad

In the early twentieth century, New Hampshire's White Mountains were laced with logging railroads. From Berlin to Plymouth, the rail lines were crowded with trains, hauling thousands of logs and pulpwood, from deep within the forest to mills around the Granite State. Over a dozen logging railroad

Flat Mountain Pond looking east from camp site

companies and hundreds of miles of tracks formed a web of rail beds that are still visible today. Logging railroads such as the Saco Valley, Wild River, Zealand Valley, Success Pond, Rocky Branch and Sawyer River ran through New Hampshire's mountain country. The best known and largest of these companies was the East Branch and Lincoln which operated from 1892 to 1947, where rail beds were laid through the rich stands of virgin forests in the Pemigewasset wilderness. The company, located in Lincoln, NH, was owned by the lumber baron J.E. Henry and his sons. As with many of these now abandoned rail lines, they no longer carry a Shay locomotive, log cars and loggers, but have become walking, biking and hiking trails that take outdoor enthusiasts deep into the forest of Northern New Hampshire.

Having read numerous books and articles about New Hampshire's logging railroads, I decided to hike to one of these abandoned rail beds of the former Beebe River Railroad. The rail bed starts in Holderness and winds its way along the Beebe River, continuing through a valley south of Sandwich Mountain and then climbing into the Flat Mountain Pond region, ending at the base of Mount Whiteface. Along the route of the rail bed one can find numerous reminders of a bygone era: log rail ties, clearings where lumber camps once stood, rusty bed frames, broken saw blades and parts of cook stoves.

The Beebe River Railroad was started in 1917 and completed in 1921. It was owned and operated by the Woodstock Lumber Company and the Parker Young Company. The Company not only built the rail line into the wilderness and an accompanying sawmill, but also constructed a village with homes for its workers, a hotel, company store, boarding house and even a movie theater. Trees harvested from the forest were turned into stock for piano manufacture, lumber and other products. Poorer grade logs were shipped to the Lincoln Paper Mill. In 1924 the Draper

Company purchased all the holdings for the manufacture of bobbins used in the cotton and woolen mills to the south. At its peak
the mill produced 100,000 bobbins per day and employed up to
350 people. Today you can still visit the small village of Beebe
River off Route 175 in Campton and see the abandoned mill, mill
pond and general store. It's truly a unique experience.

Crosscut saws left at logging camp in Lost Pass

When I planned this hike I was assuming spring would be well
underway, but thanks to Mother Nature we were hit by a snow
storm that dumped several inches of wet snow throughout portions of Northern New England. However, I wanted to keep to
my plan and I invited a couple of hiking friends with me, Steve
and Ken. Of course Reuben was assuming he would also join me,
as he always does. The plan was to hike the Bennett Street Trail,
to the Flat Mountain Pond Trail and then bushwhack into abandoned logging camps via the network of rail beds that were laid

in the beginning of the 1900s. We would then continue on the Flat Mountain Pond Trail that would take us to our waiting car at Whiteface Intervale Road. When we began our hike we encountered one of the first signs of spring: a mass of trout lilies and purple trillium sprouting up through the snow, ready to unfold their beautiful flowers. My spirit was uplifted, knowing that the snow wouldn't be around very long and we were headed towards summer.

The gradual incline of the trail followed along the bank of Pond Brook. Here we encountered roaring cascades with numerous deep pools, ideal for a dip on a hot summer day. This however wasn't summer, so we quickly moved along to the junction with the Flat Mountain Pond Trail and the Beebe River rail bed. The railroad ties are still visible. The hike from this point forward was a gradual climb along the road bed into the Flat Mountain Pond valley, so called because the pond lies between two mountains, North and South Flat Mountains. At the south end of the pond are several campsites along with a lean-to that overlooks the pond, Lost Pass and South Tripyramid Mountain. This is a picturesque setting that would make a great overnight camping experience. It was here that we took a break for lunch. A stiff, cold breeze blew across the pond, but the bright sun warmed our faces.

Following lunch we made our way along a rough trail high above the pond. We looked down and saw the old railroad ties lying underwater where they once guided logging trains up and down the mountain. The trail brought us to the north end of the pond and we followed a barely visible railroad bed that took us to a logging camp, probably abandoned in the early 1940s. The rails were torn up at that time and used to manufacture armaments for the war effort. At the site of the logging camp we found a plethora of bed frames, cooking gear, saw blades, an old cook stove and other items that were a part of everyday life of loggers. Again we reminded ourselves that any artifacts found in the area cannot be removed under the authority of the Antiquities Act of 1906. There were other camps that we would have loved to visit, including the Hedgehog Camp located at the base of Mount Whiteface, but it involved a difficult bushwhack of over a mile. We decided that we needed to begin the five mile hike down the Flat Mt. Pond Trail to our waiting vehicle at the Whiteface Intervale Road.

This is a wonderful intermediate hike of 10 miles for anyone who wants to relish in the beauty of a mountain stream, a scenic pond, breath taking vistas, explore the history of the logging industry and the associated railroads that once dominated this state's economy. For more information on this trail check out the AMC *White Mountain Guide.* Also there are several good books on logging railroads in the state including, *Logging Railroads of the White Mountains*, by C. Francis Belcher, and *Logging Railroads Along the Pemigewasset River*, by Bill Gove.

Visiting a Cold War Relic

Abandoned radar station on summit of East Mountain, Vermont

Riding our mountain bikes to the summit of East Mountain in Vermont was like entering into a set from a Stephen King movie or the Twilight Zone: eerie, ghost-like, creepy and at the same time fascinating and captivating. The skeletal remains of a Cold War relic stood before us and we were awe-struck. This was a living memory of a by-gone era when the great nations of the world were locked in a war of political, economic and social ideals. Dick, Steve, Dave and I rode our mountain bikes from East Haven, VT on Route 114, just north of East Burke, to this abandoned radar station sitting on top of a mountain in a very remote section of eastern Vermont. We stood in the midst of gigantic hulks of concrete and metal that protected the United States from nuclear attack.

From 1948 through 1991 the United States and the Soviet Union (now Russia) were locked in a war, the Cold War. It was a war of political and social ideals fought with fear, threats of nuclear war, and an overwhelming build-up of military forces that continues to this day. The Air Force base in East Haven, named North Concord Radar Station, was part of this escalation of military force, meant to provide a defensive shield against a Soviet air strike. Built in two years (1952-54) at a cost of $21 million, it was part of a nation-wide network of radar installations known as the "early warning system". Both the United States and the Soviet Union possessed nuclear weapons which heightened the tension further and made this radar system essential for defense against attack. The entire population of the United States was put on alert for possible attack. I remember drills in grade school when our teachers ordered us to hide under our desks, or sit in the hallway with our heads between our knees. Citizens were encouraged to build bomb shelters in their basements and most towns had emergency shelters stocked with water and food supplies to last months if not years. The Air Force base in East Haven was part of a network of 44 radar stations meant to provide early warning and protection. This early warning system could scramble aircraft of the Strategic

Air Command (SAC) to intercept threats detected by the radar system. In a remote section of eastern Vermont we discovered a symbol of the Cold War, a decaying reminder of a past era when nuclear annihilation hung over our heads.

Dick, Steve, Dave and I began the day by driving to East Haven, VT and heading up School House Rd. to Radar Rd. where we began the long ride up East Mountain (3,438 ft.). We had planned to spend the afternoon biking the trails of Kingdom Trails Mountain Bike Park in East Burke, VT, but little did we know the ride would last the whole day, traveling almost 18 miles, 9 of the miles pedaling uphill for over 2,000 ft. in elevation gain.

We rode our bikes, mostly uphill for about six miles, climbing the side of the mountain on what was once the main road to the U.S. Air Force base. We cycled steadily and as the road leveled out we entered the village base complex, now a maze of deteriorating buildings, with the surrounding forest creeping in from all sides. We walked around this once thriving military base where over 175 military and civilian personnel once lived. We found the mess hall, Quonset hut dormitories, gymnasium, motor pool garage, showers and other small buildings. Walls of the wrecked structures were coated with graffiti, floors covered in broken glass, metal shards, and assortment of detritus from years of neglect. It is said that many transients have used the buildings for living quarters. The Department of Defense left the base when it no longer found this radar station to be essential to our country's defense systems. Opened in 1956, closed in 1963, the base operated only eight years. It seems like a waste of millions of dollars, but the fear of nuclear attack from the Soviet Union made it an essential part of our military defense system.

After exploring the derelict buildings of the base we were itching to get to the next stage of our explorations, the radar installation. We jumped back on our bikes. The paved road suddenly became steep and our riding turned into walking our bikes. The road to the summit was still in great shape, better than most back roads in New Hampshire. It was a testimony to the engineering prowess of the military and their tendency to bar no expense when committed to military operations. Within another two miles of climbing we spied the towers and numerous remains of the once expansive complex. We explored the immense structures that served to house the radar antennas, receivers and transmitters. Dick discovered an opening into the largest of the structures. We entered and found the walls covered with interesting and creative graffiti along with lots of beer and soda cans. I envisioned many wild parties being held on this isolated mountain top. Dick continued his investigation and found a ladder that led to the roof about five stories up. Once on the roof we had a 360 degree view of the wilderness around East Mountain. There are no trails or roads in the mountains of eastern Vermont, just a vast wilderness stretching to the Connecticut River. The vista provided a sense of stark beauty as we looked at the distant mountain wilderness.

After a thorough investigation of the abandoned military complex we began our ride down the mountain. As we left I thought of the strange, mysterious and tragic history of this isolated military base: The decapitation of a snowmobile rider when he struck a chain strung across the road; the man who died when he fell from the very tower we stood on; the fire that sprang up in one of the dorms; the nine minute UFO sighting that was observed from the radar station in 1961, that coincided with the famous abductions of Barney and Betty Hill by aliens in Franconia Notch. Over the years vandals and severe weather have created a desolate and haunted landscape that is worthy of being a setting for a horror movie. It was now time to be on our way down and mountain, leaving this forsaken place.

It was a quick ride out dropping well over 2,000 ft. in 8 miles. We all used our brakes almost the entire way back to the truck. We took a side road down along the Moose River to a beautiful cascade and waterfall. When we returned to the gate we threw our bikes into my truck and headed to East Burke for dinner at Burke Public House, a great stop for some outstanding beer and pub food. We didn't get to bike the Kingdom Trails in East Burke, but we certainly had a unique experience.

Exploring the Mascot Mine

Entrance to Mascot mine shaft

I first learned about the Mascot Mine when visiting with local hikers in Gorham years ago. I had wanted to hike into the mine for some time, but the opportunity never materialized. I learned that iron ore was first uncovered in the area in the late 1800s. Subsequently, a mine was dug on the side of Mount Hayes yielding galena, the ore containing lead and a low percentage of silver. The mine, owned by the Mascot Mining Company, was in operation for only a few short years, 1881-1887. At the height of operations, the mine employed more than sixty people and produced up to a hundred tons of ore per day which was transportred to Boston, via rail, for smelting. The monthly payroll of about $2,000 added significantly to the rising prosperity of the town (Gorham, NH). (Guy Gosselin, *Among the White Hills. The Life and times of Guy L. Shorey*). The abandoned Mascot Mine was also referred to as the Galena King adit by its workers, referring to the mine opening. The site is now occasioned by rock hounds digging for galena and other minerals. Galena, also called lead glance, is the main ore of lead and a source of silver. Locals also come to picnic at Mascot Pond, located at the base of the mountainside. The mine is no longer worked by miners digging ore, but is now home to five species of bats, that at one time numbered around 2,000. With the white nose syndrome disease running rampant, the number of bats that call the mine home has been reduced to a few hundred.

I was eager to visit the mine site and with several friends, Sandy, Dave, Pam, and Dick, we set out on a beautiful spring day to find the Mascot Mine. Before the hike into the mine site we first paid a visit to the city of Berlin, via the bike/ATV trail connecting the two communities. We began the day by parking our vehicles at the ATV parking lot off Rt. 2 in Gorham. From here we mounted our mountain bikes and headed over the old railroad bridge that spans the Androscoggin River. At one time locomotives of the Whitefield & Jefferson Railroad (later the Boston and Maine Railroad) chugged across the bridge, connecting Berlin and Gorham. The bridge is now used by riders and hikers to access the trail system in and around Berlin and Gorham including the Mahoosuc Mountains Range and the Appalachian Trail. The trail, known as the Presidential Rail Trail, also extends twenty miles westward, terminating at Hazen Road, near the Whitefield Airport.

As we rode to Berlin along the rail trail we were amazed at the number of ATVs storming by us. What's the deal, I asked myself? Why so many ATVs? Later we found out it was opening day of the ATV season, when the myriad of ATV trails in the North Country open up. When we arrived in Berlin the streets were bustling with ATV traffic. More ATV's were on the road than cars. Apparently it's legal in Berlin for ATVs to travel city streets. This was the first time I saw a traffic jam of ATVs.

The ride to Gorham featured cruising along on a relatively flat grade, following the course of the Androscoggin River. The Peaks of the Northern Presidential Range, Mount Adams, Mount Madison and Mount Moriah rose up in the distance. The ride also featured a pull-off for photos at the Cascade Falls Picnic Area, where a picturesque cascade of water tumbles down the rock cliffs to the river below. After arriving in Berlin we quickly ate our lunch at a town park and headed back down the rail trail to begin our hike into the Mascot Mine site.

Before crossing back over the power canal bridge we made a left onto a path that took us along the east side of the power canal. We finally found the sign for the Mahoosuc Trail, after missing it and riding to the hydro-power dam. It was a short 0.7 miles into the mine site and Mascot Pond. When the mine was in operation there were several buildings located at the site, including a boarding house for workers and later converted to a hotel called the Mascot Cottage, a small shed on the ledge at the mine entrance and two buildings at the base of the tailings, near the pond. After arriving at the Pond we scouted for trails to find the mine openings. Now the only evidence that a mine existed was the enormous pile of tailings on the side of the mountain. While Pam, Dave and Sandy looked for trails to the mine entrance, Dick and I decided to scramble up the tailings and scree. Within a few minutes we were standing in front of one of the mine's entries into the mountain. The entrance was blocked by steel grating and a sign was posted with the following: *"The Mascot Mine is an important hibernation site of all five species of bats that winter in New Hampshire. The gate was installed to protect the bats from disturbance and people from the dangerous rotted timbers and loose rock of the mine."*

Looking into the mine I envisioned miners hammering away at the rock and hauling out ore. Now it's just a cool dark opening on the side of a mountain, a hibernation site for bats. We climbed further up the tailings and found another mine entrance that was also blocked by steel grating. This large opening stood about twenty feet high. Dick and I again spent several minutes peering into the mine, amazed at the size of the entrance and considering the fate of the bats that make their home inside the mine. The White Nose Syndrome (WNS), which I mentioned earlier, has decimated the bat population, not only in New Hampshire, but across the Northeast. WNS is a fungus that grows on the bats, causing the bat to eventually succumb to the disease. Since it was first discovered in 2006, over six million bats have died from WNS. Bats play an important role in the natural world as they eat half their body weight in insects every night. (Think of all those mosquitos that get devoured). The long term effects of WNS on the bat population is unknown at this time.

After peering into the abandoned mine shaft we began our climb out of the mine site and onto Leadmine Ledge, which offered spectacular views of the Presidential and Mahoosuc Mountains. We then found a lightly used bushwhack trail that led us back to the Mahoosuc Trail, finally hooking up with Pam, Sandy and Dave at the trailhead. Within a half hour we were back at the parking lot loading our bikes into my truck. The abandoned site of the Mascot Lead Mine is well worth the drive to northern New Hampshire. From Rt. 2 in Gorham it's an easy hike into the mine site and Mascot Pond. After visiting the mine you may want to continue your hike by following the Mahoosuc Trail to Mount Hayes (2,555 ft.) for outstanding views of the Presidential and Carter Mountain Ranges.

The Pond of Safety
A Refuge in the Wilderness

Nestled between the Presidential, Crescent and Pilot Mountain Ranges sits the Pond of Safety. The pond's name is derived from an incident involving four New Hampshire militiamen who fled into the New Hampshire wilderness to avoid arrest. Captured by the British during the outbreak of the Revolutionary War, they were interrogated and then released on the condition they would not take up arms against His Majesty's Royal Army. However, when they returned to Jefferson, their hometown, they were ordered back into the army. True to their word of honor, not to fight against the British, they fled into the wilds to avoid arrest for desertion. James Ryder, Benjamin Hicks, William Danforth and Lazerus Holmes wandered through the wilderness of northern New Hampshire and eventually came upon the isolated, desolate pond, where they found safety from arrest. For three years they lived in their wilderness home near the pond until the war ended, at which time they could return to their homes in Jefferson, where they became leading citizens of their community. In 1836 they were exonerated of all charges for desertion. The Pond was named later to honor their plight.

The story of these four men, who were bound to honor their word, always fascinated me, and I wanted to find the wilderness pond, where for three years it was their home. On a mid-summer day, when the air was thick with moisture and the clouds hung low over the mountains, I decided to find the Pond of Safety. This wasn't a day for trekking to higher elevations, as thunderstorms were predicted later in the day. I knew hiking above tree line would offer no views and pose the risk of being struck by a bolt of lightning. A hike to the Pond of Safety seemed like a good alternative.

Reuben and I drove to Randolph Hill Road, off Rt. 2, found the trailhead for the Carlton Notch Trail and began our walk that would take us over Carlton Notch, the gap between Randolph and Crescent Mountain. There are numerous trails in the Crescent Range, which offer excellent views of the Presidential Range and unusual vistas of the Pliny and Pilot Ranges. The network of trails in the area is maintained by the Randolph Mountain Club.

After a 1.5 mile hike on the Carlton Notch Trail I reached the junction with the Underhill Trail, which would take me into the Pond of Safety. Even though it was midsummer, there was a tinge of fall along the trail. Bunchberries were bright red, trillium leaves were dying, bluebeads were showing their deep rich blues, the leaves of Indian poke were wilting and the fronds of ferns were drying out and turning brown. I even found several maple leaves with brilliant red and orange colors lying on the ground. These were indications that the autumn season was approaching; a reminder of the never ending cycle of seasonal change.

The Underhill Trail made a gradual descent, through magnificent stands of birch, spruce and fir. In the early 1900s this landscape was cut over and made barren by the woodman's saw. Now the forest stands as a testament to its ability to recover. This forest also serves as a reminder of the passage of the Weeks Act and creation of the White Mountain National Forest, preserving the vast White Mountain wilderness for future generations. The Underhill Trail was named in honor of Miriam and Robert Underhill, one-time residents of Randolph. Miriam and Robert are legendary in the hiking world, and pioneering giants in mountaineering. They climbed some of the highest summits in Europe and the western United States as well as in New England. It is noteworthy to mention that Miriam was the first woman to summit all of the New Hampshire 48 in winter in the early 1960s. At this time there wasn't a managed trail system leading to many of the peaks, nor were there well maintained roads leading to trailheads. It was also a time when women weren't especially accepted in a male dominated endeavor.

The Underhill Trail, which can be difficult to follow in places, but well blazed, led Reuben and I to a Forest Service Road, and eventually to the shore line on a graded path. I sat by the Pond of Safety admiring the view of the water and the mountains rising in the distance. A cooling breeze was blowing off the water, providing an interlude to the heat and humidity of the day. The stillness and solitude were a welcome relief from the hubbub of my previous hike, last week when I climbed Mount Washington and Mount Jefferson. The trails were loaded with people squawking on their cell phones, blabbing back and forth, stopping in the middle of the trail to catch their breath and craning their necks for limited views through the cloud cover. I felt like I was in the Macy's Thanksgiving Day parade. To cope with this absurdity I joined in on the cackling, taking my time and talking to other hikers. I came to accept my plight and turned into another parade participant, marching to Mount Washington. Life is all about finding compromise.

Today was a welcomed change. I lounged next to the pond, taking in the stillness. A raven cried above and colorful dragon flies darted above the water. Reuben took the opportunity to paddle around the pond, cooling off and drinking plenty of water for the return hike. I saw not a soul for almost the entire day and had my thoughts to myself. I look forward to these solo hikes, when it's just Reuben and me. He's the best hiking companion I could have. He never complains, doesn't babble (occasionally will bark), has no cell phone, and is always ready for a hike.

After an hour of doing nothing, except eating lunch, I reluctantly started my hike back to Randolph Hill Road, this time taking the Four Soldiers Path. Obviously, the trail was named for the four militiamen who were accused of desertion and made their home in the area to escape arrest. This infrequently traveled path skirts around the southeastern slope of Randolph Mountain, climbing steadily through extensive logged areas with expansive growth of ferns, hobblebush and raspberries. In several of the cleared areas the vegetation had completely overgrown the trail, making it difficult to follow. However, the trail was well marked and wet areas were protected by numerous bog bridges. Signs of bear and deer browsing on the vegetation were evident all along the trail. After passing by a sign reading "The Eye of the Needle" we came to a spur path that led to a view of King Ravine and the Northern Presidential Range. Clouds were lowering over the high peaks, signaling a new wave of storms approaching from the southeast.

Reuben and I skedaddled from our perch on the side of Randolph Mountain and continued our journey. As the sky darkened, droplets of rain began to filter through the trees tops. We scurried along the trail, hoping to get to the trailhead before the storm caught us. We arrived just in time to beat the deluge. Once back to the truck we were ready to return home. On our way back we turned off Rt. 2 onto Durand Road, a scenic route passing many older Randolph summer homes. We also came to the site of the

Ravine House, a quintessential hotel that was a mainstay for hikers and trail builders from 1884 to 1960 when it closed. It was razed in 1963 and all that remains of the hotel today is a vacant lot, the fishing pond and an historic marker.

This circuitous route to the Pond of Safety is approximately eight miles in length, starting and ending from the parking lot at the end Randolph Hill Road. The trails are well blazed, but use care as some sections are difficult to follow, due to the overgrowth covering the foot bed. Enjoy a day hiking into history and experiencing the solitude of the Pond of Safety.

Chapter 2 - Lakes Region

I only went out for a walk and finally concluded to stay out till sundown, for going out, I found, was really going in.

John Muir

The Lakes Region of New Hampshire offers a multitude of hiking opportunities, from state parks, conservation lands, to town forests. Many hiking and biking trails are located near Lake Winnipesaukee known as the "Grande Dame" of the region, but other lakes such as Newfound, Squam, and Winnisquam dot the area. Hiking trails are numerous in the three mountain ranges that dominate the area: Squam, Belknap and Ossipee. The following represents a few of my more memorable hikes in the region where I make my home.

The Lakes Triple Crown

Preface

Maybe you've heard of the Triple Crown of horse racing — winning the Kentucky Derby, Belmont Stakes and the Preakness. There's also the Triple Crown in long distance hiking, The Appalachian, Pacific Crest and the Continental Divide Trails. In the Lakes Region we have our own Triple Crown, traversing the three major mountain ranges, Belknap, Squam and Ossipee. Traversing each range end-to-end is not only a considerable challenge, but also a rewarding accomplishment. Each traverse will take an entire day of steady, non-stop hiking.

The Belknap Range lies to the west of Lake Winnipesaukee and stretches across three towns, Alton, Gilmanton and Gilford. The highest peak in the Range is Belknap Mountain. Other lesser peaks including Klem, Mack, Straightback, West Quarry, East

Quarry, Anna and Major run from north to south. The Belknap Range Trail (13 miles) traverses the entire range from Mount Rowe in the north to Mount Major in the south. The traverse features stellar views of the Lakes Region as well as the Ossippee and Sandwich Mountain Ranges. The trail also passes along the shores of Round Pond with several campsites on the south end of the pond. The trail features distinctive trails markers (BRT).

The Ossipee Mountain Range lies across from the Belknap Range on the east side of Lake Winnipesaukee. If you were to view the Ossipee Range from above it would look like a giant circle, 40 miles around. The mountain range is what's left of an extinct volcano, the subsurface remains of the magma chamber. The center of the mountain range is the bottom of the caldera, the volcanic cone that collapsed. The traverse of the western side of the Range falls almost entirely within the Castle in the Clouds Conservation Area (Lakes Region Conservation Trust). It runs from Mt. Roberts (2,582 ft.) to Mt. Black Snout (2,803 ft.). The High Ridge Trail, which is aptly named, traverses the upper reaches of the conservation area and follows the crest of the mountain range.

The Squam Mountain Range, running east to west, is primarily a ridge of peaks rising above the northern end of Squam Lake. It is the remains of ancient volcanic action millions of years ago as the Pangea Super Continent was breaking away from what is now North America. The major peaks are Doublehead, Squam, Percival, Morgan, Webster, Livermore and Cotton. The entire ridgeline has outstanding views and also features rock scrambles, ledges, summit ponds and waterfalls.

The Belknap Range Traverse

Belknap Range Trail marker

On a beautiful summer day my dog Reuben, and I met four close friends to traverse the Belknap Range using the Belknap Range Trail. The hike would take us from Mount Major to Mount Rowe, a thirteen mile trek across the entire range. The clear day was a welcome relief from the rain that we experienced the past few days and I was fortunate to have good friends along for the day. This was truly a day to appreciate the mountains which are a gift to those who live in the Lakes Region.

The Belknap Range traverse or BRT is a challenging all-day hike that is not recommended for the beginner hiker or families with small children. It crosses the summits of eight mountains: Major, Straightback, Anna, Mack, Klem, Belknap, Gunstock and Rowe. The entire length of the trail is marked with BRT signage as well as blazes. Be sure to watch for the BRT signs and stay on the trail as there are several other trails that join the BRT. Many hikers have taken one of these trails and ended up miles from their intended route. The Alton Fire Dept. and N.H. Fish and Game Dept. can readily attest to this fact, as they have made numerous rescues of lost hikers each year. It's essential that you have a map of the Belknap Range. Maps can be purchased from many local libraries or down loaded at (*belknaprangetrails.org/belknap-range-trail-map*). You can also purchase the AMC Southern New Hampshire Trail Map and the Lakes Region Conservation Trust, Belknap Range map at area stores. It's also important to have a compass and know how to use it in conjunction with the map. The hiker should also have at least two liters of water, plenty of food and snacks, proper footwear, and appropriate clothing for the 13 mile hike. It's also necessary to have a car parked at the end of the traverse or have someone pick you up and drive you back to your car where you started.

We began our hike at the Mount Major parking lot. The BRT starts from the right side of the parking lot and is marked with blue blazes. At 1.4 miles we reached the ledges and several spectacular viewing points looking east to Lake Winnipesaukee and the Ossipee Mountains. Soon afterward we were standing on the Mount Major summit and spied the foundation of a cabin that once stood there. From this point we found the BRT signage and blue blazes. There are several trail intersections that can lead you off in another direction, so be sure to follow the blue blazed BRT signs. At 2.7 miles we arrived at the summit of Straightback Mountain. Here we found open rock ledges that offer stunning views to the west. After a short snack break we descended from Straightback, continuing to follow blue blazes. The trail is well marked and winds through a beautiful mix of hardwoods. At 3.6 miles the Precipice Trail diverges left, and soon after we found the summit of Mount Anna. There are no views from the summit, but a short spur or goat path leads to an old pasture that provides views to the south and west. We continued on the trail, dropping down off Anna and climbing to Mount Mack at 5.2 miles.

After having lunch on Mount Mack we followed the trail along the ridge to Mount Klem, following red diamond markers. The ridge offers impressive views to the east. We then dropped down to Round Pond, a beautiful mountain pond occupied by a thriving beaver colony. We followed green blazes and at 8.2 miles we arrived at the junction with the Boulder Trail (blue blazes). We made our way up a steep incline through an extensive rock slide and boulder field and at 8.5 miles the trail merges with the East Gilford Trail (yellow blazes). Within a half mile we ate our lunch at the summit of Belknap Mountain, beneath the iconic fire tower. All along the way were fields of blueberries just starting to ripen. We had the pleasure of munching on a few berries and within a couple weeks the fields would be filled with ripe, succulent berries.

After a snack break we continued on to Gunstock. Just before the climb to the summit of Gunstock, we diverged left onto a white blazed trail that skirts around the ski slopes. From this point the trail begins its final leg to Mount Rowe along the newly constructed trail following the western slope of Gunstock and arriving at Mount Rowe. The BRT follows a service road down to the ski area and the parking lot where our cars were waiting for us.

Our traverse covered 13 miles (Mount Major to Gunstock parking lots) and took us 9 hours at a leisurely pace. At the cars we said our farewells and looked forward to our next adventure in the mountains of the Lakes Region. I hope some of you will take the challenge and hike the traverse. It's an experience that you'll long remember.

The Squam Range Traverse

Tom, Karen, Sandy, Karen and Fran looking east from Mount Squam

Under beautiful bright blue sky, Reuben and I met five close friends. Our plan was to traverse the Squam Mountain Range, from Sandwich Notch to the terminus of the Cotton Mountain Trail on Rt. 113, 13.1 miles with some of the most breathtaking views in the area. After meeting Karen, Tom, Karen, Fran and Sandy, we drove to the Cotton Mountain Trailhead. Since this is an end-to-end hike we had to leave a car at this parking lot and then drive to the start of our hike at the Mead Base Camp, just off Sandwich Notch Road in Sandwich. We arrived at 7:30 am. Parking here offered plenty of room for several cars, plus the added attraction of hiking 0.6 miles on the Bearcamp River Trail. The trail passes Beede Falls, a 37-foot high cascade that plunges into a shallow, sandy pool. The trail also took us past Cow Cave, an interesting rock formation. It's alleged that a cow strayed from a nearby farm and was lost for days. When the local gentry found the cow it was hiding in this cave, protected from the harsh New England weather.

We then turned right, heading north on Sandwich Notch Road and after a half mile we hit the northern terminus of the Crawford-Ridgepole Trail, the main trail that would take us across the Squam Range. Soon after starting on the Crawford-Ridgepole trail we encountered several steep climbs out of Sandwich Notch. This was the beginning of numerous rock climbs, which reminded me that this range isn't particularly high in elevation, but is very rugged in sections and hikers should wear proper hiking footwear (no sandals, flip-flops, crocs or high heels). It always amazes me when I see people wearing the most inappropriate footwear when hiking in the mountains. At 1.4 miles, just below the summit of Doublehead Mountain we came to our first viewpoint to the North. We descended steeply down a rock face coming to the junction with the Doublehead Trail, which travels south to its terminus just off Route 113.

We continued our journey hiking over Mount Squam (2,223 ft.) and then onto Mount Percival (2,212 ft.) at 5.5 miles and Mount Morgan (2,220 ft.) at 6.5 miles. This stretch of trail between Doublehead and Morgan was surprisingly rugged, with many scrambles over rock ledges, but we were blessed with amazing viewpoints to the north and south. We stopped for a short water and snack break at the "potholes", an interesting geological feature left behind from the last ice age. Karen remarked, "It's worthhiking up here for this beautiful treasure." Reuben agreed and decided to take a well-deserved swim in the water that fills the potholes. On Percival, which has outstanding views of Squam Lake, and the Belknap and Ossipee Mountain Ranges, we encountered numerous trekkers, hiking the Morgan-Percival Loop Trails. This is a very popular day hike for those who want a short, but strenuous hike with breathtaking views of the Lakes Region.

After a lunch break on Morgan we resumed the traverse heading to Mount Webster (2,076 ft.). It's interesting to note that so many locations (towns, mountains, trails, roads) are named for our illustrious and most famous N. H. statesmen. Continuing on over Mount Webster at 8.45 miles, we came to another of many viewpoints that afforded us vistas to the south and east.

From this point forward the trail became softer, winding through beautiful groves of hemlock and balsam fir. After hiking over nine miles the path offered a welcome relief to our sore feet. As the day wore on we felt ourselves becoming weary and looking forward to the end of the trail. However, we knew that we had another five miles to go before the end of our journey. We reached Mount Livermore (1,500 ft.) at 11.3 miles and continued on with few breaks until we got to the base of Cotton Mountain, the last summit to stand between us and Rt. 113. This was a surprisingly hard climb at the end of the day, as we trudged uphill to the top of a rock stairway and the summit of Cotton Mountain (1,200 ft.). After summiting Cotton Mountain it was a short one mile hike to the parking lot. We knew it must have been a long day of hiking because Reuben laid down and went to sleep next to our car. Even though our feet and legs felt like lead and our backs were sore, our spirits soared with the thought of returning to Sandwich to pick up our cars, and better yet, having some cold refreshments at the Corner House Inn.

The Ossipee Range Traverse

Reuben gazing toward Lake Winnipesaukee

The Ossipee Range traverse follows the western ridgeline of the Ossipee Mountains and is located within the Castle in the Clouds Conservation Area, a 5,381 acre property owned and stewarded by the Lakes Region Conservation Trust. The trails are maintained by a group of dedicated volunteers who spend hundreds of hours mowing, clearing blowdowns and brushing vegetation from the footpath. Almost the entire system of trails of over 28 miles is made up of old carriage roads. They were constructed in the late nineteenth century by Thomas Gustave Plant (1859-1941), who made his fortune in the shoe manufacturing industry, retiring as a millionaire at age fifty one, focusing his time and money on building this palatial "country" estate. Prior to Plant's ownership, much of the current property was owned by B.F Shaw who operated a hotel. Mount Shaw, the highest mountain in the Ossipee Range, is named in his honor.

Most hikers interested in hiking the Ossipee Range begin by parking at the end of Ossipee Park Road directly off of Route 171. Sandy, Dave, Fran and I began our hike on the Mount Roberts Trail, which is a 2.5 mile climb to Mount Roberts, a 1,269 ft. elevation gain. This trail took us over several rock outcrops with wonderful vistas. From the summit of Mount Roberts (2,582 ft.) we began a long ridge walk of 5.3 miles to Mount Shaw. The High Ridge Trail is mostly a level, easy walk, following an old carriage road. At about 1.3 miles from Mount Roberts, we found an old road that took us to the summit of Faraway Mountain, and a cell phone tower. Along the route we discovered old machinery that may have been used long ago to maintain the system of carriage roads found throughout the property.

As we approached Mount Shaw (2,990 ft.) we began a steady ascent to the summit. The temperature and humidity continued to climb and we were thankful to reach the summit and find a cool breeze blowing. As we ate our lunch, we looked out over the eastern section of the range. We remarked that there are numerous other trails to hike with access from Routes 25 and 16. After finishing our lunch we proceeded down the Black Snout Trail, 0.4 miles, to a precipice called Black Snout (2,803 ft.) which provided hazy views of the mountains to the south and west.

We then began our decent down the ridge on Turtleback Mountain Trail which consists of numerous switchbacks on carriage roads, until we reached the summit of Turtleback Mountain (2,200 ft.). The peak of this mountain is made up of columnar basalt and resembles the shell of a turtle, thus the name Turtleback Mountain. We also found the remains of an old observation tower constructed by Thomas Plant for guests to view the mountains and beyond. After taking in the views we worked our way over to the Bald Knob and the Bald Knob Cutoff Trail for our final decent, down to the Shannon Brook Trail and back to our car. Along the Bald Knob Cutoff Trail we found the famous basalt columnar formations, which are lava deposits that form various geometric columns. Similar formations in much greater quality and quantity can be found at Devil's Post Pile National Monument in California. However, we have our own devil's post pile right here in the Lakes Region.

When we returned to the car we were surprised at the mileage we covered, 18.8 miles. We were weary but happy that we completed the "Winni Triple Traverse." The trail system in the 5,381 acre property of the Lakes Region Conservation Trust offers not only the trails we took, but many more on carriage roads and foot paths well-marked and easy to follow, with varying degrees of challenge and difficulty. A guidebook and map of the hiking trails can be purchased from the Lakes Region Conservation Trust by calling 603-253-3301 or visiting their web site (*lrct.org*). All proceeds go to benefit the stewardship of this conservation area. Many thanks to the Lakes Region Conservation Trust for their work in stewarding this land for our enjoyment.

The Three Ponds Trail and Beyond

Come forth into the light of things
Let Nature be your teacher.

William Wordsworth

The sign on the Kiosk at the trailhead reads, "Welcome to the quieter corner of the White Mountains. The Three Ponds Trail and the surrounding area offers, beauty, challenge and varied recreational opportunities." This yellow blazed trail serves as a gateway to other trails leading to Carr Mountain (3,440 ft.), Mount Kineo (3,313 ft.), the Hubbard Brook Trail and the Hubbard Brook Experimental Forest. The trail is accessed from Stinson Lake Road in the town of Rumney, 6.9 miles from Rt. 25. The trail mostly follows old logging roads and recently constructed snowmobile trails.

Trailhead of Three Ponds Trail on Stinson Lake Road

On a lovely, warm and sunny day my wife Nancy decided to join me and our dog Reuben on a short 2.3 mile hike to the Three Ponds Shelter, which sits above the largest of the three ponds the trail is named for. I have hiked this trail and the other connecting trails many times in the past and have always appreciated the solitude of the experience in a "quieter corner of the White Mountains."

We decided to only hike to Middle Pond and the shelter. However, for those who would like an easy five mile day hike you can take the Three Ponds Trail, returning to the parking lot via the Donkey Hill Cut-Off and Mt. Kineo Trails. This mostly level loop will take you past scenic ponds, beaver flowages and wetlands. If you are interested in a longer, multiday hike of twenty miles take the Three Ponds Trail to the Hubbard Brook Trail returning to the parking lot via the Mt. Kineo Trail. A primitive campsite is available along the trail.

As we began our hike up a moderate grade I was reminded that this section of the trail, as well as other sections, were obliterated by Hurricane Irene in 2011. The US Forest Service has done a remarkable job in reconstructing the trail. I also reflected on the fact that the U.S. Forest Service does a remarkable job in trail construction and maintenance, given their limited resources. It seems that over the course of several years Congress continues to cut funding for this agency, yet they are able to manage The White Mountain National Forest for a variety of interests and needs.

At 0.1 mile the Mt. Kineo Trail diverges to the right and at 0.5 mile the Carr Mountain Trail cuts to the left. The Carr Mountain Trail leads to a side path, gaining the summit of Carr Mountain at 2.9 miles. At the summit are the remains of an old fire tower. Sweeping views of the Baker River Valley can be taken in by perching on several rock outcrops. This trail continues north for three miles, ending at the New Hampshire Fish Hatchery in Warren.

Continuing along the Three Ponds Trail we encountered two inactive beaver ponds, and watched a flock of Flycatchers and Cedar Waxwings swooping and fluttering around the dead trees in the beaver bog. The world around us was full of life, yet we stood in the stillness and solitude. The trail meandered along the right side of Sucker Brook. The brook was crystal clear with many deep holes for wading or swimming, which Reuben enjoyed doing several times. I also remarked to Nancy that the gentle sound of the brook is mesmerizing as we walked along in silence. Thanks to the local and state snow mobile organizations, bridges provided safe and dry crossings of all streams. After a gradual climb of about two miles we began our decent to the largest of the three ponds. At 2.3 miles on the south end of Middle Pond a side trail led up to a six-person shelter. While we sat on the shore and had our snack we noticed a canoe at the far end of the pond. It was probably a couple of folks staying at the shelter who may have brought their canoe with them. While we were resting and enjoying the view we met our first fellow hikers, a family from Norwich, Connecticut enjoying the day just as we were.

After our break we headed back down the trail to the parking lot. It was a leisurely walk mostly downhill to our waiting car. As we drove down Stinson Lake Road towards Rumney, we considered stopping for coffee at the Common Tavern, but thought better of it as we needed to get home so we could finish daily chores. This half-day adventure was a welcome respite from the tasks and responsibilities we encounter daily. We are fortunate to live in the mountains of the Lakes Region.

Bald Ledge and the Winona Legend

When the blood in your veins returns to the sea, and the earth in your bones returns to the ground, perhaps you will then remember that this land does not belong to you, it is you who belongs to this land.

Native American teaching

Located close to my home in New Hampton lie a series of ledges known as Bald Ledge. These cliffs sit high above Winona Lake and offer outstanding views of Lakes Winona and Waukewan, as well as the Sandwich, Ossipee and Squam Mountain Ranges. The ledges and surrounding property are owned by the town of New Hampton. The trail and views from the ledges are maintained by the New Hampton Conservation Commission. The trail can be easily reached via a class VI road starting from Sky Pond Road and Sky Pond, a spring fed pond that is well known by fly fishermen.

One day I received a phone call from Frank, an old friend, who wanted to get together for a short hike in the area. Bald Ledge was the perfect answer to his request. These ledges are part of the Beech Hill Ridge that extends from close to the Pemigewasset

View of Winona Lake from Bald Ledge, New Hampton

River to Winona Lake. In precolonial times, this ridge served as a transportation route for Native Americans. It allowed them a safe and direct pathway between the Pemigewasset River and Lake Winnipesaukee to trade and barter for food and clothing at the fishing weirs, located at what is now Weirs Beach. Along this ridge, in an area that was known as Indian Mortar Farm, is a mortar sunk into the surface of a rock cliff. The mortar was used to grind corn or other plants and seeds into a useable food source. The mortar pestle is said to have been destroyed when some ruffians threw it over the cliff and it shattered into several pieces.

Legend also has it that an Algonquin Princess, Winona, was sitting atop Bald Ledge one winter's day, when members of a warring tribe found her and tried to take her prisoner. She escaped down the cliff and began to run across the frozen lake. But to her misfortune she fell through the ice and drowned. As this story became more commonplace, the lake, known previously as Long Pond, was renamed Lake Winona in honor of the fallen princess.

Bald Ledge also holds an important place in local history, especially for the Town of New Hampton. The ledge was the site of New Hampton's first Old Home Day in 1898. In those days, before autos ruled the transportation world, people walked or drove horse-drawn wagons to the site. On that first Old Home Day, town residents made their way to Bald Ledge on foot or in wagons. Today Frank and I likewise would be on foot, taking the same route.

So enough of these history lessons, and back to the hike. Frank and I met in New Hampton and drove up Dana Hill Road to Lower Oxbow Road. At the intersection there's a canoe launch sign that directs motorists to Sky Pond. Follow Lower Oxbow Road to Sky Pond Road on the left and after a short distance you will find a well maintained parking lot. The pond is well regarded in the fishing community as a premier trout pond, for fly fishing only.

After parking the car Frank and I began our hike by heading up the woods road that leads to Sky Pond State Forest. It's possible that this woods road was once a section of the Old Province Road, one of the earliest highways in New Hampshire. It was authorized in 1765 as a supply route from the tidewater port of Durham to the colony's northern settlements in the Coos. Sections of this colonial highway are still used today, Routes 4 and 107. Other sections have been lost to farmland and the wooded countryside. However, this section of the road can still be used by hikers and leads to Beech Hill Road in New Hampton.

Within a quarter mile, the trail takes a sharp left at a gate. On the corner we found a substantial cellar hole and barn foundation that was once the farmstead (1828-1880) of Orlando Huckins. Following this woods road, that is being overtaken by vegetation, Frank and I entered an older stand of trees and began looking for the small trail sign nailed to a tree. Upon finding the sign we turned right onto a well-groomed path leading us to the overlook of Bald Ledge. Frank was amazed at the views we had after hiking for less than a mile. Directly below the ledge sits Winona Lake and farther out we viewed Lakes Waukewan and Winnipesaukee. To the north we could see Squam Lake and the entire Sandwich and Ossipee Mountain Ranges. After a brief respite for a snack and water, we headed back and within a less than an hour we completed our short hike.

The Bald Ledge area can also be reached by the Lake Road that runs off of Winona Road. Follow the Lake Road along the perimeter of Winona Lake. As you near the end of the road there is a small sign that directs you to the trail, taking you to Bald Ledge. This trail is somewhat longer and steeper, and not recommended for a leisurely walk. Either way you choose, a hike to Bald Ledge will be a memorable experience. This is a gem in the lakes region that should not be missed.

A Cardigan Mountain Adventure

You need mountains, long staircases don't make good hikers.

Amit Kalantri

When Annemarie and I reached the trailhead of the Holt Trail we stopped for a few minutes to read the warning sign: *This is the shortest but most difficult trail to the summit of Mount Cardigan. The upper ledges are steep and the scramble up the ledges is much more difficult than any other trail in this section and one of the most difficult in New England.* This trail was for us! Annemarie, my youngest daughter, was visiting from her home in Bozeman, Montana. She had moved there, with her husband Derek to hike in the Rockies and fish the mountain steams close to their home. Even though Cardigan is not a 10,000 foot peak

Annemarie and Reuben on the summit of Cardigan Mountain

as Annemarie is used to hiking (it's slightly over 3,000 feet) it offers spectacular 360-degree views at the summit and the Holt Trail would provide a challenge equal to any.

We began our hike on the Manning Trail, and soon reached the intersection with the Holt Trail, where we read the sign that warned us of hiking this steep trail, especially in wet or icy conditions. As we began our climb, the trail became increasing precipitous. I had hiked most of the trails of Cardigan, but never the Holt. I was looking forward to reaching the summit with terrific views of the Sandwich Range, the White Mountains, Mount Monadnock, Camel's Hump in Vermont and Pleasant Mountain in Maine.

As we made our way up the Holt Trail it became increasingly difficult with vertiginous ledges to maneuver over and around. The trail leads directly to the summit and is not to be taken lightly. It should not be climbed by families with small children or anyone who is not used to scrambling up rock ledges. Nor should this trail be climbed in rainy and/or cold temperatures. Fortunately for Annie and me it was a dry, warm day and the conditions were perfect for rock climbing. Reuben, my dog, is always looking for alternative routes, other than the rock faces, but in some sections of the trail there were no alternatives and he had to be boosted up the ledges. We were careful to stay on the trail. At times we veered away from the blazed path, at what looked like an easier route, but these paths turned into dead-ends with 50 and 60 foot drop-offs.

At last we reached the summit. The Holt Trail, which is just over a mile in length, was a challenging but rewarding climb. I was surprised that it took us over an hour to hike this one mile section of trail. When we arrived at the fire tower we were greeted by the crisp, cool air of autumn, and a brisk wind was gusting over the rock face of the mountain. We layered up and I was glad we brought extra clothing. So many times I've been fooled by the weather on the summits. It may be 60 or 70 degrees at the base of the mountain but much cooler at the summit with biting winds, making the wind chills below freezing.

Most mountains that are 3,000 ft. are not above tree-line, but in 1855 fires swept over Cardigan Mountain destroying the forest. Without vegetation to hold the soil in place, it was washed away by wind-driven rain and melting snow. Even though forest fires have destroyed many mountain top forests, they have given us some of the most memorable views in New England (The Baldface Peaks in Evans Notch, Mount Major in Alton). However, given the fact that the summit ledges of Cardigan are above tree line there is a significant risk for hikers to become lost on the summit in fog, rain or snow. With very few trail markers above tree line, many hikers become disoriented in bad weather and find themselves lost and have to phone the Cardigan AMC Lodge for help or even call in a rescue. After eating our lunch, admiring the views and chatting with other hikers, we began our way down the mountain, not by way of the Holt trail (not recommended for descent), but taking a more leisurely route back to the parking lot via the Clark Trail. As we began our ride home we looked forward to stopping at Cardigan Mountain Orchard to purchase apples and cider. What could be better than a day spent with my youngest daughter and my dog Reuben on a beautiful mountain hike in Central New Hampshire and finishing the day with a drink of freshly pressed apple cider!

Rock Around Rumney Rocks

Those who contemplate the beauty of the earth find reserves of strength that will endure as long as life lasts. There is something infinitely healing in the repeated refrains of nature — the assurance that dawn comes after night, and spring after winter.
Rachel Carson

Steve hiking to the summit of Rattlesnake Mountain

In Rumney, New Hampshire you can find some of the best hiking trails and rock climbing in New England. Yet it is an area few people are aware of, except the rock climbing community and the locals. When I mention Rattlesnake Mountain, most people reply, "Oh ya, that short hike in Holderness, which has a beautiful view of Squam Lake." I say, "No, the other Rattlesnake in Rumney." They then give me a puzzled look and respond, "Where's Rumney"? Usually, most outdoor adventurers are looking toward the summits of the Whites and speed up I-93 to tackle the "big mountains." Little do they know that Rumney, just west of Plymouth holds great opportunities for hiking.

The cliffs on Rattlesnake Mountain, called Rumney Rocks, are well known by the rock climbing community. During the summer months the parking and camping areas on Buffalo Road are filled with enthusiastic rock climbers. It's one of the premier rock climbing destinations in New England. Climbers from all over the area visit during the fall season. It has become a focal point of sport climbing, which is a term used by climbers that refers to using permanent anchors fixed to the rock. It's truly amazing that there are over 40 different rock climbing routes on these cliffs.

Rumney, just off the beaten path, is the quintessential New England town. It was settled in 1765 and was once the home of many mills and tanneries located along Stinson Brook, flowing out of Stinson Lake. The town square is bounded by colonial homes, churches, a library, inn, pub and coffee shop.

Three mountains dominate the area, Rattlesnake (1,594 ft.), Carr (3,453 ft.) and Stinson (2,900 ft.), which can be climbed via well marked trails. A fourth mountain, Kineo (3,313 ft.), is trailless, but the base of the mountain is accessed following the Mount Kineo Trail to the height of land. One can then bushwhack to the summit. Both Stinson and Carr mountains were once the site of fire towers and the remnants of these towers are still evident today. All four mountains rise at an angle between the Pemigewasset and Baker Rivers. The trailheads are all within a 45 minute drive from my home in New Hampton.

Steve and I, along with our dogs Skipper and Reuben, began our climb on a clear, cold afternoon, with winter knocking at the door. We wanted to hike for half a day, knew that Rattlesnake was less than three miles round-trip and offered outstanding views of the Baker River Valley. The parking area for the trailhead is located off Buffalo Road, about three miles from the town square in Rumney. As we were nearing the trailhead we passed the large parking area for rock climbers thinking that this was where we could park, but further on we found a small open area that marked the beginning of the Rattlesnake Trail.

We commenced the hike along a stream that was beginning to freeze with the coming of colder weather. There was minimal snow and ice on the ground, so it made for easy walking, with no need for trail crampons or other traction on our feet. We followed an old logging road that was probably used to haul timber off the mountain. We made our way along this well-defined path until it started to climb steeply to the ridge that would eventually lead us to the summit. Within a mile we came to a fork in the trail. This marked the section of trail that makes a loop over the cliff face of Rattlesnake. We chose to take the left-hand path and began our final thrust to the summit. It was a clear day with only a few wispy clouds in the sky. As we neared the summit, Stinson Mountain dominated the view to the east. We could also see the summit of Carr Mountain in the west. We continued along the cliff edge, taking in the views and looking down at the cliffs below hoping to see rock climbers working their way toward us. There were none to see, so we began our hike down the mountain and back to the trailhead. On our way off the summit we noticed several dead trees, blackened skeletons standing upright, reminding us of the forest fire that swept across the mountain several years ago. It appeared that the area was bounding back to its natural state, demonstrating how nature has a way of recovering from the devastating effects of fire.

Little known Rattlesnake Mountain would make an enjoyable day hike of about two to three hours for the entire family. The rewarding views and moderate hike to the summit offer a wonderful opportunity to explore an area that many people miss. You may also want to follow the rock climbing trails to the base of the mountain to watch rock or ice climbers scaling the cliffs. On the way back to the Lakes Region you may also want to stop at the Quincy Bog Natural Area located on Quincy Road, just off Rt. 25 for a one-mile hike around the fen.

Another Day in the Belknap Range

The crow sees me.

They stretch their glossy necks

In the tallest branches

Of green trees. I am

Entering the Kingdom.

Mary Oliver

After spending the summer and fall hiking in the Adirondacks of New York State, the White Mountains and other ranges, I decided to return to the Belknap Range. I hadn't hiked in the Belknap Range since early June, and there are so many interesting trails to explore. I needed to reacquaint myself with this great system of trails. I checked out the map I had purchased at the Gilford Library and elected to take a circuitous route starting from Glidden Road in Gilford, taking the Dave Roberts Trail to West and East Quarry Mountains, and continuing to South Straightback, Anna, Mack, Klem and Rand Mountains. This route would bring me back to Glidden Road.

Trail signs on summit of Straightback Mountain

It was a wonderful fall day, with plenty of brilliant sunshine. However, the days were getting shorter, so Reuben and I needed to get an early start. I drove to Glidden Road, off Rt. 11A. This is a dead end road with limited parking. Since I have a 4-WD pickup I continued up Old Clough Road, a Class VI Rd. After a few hundred yards of a very rough ride, I found a large open area where I could park. From here Reuben and I began our day.

We followed an old logging road for about 0.5 mile that ran between West Quarry and Rand Mountains. We then came to the junction with the Dave Roberts trail (white blazes). We turned left and began our schlep up to the summit of West Quarry. The Dave Roberts Trail is named for the avid hiker who cut and blazed many of the trails in the Belknap Range. Dave single-handedly built 30 to 50 miles of trails. He also drew up the first trail map of the area and those of us who hike in the Belknaps have Dave to thank for the trail system we cherish today.

The trail to West Quarry led us through a stand of hardwoods and then to the base of West Quarry. Here I found the remains of an old granite quarry. This small quarry was active in the late 1800s. On this site the rough granite was cut and worked into building blocks. Many of these cobbled stones were used to pave the streets of Laconia in the late 1800s to early 1900s. Cut stone was also shipped to Concord and Boston, used for foundations, cemetery markers, fence posts and outdoor entry steps. At the site there are still tools and equipment, such as cables, articulated iron rods, drills, wedges and even a winch used to quarry the stone.

After exploring the site we began a steep assent up West Quarry. I needed to climb carefully as the blazes were faded and not easily seen. We reached the first viewpoint that looks toward Mounts Rand and Gunstock. After this steep rock scramble the trail leveled off and looped through a stand of majestic hemlocks. Upon reaching the summit of West Quarry (1,894 ft.), which is located just off the trail, we continued on to East Quarry. The trail descended sharply into a col and then rose precipitously to the summit. Here we encountered a view of the southerly Belknap Range and Lake Winnipesaukee. I was intrigued by the sign that read "caves". It pointed to a cliff, with gigantic boulders strewn down the mountain side. The Belknap Range is noted for the many porcupines that inhabit these rock outcroppings and I was concerned that Reuben in his curiosity would encounter one of these prickly varmints, so we hustled off toward South Straightback Mountain. After a very steep climb, we hiked over rock ledges until we reached the junction with the Belknap Range Trail (BRT). Here we turned right following the BRT, marked with blue blazes, and continued on our journey onto Mounts Anna, Mack and Klem.

The trail to Anna was difficult to follow, because of a thick covering of leaves that obscured the trail. This is a precaution that any hiker needs take when hiking late in the fall and early winter. The trail is often hidden by a thick carpet of downed leaves and one must be careful to stay on the trail by following the blazes. It's important to keep an eye out for the blazes, look for cut logs and branches that border the trail, and always carry a map and compass. Of course knowing how to use them is critically important. Because of the shrinking daylight hours, hiking in the late fall also carries with it two other important safeguards: a headlamp or flashlight with spare batteries, and extra clothing for warmth when the sun begins to set and temperatures fall quickly.

The walk to Mount Klem is one of my favorite parts of the trail. It follows the ridge connecting the two mountains, Mount Klem and Mount Mack, and winds through beautiful stands of spruce and fir with several views of the distant mountains and lakes along the way. When I checked my watch I found that Reuben and I had made excellent time, stopping only to take in views and eat a light lunch. Mount Rand was the last summit standing between us and the finish. Following white blazes, we climbed down into a col, then made another challenging climb up a rock face to the summit of Mount Rand. Reuben bounded up the cliff face and then looked down at me, as I struggled to find solid footing. I'm sure he was saying to himself, "Why is he so slow climbing up the rock wall".

We finally made it to the summit and began the trek down off Mount Rand, bringing us back to where we began the day, the trail junction of Old Clough Road and the Dave Roberts Trail. After Reuben and I returned to the truck there was one last area I wanted to explore: The 1812 Lamprey Cemetery which lies just off Old Clough Road. The trail into the cemetery is not well blazed, but after a quarter mile walk we found this very old and large cemetery that marked an area where once stood many small farms, roads, pastures and most likely a church and school. The only landmarks remaining of this historic mountainside community are the cemetery, stone foundations, rock walls and the granite quarry we visited earlier in the day.

Double Your Pleasure with Prospect and Plymouth Mountains

The journey is the destination.

Appalachian Trail Conservacy

*Steve and Beth on the summit of Prospect Mountain,
looking south*

Prospect Mountain (2,064 ft.) and Plymouth Mountain (2,197 ft.) sit a few miles from each other and provide an opportunity for hiking enthusiasts to enjoy a trek of two summits in one day. The trailhead of Plymouth Mountain is located within a few miles of Main Street, Plymouth and Prospect Mountain, in the town of Holderness is only three miles from exit 25 off I-93. It's worth noting that there is another Prospect Mountain in Lancaster located in Weeks State Park, which is also an interesting climb, but for this trip we will stay close to home.

I had no knowledge that these two mountains even existed or that they had well maintained trails to their summits until my good friends Steve and Beth invited me to climb Prospect Mountain. I leaped at the opportunity to get out of the house for a day with Reuben. We met them at our usual rendezvous spot, I-93 exit #23 Park and Ride. After a 15-minute drive on I-93, we left the highway at exit 25, turned onto Holderness Rd. toward the Holderness School and at the hockey arena turned left onto Prospect Mountain Road. From exit 25 it was only a three mile drive until we found the trailhead at a small turn-off where we could park our cars. Located across the road was a small white farm house with a red barn.

We began our hike on an old tote road. There was a slight covering of snow and ice on the trail so we donned light boot traction and climbed leisurely past old stone walls and through stands of oak, maple and birch. The wide pathway, which was once a wagon road, gradually narrowed to a foot path. It followed the ridgeline, leveled off and came to an outcrop of rock that provided a clear view of Squam Lake and the Ossipee Mountain Range beyond. After a short walk the trail took us over another rock outcrop that had wonderful views of the valley below. We reached the summit a short time later and found a canister nailed to a tree that marked the summit of Prospect Mountain. We signed in, had a bite to eat and explored a trail that appeared to head down the other side of the mountain. Not wanting to descend off the mountain too far, we backtracked to the loop trail that led us down the mountain. On our way off the mountain we found several alternative trails which led us through other sections of the mountain. One could easily get disoriented and lost by taking this alternate system of trails which appeared to be single-track mountain bike trails. So, hikers should be sure to stay on the well-trodden main trail. I made a note to return here in summer, with my bike in tow to continue my exploration of Prospect Mountain.

For many years Plymouth Mountain was climbed using the Plymouth Mountain Trail off of Rt. 3A in Hebron. A newer and better marked trail provides a slightly longer, but more satisfying ascent than the traditional route and provides access to a knob called "Pikes Peak" which has outstanding views to the north and east. This trail begins off Old Hebron Road in Plymouth. There is ample parking in the large clearing and a kiosk marks the beginning of the Fauver Link Trail, which winds through the Fauver Preserve, land that's protected by a conservation easement.

On the day Reuben and I hiked Plymouth it was overcast, with rain predicted later in the day. As I began my hike it was clear I would need foot traction (trail crampons). The trail was covered with frozen water flows, making walking without traction extremely dangerous. After reading the information on the kiosk we began on the Fauver trail, marked with yellow and blue blazes. The trail climbed moderately on an old woods road and then turned onto a narrow footpath. At 0.4 mile I crossed a large logging road and found the beginning of the Sutherland trail on the other side of the clearing. This trail crossed conservation land and was also marked with yellow blazes. We followed the Sutherland trail through beautiful stands of hemlock, interspersed with some hardwoods. There were numerous beech nuts laying on the ground. I'm sure deer, rabbits and other varmints have feasted on these tasty morsels. At 0.9 mile I reached a side path which led to a rocky knob and provided restricted views. Continuing on my journey, the trail began to climb more abruptly, crossing several rock outcrops and at two miles I came to the outlook called "Pikes Peak". I continued my scramble over several ledges, treading carefully, due to the extremely dangerous ice pack on the trail. There were several locations where I needed to bushwhack to avoid some of the more difficult sections of ice. Within a half mile I found the summit of Plymouth Mountain, which offered limited views. After exploring the summit and other rock outcrops nearby I made my descent back to the car.

Both hikes of Plymouth and Prospect Mountain can be completed in one day and offer a fun-filled adventure for the entire family. Children would especially love scrambling over the many rock out-crops on Plymouth Mountain. A good lunch at noon can also be found at several restaurants in Plymouth.

Hiking in the Three Ponds-Kineo Region

Because in the end, you won't remember the time you spent working in an office or mowing the lawn. Climb that goddamn mountain.

Jack Kerouac

Dick crossing beaver dam while Sandy and Fran look on

Sandy contacted a few of her trekking buddies and suggested a hike on the Three Ponds – Kineo loop Trail, starting and finishing at the trailhead off Rt. 118 on Forest Road 211. You may wonder why Sandy would want to hike these obscure and almost abandoned trails in the Rumney region. Well, Sandy is working on a list called "Redlining". Redlining means hiking all the trails found in the AMC *White Mountain Guide* (over 1,000 miles of trail). Sounds like a crazy list but I know people who have completed it, or are working on it. I joined her because I have hiked in this area before and wanted to return and bushwhack to the summit of Mount Kineo. Fran and Dick also jumped on board and we set out on a beautiful warm spring day.

The Three Ponds area and Mount Kineo lie north of Rumney and west of Thornton. The trails in this section of the White Mountains offer delightful opportunities for day hikes to Stinson, Rattlesnake and Carr Mountains. Both the Carr and Stinson summits were once the sites of fire towers and the remains of these towers are still evident today. The trails in this area also provide a pleasant day hike starting from Stinson Lake Road to the shelter on the shores of Three Ponds. The hike we chose to embark on is less well-traveled and very obscure in some sections. The AMC *White Mountain Guide* does not recommend this trail for inexperienced hikers. A map and compass are essential and a GPS can be helpful.

We began our hike at the gated National Forest Road, 211. This USFS road merges with the Hubbard Brook trail which leads to Hubbard Brook Road and into the Hubbard Brook Experimental Forest. The U.S.D.A. Forest Service Research Station was established in 1955 as a major center for forest hydrologic research in New England. In 1988 it was designated as a Long-Term Ecological Research site by the National Science Foundation. The first documentation in North America of the long-term effects of acid rain on vegetation and water quality were done here. The area is still active in doing cooperative research in the fields of soil physics and forest hydrology. The research will also help in the understanding of climate change and its effects on forest ecology.

We began our hike on the Three Ponds Trail, which took us over Whitcher Hill, named after one of the first settlers in the town of Warren. As we progressed along the trail, it became difficult to follow and the treadway became obscured with hobblebush. Hobblebush is a very appropriate name for this shrub as it grows throughout the openings on the forest floor, tripping and ensnaring hikers in a web of branches. Even though hobblebush is bothersome to hikers, it throws out beautiful white and pink flowers in the spring. Thankfully, we were able to follow the trail because surveyor's tape had been placed on trees along the supposed route. Without the tape we would have had a difficult time finding our way. Many wildflowers were in bloom throughout the forest floor and they gave us notice that spring had arrived and summer was fast approaching. All along the trail were hepatica, purple and pink trillium, spring beauties, wild oats, bedstraw, Indian poke and goldthread. Trout lilies were everywhere, shooting up their delicate flowers, signaling the beginning the trout fishing season. The oak, maple, birch and beech trees were throwing out their new leaves to bathe in the warm, spring sunlight. It was the perfect, idyllic spring hike in New Hampshire, with no blackflies (yet).

After crossing Whitcher Hill we descended into the depression that holds the three ponds. We passed by Foxglove Pond (no foxgloves in bloom) and in a swampy area we found a number of pitcher plants waiting for their spring meal. This plant grows in wetlands and is unique in that it doesn't look like a normal leafy plant. It's carnivorous, just like many of us, and devours insects by attracting them with a sweet nectar and then digesting them with a fluid that is similar to the juices in our stomachs, amazing!

After stopping to admire the view we continued on our journey to Three Ponds, crossing a beaver dam and onto the Donkey Hill Cutoff. From this trail we then swung onto the Mount Kineo Trail which started as a snowmobile trail and reverted back to a wilderness pathway. We lumbered up the side of Mount Kineo (3,313 ft.), until we reached the height of land where we began the bushwhack to the summit. This was about a two mile round trip diversion from the trail, but Kineo is on the NH 200 highest summits list, so why not grab it. Returning to the Mount Kineo Trail we began the long descent to Hubbard Brook and Hubbard Brook Trail.

However, this adventure was far from over. Our hike off Kineo Ridge took us into a beautiful valley and as we made our way along the trail we began to encounter a series of beaver communities. The beaver flowage and dams were extensive, flooding the trail in many sections. At one point we noticed a trail marker on a tree sitting in the middle of a beaver pond and we had to make several detours. The trail from here on out was not marked and the footpath was non-existent. I believe the only ones using this trail are moose, deer, fox and coyote. We continued to be enthralled with the wildflowers blooming around us and the many beaver ponds that were active or dried up. Upon leaving the valley we finally arrived at the junction with Hubbard Brook Road, which turns into Hubbard Brook Trail. As we neared the end of our hike we encountered a barred owl, calling to its mate. We looked up and there he was overhead, sitting on a branch of a tree. We watched him for several minutes as he flew from tree to tree, staying close by. As we continued our hike he flew along overhead, perching on tree limbs and watching us, seeming to say, "I'm keeping an eye on you invaders!" After taking many pictures of this guardian of the forest, we left him and his mate, listening to their familiar call, "Who cooks for you, who cooks for you."

As we ended our day, after hiking a total of 16 miles in 12 hours and nearing nightfall, we looked forward to a cold drink. On our way down Rt. 118 we spotted a very large black bear roaming along the highway. We pulled over to watch him ramble along, stopping occasionally to watch us. It was the perfect ending to a day spent in the wonders of nature and being a part of the beauty that is all around us when we are on the trail.

Fletcher's Cascades and the Lure of Waterfalls

There is a hidden message in every waterfall. It says, if you are flexible, falling will not hurt you!

Mehmet Murat ildan

View of the Fletcher Cascades from the terminus of the trail

I was sitting at the base of one of the upper falls of Fletcher's Cascades on a warm summer day, watching the water spray in the sunlight as it fell from the stream 90 feet above my head. I contemplated the attraction we as humans have to falling water and in particular waterfalls. Many of the best known landmarks in America are waterfalls such as Niagara in New York, Bridal Veil in Yosemite National Park, Lower Falls in Yellowstone, Amicalola in Georgia, and Multnomah in Washington. In New Hampshire there are well over fifty waterfalls and cascades visited each year by hundreds of hikers and tourists. Some of the more well-known are Diana's Baths in Bartlett, Flume Cascade and Georgiana Falls in Franconia Notch, Sabbaday Falls off the Kancamagus Highway, Zealand Falls near the Zealand AMC Hut, Thoreau Falls off the Ethan Pond Trail, and Nancy Cascades on the Nancy Pond Trail in Crawford Notch. A listing of all the notable waterfalls and cascades in New Hampshire can be found in a guidebook entitled, *New England Waterfalls*, by Greg Parsons and Kate Watson.

What is it about water falling over rock walls from extreme heights that lead so many of us to seek out these places? Just visit Diana's Baths or Sabbaday Falls on any summer day and you will find crowds of people with cameras in hand gazing at the water tumbling over and down rock walls, plunging into shallow pools below. I am one of those seekers of falling water who has visited many of these places. I ask the question, "Why am I drawn to waterfalls like so many others?" There must be some innate quality in the human condition that draws us to these special places. With these thoughts swirling in my head I ended my respite at the base of the upper falls and continued my trek to find the beginning of the Fletcher's Cascades, which required that I climb off-trail to the steep cliffs above my head.

Earlier that day I was planning to meet Dick and Fran for a drive to Dixville Notch and bushwhack to the summit of Kelsey Mountain. Plans changed suddenly when Dick called off the hike due to illness. My bushwhacking knapsack was all packed for the day. The sun was brilliant, the day was warming so why not come up with an alternative plan. Earlier in the year, near the end of winter, I had hiked the Drakes Brook trail to climb Sandwich Dome, the last of the mountains I needed to complete the New England Hundred Highest in winter. On my way up the Drakes Brook Trail, not far from the parking lot off Rt. 49 in Waterville Valley, I noticed the trail sign for Fletcher's Cascades. I hadn't heard of these cascades before and felt drawn off my mission to climb Sandwich. But I couldn't be deterred from the goal since the end of winter was close at hand. However, I made a note to myself to return to this spot and hike to the cascades, drawn by a mysterious calling. So, today was a perfect day to return to Fletcher's Cascades.

The cascades originate on the northwest side of Flat Mountain and are most likely named for Ebenezer Fletcher of Concord, NH, who in the 1870s settled in the Waterville Valley. The trail to the cascades was probably cut around this time, but extensive logging in the late 1800s wiped it out. The trail was reopened by the U. S. Forest Service 1951 and now the cascades are located within the Sandwich Range Wilderness.

Reuben and I pulled into the parking lot off Rt. 49 at the trailhead for the Drakes Brook Trail. The Sandwich Mountain Trail also starts from this same area. I followed a bike-ski trail for 0.4 miles until I found the trail sign for Fletcher's Cascades. The trail climbed gently along Drakes Brook, named after Arnold Drake who settled in this area around 1840. The trail gradually moved away from the brook and began to climb more steeply to the foot of the cascades. I could see swirling water below the trail as I climbed higher, finally reaching a beautiful pool at the base of the first major cascade. Here Reuben enjoyed a long swim in the crystal clear water. At the end of the marked trail (blazed yellow), I noticed an arrow pointing to the base of the 90-foot waterfall.

Reuben and I stopped to rest and contemplate my calling to falling water. The mist from the falls blew over my face and felt refreshing on this very warm day.

While sitting below the falls I wondered if there were more cascades above. Curiosity and the urge to explore this beautiful sanctuary led me to begin an off-trail climb up the steep rock cliffs, through blowdowns, and dense forest. I found a fairly well defined herd path that led me to an outlook where I had a clear view of Mounts Welch and Dickey. Reuben and I continued our scramble through fairly open woods, finding the ridge summit and a number of small streams and seeps that marked the beginning of the water flow to the cascades below me. I was tempted to keep climbing to the ridgeline of Flat Mountain, but thought better of it as I needed to be home soon. I retreated back down the cliffs staying close to several small streams feeding the cascades. On my way back to my car I was amazed that there were no other hikers on the trail on this very warm and humid day. Maybe this lesser known cascade in New Hampshire is not visited very often; I wonder.

The 1.8 mile trail to the upper cascades would be an ideal half day hike on a hot sunny day for the entire family. Take a lunch or snack and spend time admiring the cascades and cool your feet in the pools of crystal clear water falling from the mountain ridge above. This hike could also be combined with the Welch-Dickey Loop Trail for a full day of adventure. Welch-Dickey is a classic New Hampshire above tree-line loop trail which climbs over two mountains with several rock outcrops providing unmatched views of the White Mountains. The Welch-Dickey Trail lies within only a few miles drive from the Fletcher's Cascades trailhead, so these two hikes could be combined into a one day adventure for the hearty trekker.

Blueberries and the Silent People of Finland

There are eyes, to be sure, that give no more admission into the man than blueberries.

Ralph Waldo Emerson

Blueberry barrens on Straightback Mountain

Anyone for blueberry pie, blueberry jam, blueberry cobbler? The wild blueberry (*vaccinium angustifolium*) season was upon us and picking was in full swing. With my friends Karen and Tom, along with Reuben, I headed to the Belknap Range where the wild blueberries grow in abundance. On the side of South Straightback Mountain we found an incredible field of blueberries, hanging off their slender stems like grapes. In an hour we filled our pails and mouths with hundreds of the beautiful blue fruit.

Earlier in the summer I hiked to the summit of South Straight-back Mountain via the Jesus Valley Road and the Straightback Mountain Trail. There I encountered field upon field of blueberry blossoms. I knew that in a few weeks the mountainside would be covered with the gorgeous fruit. I put out a notice to friends who I thought would be interested in harvesting a crop of berries, along with hiking some of the best terrain in the Lakes Region. Tom and Karen leaped at the proposition of hiking a section of trails in the Belknap Range and picking blueberries along the way.

On a very hot and humid day we set out for the Jesus Valley Road Trail, just off Rt. 11, to begin our trek up Straightback Mountain via the Blueberry Meadow Trail. As we approached the ridge running over to Mount Major we beheld a beautiful sight: an Elysian field of blueberries. It was like magic when we spotted the endless meadow of low-bush berries full of ripened fruit. It seemed as though a magnet just sucked us into this meadow. Within an hour we had filled our buckets and our stomachs with this delicious fruit. Reuben laid beside me in a meadow filled with wildflowers and berries. A slight breeze was blowing and provided a welcome relief from the heat and humidity of the day. I felt as though I was laying in Elysium, the beautiful meadow referred to in Homer's Odyssey, the ultimate paradise where men lead an easier life than anywhere else in the world. I found my own Elysium where the berries hung like grapes from the vine, just waiting to be picked. If you have never tasted a wild low-bush blueberry, then you have never lived. Forget those propagated high-bush berries or better yet, throw out those frozen berries from the grocery store and head to the hills with your bucket in hand and begin picking.

As we filled our canisters with berries, the wind began to pick up and the skies turned cloudy. The weather report for the day pre-dicted severe storms that would be moving in by afternoon.

We decided to pull stakes and continue on our hike along the Belknap Range Trail, hoping to be off the mountain before the storm hit. As we hiked the trail at a brisk pace we couldn't resist the temptation to stop and scoop up a handful of berries as they dangled from bushes along the trail. We even had a contest to see who could grab the most berries in one swipe. I think Karen won with nine! As we neared Mount Anna we decided to head down the Precipice Trail into the valley below.

We wound our way along the ridge of Straightback Mountain, traversing sheer cliffs that provided exceptional views to Piper Mountain and Hill Pond below. Upon reaching the Cascade Brook waterfalls we descended carefully. Reuben took advantage of the small pools of crystal clear, ice-cold water that were dammed up behind blocks of granite. I'm sure it was a welcome relief for him in the sweltering heat of the day. Karen, Tom and Reuben zipped down the rock-strewn cliff as I stumbled downward on my two metal replacement knees. When we arrived at the base of the cascades, we followed the trail out to Old Stage Road, or so we thought.

We followed this woods road, which also serves as a snowmobile trail, for about a mile until we came to a housing development on a lake. We were confused. We thought this path would take us back to the Jesus Valley Rd. Instead we were wandering aimlessly around, looking for a clear way back to where we started our trek. Tom took out his trusty compass and Karen her map. They came to the conclusion that we were headed in the wrong direction. However, Reuben being the smart dog that he is, began leading us along a trail that led to an open field filled with what we thought were scarecrows. There were a dozen of these fixtures planted in an open field in the middle of nowhere, at least this is what we thought. It was surrealistic. It was as though we had entered the twilight zone, with these stick creatures eyeing us. After my initial

The Silent People of Alton and Reuben barking with delight

shock I noticed a sign on a post that read: "*The Silent People of Finland was created by a Finn who lives in the area. No one knows the artist's idea behind the Silent People. He feels the viewer should come to their own conclusion. Some (people) view it as a state of psychological withdrawal, some as forgotten people.*"

After spending a few moments contemplating the display we continued on our journey, hoping to find Old Stage Road and the way back to our waiting vehicles. After walking for some time on a snowmobile trail we finally found, to our surprise, that we were on the Old Stage Road and would soon be back at the Jesus Valley Road trailhead. When we did reach the parking area we were relieved to know we didn't have to spend the night in the woods or have to call the Alton Fire Department for a rescue. We could drive home to the comfort and safety of our own homes. What a day it was, beginning with the Idyllic Elysian Fields of blueberries and ending with the Silent People of Finland, representing the tragedy of war. Hiking the Belknap Range never lets me down.

Footnote:

Several days after returning from the hike, I received an email from Charles Weston who, along with his wife Sandy, created the Silent People Memorial. I was anxious to learn more about the Silent People and I decided to meet Charles at his home in Alton. He shared with me the following story: He was born and raised in Marquette, Michigan on the Upper Peninsula. (He proudly admitted he's a "Yooper", a native of the U.P). He met his wife Sandy while they were students at Finlandia University. Sandy was of Finnish descent, and Charles Swedish. After graduating from Northern Michigan University, Charles taught in public schools and later worked for the Ford Motor Company. Sandy was an artist. After retirement they moved to Alton, NH and in 1997 purchased property on Hill's Pond.

In 2002 Charles and Sandy travelled to Finland for a family re-union. While there they took a road trip through rural Finland with Sandy's cousin Seppo. After travelling a number of miles through the forested landscape on Highway 5 outside of Suomus-salmi, they came to an open field filled with over 1,000 Silent People. They were awestruck by the sight. They learned that the display, created by artist Reijo Kela, is interpreted by some as a memorial to the thousands of Finnish soldiers and citizens who were killed in the Russo-Finnish War of 1939-40. The war was fought on Finnish soil as the Finns defended their country from Russian invasion and an attempt by Stalin to take control of the country. The Finns fought valiantly and ultimately drove the Russians back to their Homeland. During the conflict Sandy lost two cousins. The Silent People Memorial took on a personal meaning for Sandy and Charles.

Sandy was particularly moved by the display, not only because of her Finnish descent, and her loss of family members to war, but to the ongoing war in Iraq at that time. When Charles and Sandy returned to their home in Alton they felt moved to create their own Silent People Memorial as a symbol of their opposition to senseless wars. Charles stated that Sandy had something called sisu. Sisu is a unique Finnish concept. It can roughly be translated into English as strength of will, determination, perseverance and acting rationally in the face of adversity. Sandy acted with sisu and was determined to build a replica of the Silent People Memorial she saw in Finland, her homeland.

In 2003 Sandy along with Charles began erecting the New Hampshire version of the Silent People in a field adjacent to their house. The field, known as Joe's field, was used to raise potatoes. The field that once was used to feed a family was now going to be used to remind people of the human toll of warfare.

Sandy died of breast cancer in 2012. Charles has moved on with his life. Many people have passed through Joe's Field and stared at the Silent People: hikers, snowmobilers, and people just interested in the display. Some bring their shirts to place on the cross, others significant items, and some like myself just look and contemplate the powerful message of the Silent People.

Ahern State Park
A Jewel in the Lake City

Home is behind, the world ahead,
And there are many paths to tread
Through shadows to the edge of night,
Until the stars are all alight.

J.R.R. Tolkien

Walking along the shores of Winnisquam Lake in Ahern Park I reflected on my past work at Laconia Sate School. When I worked at the institution from 1977-1991 I would often jog to the lake on my lunch break and take a dip in the beautiful clean

Small sand beach on Lake Winnisquam

water. As I meandered along, memories of this past rushed through my head: the wonderful people who lived there, the dedicated, committed staff who gave of themselves to make life better for people who were rejected by society. Now most of the buildings and grounds lie abandoned, being swallowed up by time. It's an ugly scar within the City of Laconia. The state has neglected the property for years. What the future holds is anyone's guess. But for the moment I live in the present, thankful that Ahern Park belongs to the people of New Hampshire and is located in Laconia.

A short distance from the abandoned grounds of Laconia State School lies Ahern State Park, an oasis of beautiful woods, sandy beaches, biking/hiking trails, and remarkable views of Lake Winnisquam. The Park is named after William J. Ahern, a prominent New Hampshire legislator from 1895-1927, and the first

Chairman of Board of Trustees for the Laconia School for the Feebleminded (Laconia State School).

I return often to my former stomping grounds. I love to hike the numerous trails that wind along the hillside of the lake, take in the views and watch Reuben prance along the shore, sticking his nose into the crevices of rocks. When he gets the urge, he'll jump in the water to cool off and chase the sparkling sunbeams reflecting off the water. Ahern provides a place for solitude and reflection. I wonder why so few people visit this state park. Every time I'm here I see only a handful of visitors: people walking their dogs or sitting on the beach. This is a gem in the city of Laconia. Nothing exists like this park in the entire Lakes Region. Yet it appears to me that it's similar to the abandoned institution on the hill above, desolate and forgotten.

The sign, "Ahern Park" is like other state park signs, but the feeling driving into the park is one of rejection. I parked my truck at the upper gate and began my hike on the Alcatraz Trail. The trail system was built primarily for single track mountain biking. The trails take many twists and turns and I needed to study the trail map on the kiosk carefully to plan my hike. I then noticed the plaque stating "Ahern Park" was missing. It was once anchored to a large rock and now is missing, perhaps stolen by a souvenir seeker.

The park is comprised of 128 acres and has 3,500 ft. of shorefront on Winnisquam Lake. When the Laconia State School closed in 1991, shortly afterward it was converted to a state prison. The prison closed in early 2000 and the state was left with a decision, what to do with the land and buildings. In 2017 the New Hampshire Legislature enacted legislation, Chapter 240, HB 340, to establish the Lake Shore Redevelopment Commission to study the former Laconia State School land and buildings and identify potential development alternatives. Fortunately in 1994 the state determined the 128 acres of Ahearn Park should be set aside as a state park and will not be affected by future plans for the State School property.

As Reuben scampered ahead of me along the Alcatraz Trail I was amazed at the immense white pine, beech and oak trees rising above the trail. Perhaps this forest never heard the sawyer's ax or the buzzing of a chain saw. John Muir came to mind, *"Between every two pines is a doorway to a new world."* Continuing on the trail I came to an intersection and I recognized the old tote road that led to the grounds of the State School. I followed this road until I came to a clearing near the Spear Building. The building was named after Eva Spear, a prominent citizen in New Hampshire politics and social services. I stood overlooking the other large brick buildings that housed hundreds of devalued people: Baker, Blood, Keyes, Felker, King, Dube, Dwinell and Powell in the distance. My thoughts brought me back to the 1980s when I worked in the Blood Building. Memories shot through my mind, most good, others not so good. After pausing for several minutes to reflect on my work at the institution, I resumed my journey. I wandered over to what remained of the upper farm, called the Brown Farm: old storage sheds and chicken coops are all that remain.

The State School property once belonged to William Crocket. He and his family settled here in 1770. They built their first home, a log cabin, close to what is now the corner of Old North Main and Parade Road. The log cabin was replaced later by a framed farm house, built by William's son Joshua. Over the years the Crocket family lost interest in farming and moved away. In 1901 the state was looking for land to build The New Hampshire Home for Feebleminded. They found the perfect spot, 250 beautiful acres of farmland. In 1901 the NH legislature allocated $60,000 to purchase the property, construct a residential hall and a school house. The institution opened its doors in 1903 and until 1991 it warehoused thousands of children and adults with disabilities. If you are interested in learning more about the Laconia State School you can view the documentary film, *Lost in Laconia,* written and directed by me and Bil Rogers of 1LMedia, LLC.

I left the farm buildings behind and made my way down the old tote road to the waterfront, arriving at Cottage Beach. The small cottage that once stood here has disappeared and the beach is growing in with weeds. The cottage was once used as a rest camp for employees, later for residents of the State School to enjoy a swim, picnic and spend a day away from the crowded conditions of institutional life. It was alleged that the restless ghosts of two nurses, murdered by a lunatic employee of the institution in the 1920s, haunted the cabin at night. (This story is true and a full account of the incident can be found in the records of the *Laconia Democrat* located at the Laconia Public Library). No wonder the cabin was taken down.

I continued my ramble along the shore road leading to the much larger Sandy Beach. I thought the beach would be crowded on this hot and humid day, but there was no one in sight. I continued my journey along the perimeter road running along the shore and then headed into the woods on the Backbone Trail. This trail would eventually lead me back to my truck. This short jaunt of 2 hours was as enjoyable as ever and offered me a time to reflect on bygone days. John Muir stated, *"In every walk with nature one receives far more than he seeks."* I hope others will take the opportunity to explore the trails of Ahern Park, whether it's on bike or on foot. It's a gem waiting to be discovered.

A Haunting Hike to Devil's Den Mountain

If a child is to keep alive his inborn sense of wonder, he needs the companionship of at least one adult who can share it, rediscovering with him the joy, excitement, and mystery of the world we live in.   Rachel Carson

Gordon entering the Devil's Den with Reuben looking on

I was perusing through our family library, looking for *A Sand County Almanac* by Aldo Leopold, when I came across an interesting book entitled *Haunted Hikes of New Hampshire*. It was tucked away in a corner of the bookcase and I had forgotten that my son Matthew had given me this book as a Christmas present back in 2009. Written by Marianne O'Connor, educator and writer from Nashua, NH, this small paperback has a number of attention-grabbing stories of hikes that have a unique and fascinating history. The book is filled with stories that will capture your curious mind. As I scanned through the table of contents one particular hike caught my attention, "Devil's Den, Chasing Satan." Halloween was approaching and it seemed that this would be a fitting hike for the season of ghouls, ghosts and goblins,

I called my friend Steve to see if he wanted to find the "Den of the Devil" with me. He leaped at the opportunity to hike into this mysterious area located in New Durham, near Merrymeeting Lake. We began the day by driving along Rt. 11 to the rotary in Alton, where Rts. 11 and 28 merge. At the rotary we turned onto New Durham Road and drove a few miles to Merrymeeting Lake Road, turned left, following the sign for the New Hampshire Fish Hatchery. We continued on this road until we reached a sharp turn where North Shore Road made a sharp turn to the right and Devil's Den Mountain Road swung to the left. At this point we needed to make a decision. The road from this point forward is a class VI road, heavily rutted and filled with rocks and large boulders. Since I have 4-wheel drive and a high clearance pickup we decided to drive the road. However, it's advisable that you park your car at this road junction. There is plenty of room for several parked cars. After a rough and tumble ride of about a mile we found a large clearing to park the truck. If you choose to walk the road it is a pleasant hike through beautiful stands of hardwood. There's a large cellar hole you can explore as you make your way up the road to the trailhead, which is about 1.5 miles from North Shore Rd. parking area. Be on the lookout for ATVs, as the road is frequented by thrill seeking riders.

After parking the truck we headed up the road to the beginning of the Devil's Den Mountain Trail. We passed a beaver bog that had long been forgotten by beavers, but provided us with an interlude to our walk in the woods. Shortly after the passing the bog we found the trailhead on the left marked with a "T" painted on a rock. This is where we began our journey to find the cave. We continued on this well-defined trail until we eyed the steep rock face of the mountain. We noticed many side paths as we climbed toward the mountain, but we found the trail to be well marked with frequent red blazes painted on trees. The trail then swung to the right and we began our final short ascent to the summit. The barren rock face provided a few semi-obstructed views of Lake Winnipesauskee and Merrymeeting Lake. The mountainside is a good example of how the ancient glaciers of 10,000 years ago scoured the mountain, leaving behind this bare granite mound of rock high above the forest floor. After taking in the views and peering over the side of the precipitous cliffs, we began our excursion to the other side of the mountain to find the den of the devil. The red blazed trail led us down the mountain, over several rock scrambles to a split in the trail.

Now the real fun began! We turned left, climbing over large boulders that had fallen from the cliffs above. Noticing a red blaze on a large boulder we hoisted ourselves and Reuben onto a rock ledge where we encountered the entrance to the cave. No doubt this was the Devil's Den. We dropped our packs, hiking poles and strapped on our headlamps. Steve entered the cave first. I hung back, playing "chicken", not wanting to stir up the spirits of those who were buried in the deep recesses of the mountain. There are many tales and legends of the cave. Some say it was used as a burial site for native peoples. Others have claimed that the cave was once used by early explorers as shelter from winter storms and some died in the cave, trapped by winter-long snow storms. I noticed iron hinges on the rock at the entrance to the cave where once hung an iron gate. Legend also has it that the cave was used in early colonial days to imprison witches who lived in settlements across the region. It's rumored that you can hear the voices of the dead as you enter the cave. Reuben sniffed around the entrance not wanting to go in. Steve tried to coax him but he staunchly refused, stiffening his back, hair standing on end, tail between his legs and whining softly. Did Reuben sense something foreboding and sinister inside the cave?

After calling out to Steve I heard his faint voice respond, "It's OK, come on in." I attached my headlamp to my head and began to carefully enter the cave. I had to crouch low and wiggle through the entrance. The air felt cold and damp. I thought to myself, "This is not a place for anyone who is claustrophobic". Once inside the cavern it opened into a narrow room, with what looked like ancient writings on the wall. I also noticed streaks of red. Could this be dried blood? I met up with Steve after my carefully and cautiously placed feet led me to the end the cavern deep inside the mountain. Here we found a ladder that led to another entrance to the cave from the cliffs above. We dared not climb the ladder as it was wobbly and several rungs were missing. Having satisfied our curiosity, we turned around and made our way back to the entrance where Reuben was anxiously waiting our exit. Thank goodness we heard no strange noises or felt any bony fingers poking us in the back.

We finished our exploration and began our hike back around the mountain by scrambling along a series of cliffs. We looked up and saw rope anchors that indicated the mountain is a popular destination for rock climbers. We found our way back to where the truck was parked and headed home. When I returned home and unpacked my gear I found my camera was missing. It strangely disappeared from my pack and I didn't know how. The next day I raced back to the cave to see if I dropped it along our route. The camera was mysteriously gone, nowhere to be found. It simply disappeared. How could this be? I wondered, "Was this the work of some imp or mysterious spirit lurking in the den and taking revenge for entering their home, Devil's Den?" I considered my camera lost forever.

About a week later I received a phone call from a jogger who was running in the area of Devil's Den Mountain. He found my camera lying in the road, the road I had walked several times in search of my lost camera. How come I didn't notice it earlier? My explanation:

some ghoulish creature was playing tricks on me by stealing the camera from my pack. He was letting me know not to tread into the cave again. The Halloween season may be a good time to hike into Devil's Den Mountain and find the cave, if you dare. It is a four-mile round trip of about 2-3 hours. However, you may like to leave yourself more time to explore the cave. Remember to keep a close eye on your possessions, as there may be some ghostly creature waiting to play a trick or two on you.

Redlining the Belknap Range

To those devoid of imagination a blank place on the map is a useless waste; to others, the most valuable part.

Aldo Leopold

Goat Pasture Hill Trail leading off of Mount Anna,
Reuben leading the way

I was hiking the Anna-Goat Pasture Hill Trail with Reuben when I heard voices. I thought no one else would be on this isolated trail, but I was wrong. I was surprised at the jabbering ahead of me and was curious to find out who it was. I soon saw two guys dressed in brightly colored garb (it was hunting season) sauntering along, gabbing away. We stopped and chatted for some time, sharing information about the trail ahead and swapping hiking stories. I learned that one of the trekkers, Joe, was finishing the Redline List of the Belknap Mountain Range. He was really animated about his Redline finish and his partner, John was equally excited. Both shared their love for the Belknap Range and the trails that crisscross the mountains. I was also on the quest to redline, with only a few miles left to complete the goal. Following our extended encounter we parted ways, equally enthused to be out hiking on this beautiful fall day after heavy rains of the past week.

If you are wondering about redlining, it's a goal of trekkers to hike every marked trail in a given area. The term "redlining" came about from the goal that was created several years ago by hiking enthusiasts to trek all the trails detailed in the AMC *White Mountain Guide,* 1,440 miles. The trails on the maps are marked in red, hence the term redlining. This term has now been applied to hiking other areas that have a series of trails, such as the Belknap Range. The Belknap Range has 65.5 miles of sanctioned trails and is a much more doable goal than that of White Mountain list. The Belknap Range Trail Tenders (BRATTS) have created a patch for those who complete this goal. Now Joe was about to join this distinguished group of Belknap Range Redliners. If you are intrigued by this challenge check out (*bratts.org/category/redlining*) where you'll find a list of the trails, maps and instructions on ordering the Belknap Redline Patch.

I began the day by driving to the Boy Scouts of America, Daniel Webster Council's Griswold Scout Reservation, Hidden Valley and Camp Bell, located in Gilmanton, NH. I took Rt.140 to Crystal Lake Road, and followed signs to the B.S.A. Camp. The property consists of 3,270 acres which is open year-round for passive recreation such as hunting and back country hiking. I was surprised to find this expansive camp so open and accessible. I parked my truck in the lot adjacent to Lake Eileen, which was once known as Woodsman Pond. However, not being familiar with the trails in the area I wandered around for a while before finding the trail to Goat Pasture Hill. The trail marked with red diamond blazes led me through campsites and along Sunset Lake. Bright sunshine reflected off the lake and the water sparkled in the sunlight. Leaves covered the trail in hues of colors. This display of fallen leaves can be beautiful but also problematic, in that they often obscure the foot bed, leaving the trail difficult to follow. One must be ever diligent in watching for blazes marking the trail.

Winding my way along the lake, I arrived at the junction with the Old Stage Rd. leading to Mount Anna. I decided to continue following the red trail to Goat Pasture Hill. I soon came to West Brook, which normally would be an easy crossing, but with an unusual amount of rain earlier in the week the crossing proved to be a significant challenge. I had to hike upstream for several hundred yards before I could find a safe crossing. From here I continued my climb and nearing the summit of the hill I noticed numerous stone walls which at one time held herds of sheep and goats that grazed here in the early 1800s. From the top of the hill I gazed across the valley to South Straightback Mountain. As Reuben ran ahead, down the trail to Old Stage Road, I heard the roar of the waterfall of Suncook Brook. It's truly one of the premier sights in the Belknap Range. I found a spur trail, blazed purple, which led us to the Precipice Path and the spectacular waterfall rushing full force due to the recent rains. Reuben raced up the escarpment while I slowly scrambled after him. Reaching the apex of the cascades, we took in the view and then slowly and carefully scrambled down the wet rocky trail.

We then continued our climb to Mount Anna, passing a spur trail to Carbonneau Cave. We explored the fallen rock zone which created the cave and also came upon a massive pine tree. At the summit of Mount Anna we rested and had our lunch, or better stated, where Reuben had my lunch. After I set my sandwich on a rock to get a drink I found my lunch had disappeared. I looked at Reuben and he had a goofy, guilty looking smile spread across his snout. He has a reputation as a food thief, and I should have kknown better then to leave my lunch unattended. After this short rest we found the Old Stage Road/Mount Anna Trail, blazed with blue diamonds. Leaving the Mount Anna summit the trail took us to a rock outcrop with magnificent views to the south and west. The trail turned into what was at one time a carriage road. This wide trail wound through a beautiful stand of hemlock along the edge of a steep gorge, holding the stream that connects to a large beaver pond. Upon arriving at a rock outcrop high above the beaver pond, Reuben and I sat for quite some time. We marveled at the beauty below us: the rippling waters, the fading colors of autumn, the standing dead trees sitting in the pond, chickadees, robins, and juncos darting in and out of the brush below, while a pileated woodpecker hammered away on a dead hemlock in search of ants for dinner. It was an idyllic moment, far too short, knowing I had to be on my way before darkness set in.

The climax of my journey was reaching the summit of Shannon Mountain, a small hump standing above the scout camp and Lake Eileen. I met the two "redliners", Joe and John, on their return to the Jesus Valley Road. Joe had just finished the Belknap Redline List and was elated over his accomplishment. I asked him, "What's next?" He shrugged his shoulders and replied, "Um, I'll have to think about it." After our brief encounter I continued on my way to the summit of Mount Shannon. As I reached the rock face of the mountain I was stunned by the views. This little known mountain (it's really a hill) has one of the best views in the Belknap Range.

When I returned to my truck, with Reuben close behind, I reviewed the Belknap Redline List and realized I was almost done. I needed only a few small sections of trail to meet the goal. I look forward to returning to Camp Bell and hiking the trails from the southern side of the range. If you haven't hiked these trails leading out from Griswold Scout Reservation, I recommend you put them on your hiking bucket list. The trails are well marked and less traveled than those situated on the north side of the Belknap Range. During the "off-season", September through May, no permission is necessary to park at either Camp Bell or Hidden Valley. Parking is available in the main parking lot at either camp. The scouts do ask hikers to leave a basic trip plan in the window of your vehicle, along with an expected time of return. This serves as a safety net in case a hiker is overdue and potentially in need of assistance. Name and phone number are also helpful. They ask that all vehicles remain in the parking lot and not drive on camp roads. Remember, wear hunter orange during the hunting season. It's equally as important for your dog to be dressed in hunter orange as well, just ask Reuben.

Mount Cardigan and Welton Falls

Let it be known there is a fountain that was not made by the hands of men.

Robert Hunter

I reached the river crossing on the Lower Manning Trail and found myself stuck. I could go no further. Winter temperatures had been set in motion and ice was forming along the banks of the Fowler River. No way could I cross to the other side, where the trail continues, without risking life and limb. One slip on a rock and I would find myself tumbling downstream; worse yet my head could possibly be smashed to smithereens. My destination hike to Welton Falls was now in jeopardy of being aborted.

However, I was not to be denied by a river crossing strewn with ice covered rocks and boulders. I was determined to find safe passage. I searched for a crossing, striding ceaselessly up and down the side of the river. All that I could see was ice-covered rocks and boiling water. I was getting discouraged and ready to turn back, when I suddenly spotted a series of boulders with no ice. They rose up out of the stream, like sentinels guarding the river. This was the place for safe passage. I felt like Frodo Baggins of *Lord of the Rings* making his way through the Old Forest. The boulders could be used as stepping stones and with any luck they will get me across the river. I lowered myself down the bank onto the first gigantic rock. I stepped gingerly across the rushing stream, one boulder at a time, watching carefully for any ice covering the foothold. I looked down once, noticed the swirling eddies below and raised my eyes quickly, focusing on the dry boulders ahead. At last I was across the river, where I rested on terra firma. I could now continue my journey to Welton falls.

This is the shoulder season, when fall is fading and winter is close at hand. The morning began under cloudy skies and cold temperatures. A chilling breeze sent icy fingers through my outer jacket. I was on this hike as part of a writing assignment for a conference I was attending, "Writing From the Mountain", sponsored by the Appalachian Mountain Club. We were spending the weekend at the AMC Cardigan Mountain Lodge. The lodge is nestled near the foot of Cardigan Mountain, at the end of peaceful Shem Valley Road on a 1,200 acre reservation in Alexandria, NH. The valley was carved out by the glaciers 12,000 years ago. The summit of Cardigan is composed of three main peaks: South Peak, Cardigan Peak and Firescrew. In 1855 a massive forest fire raged over the mountain, denuding the entire summit of vegetation. The fire was so intense it threw flames hundreds of feet into the sky.

Firescrew Mountain was named for the spiral of fire and smoke that rose from the peak. The summits have never recovered, but the valley has recuperated from the devastating inferno. Nature has a way of healing its wounds and marvelously restoring the forest to its former self. Cardigan is a place where you can find a challenging climb, as well as a leisurely woodland walk. The mountain preserve is also a favorite destination for backcountry skiers and has a plethora of ski trails for a wide range of abilities.

The Lower Manning Trial begins adjacent to the Cardigan Lodge. The trail wanders through several camp sites and then enters the Welton Falls State Forest. Here I encountered a forest of gigantic hemlocks and beech. Brown leaves scattered along the trail swirled around my feet as I bustled along. I felt like Aldo Leopold when he wrote, *"What great satisfaction there is in plowing through the rich brown autumn leaves of the woods on a fine sunny day."* I soon found myself hiking along the Fowler River. The trail overhung the river in several places, where the Fowler had undercut tree roots and soil. With each storm and spring runoff the banks of the river are pushed wider, trees become imperiled, eventually falling into the water.

After making my risky crossing of the Fowler I continued my trek to Welton Falls and encountered "clear sailing". No more rushing streams to cross. Within a matter of minutes (0.2 miles) I noticed a cable fence in disrepair, guarding the trail, keeping onlookers from tumbling into the boiling waters below. Looking over the precipice of the roaring cascade, I was struck by the stark beauty of this waterfall, walls of granite rising up from the foaming water. It was easy to see where the glaciers, as they melted, sent tons of water, rock and debris down the river carving out the chasm below. Blocks of ice clung to the sidewalls of the gorge. I found a resting spot to contemplate the stunning

Welton Falls from trail overlook

beauty around me and I tried my feeble best to capture the moment in this poem:

Water rushing by underfoot,
Signs of high water lay about: trees, boulders, sand, and silt.
Sheets of ice cover the river and the granite cliffs,
Winter closing in.

Ancient broken trees cling to the ledge,
Tree trunks riddled with holes from woodpeckers
Searching for a tasty delight.

Roots undercut by the rushing water.
Ancient rotting branches
Reaching with outstretched arms for sunlight,
Trying to stay alive.

Beech tree pocked with warts,
Moss crawling up the trunk;
Shelf fungus taking hold
Of the rotting bark.

I notice a small hemlock seedling
Emerging from the dying tree.
Green needles show off brilliant color,
As they rise like a phoenix.

A sign of new life,
Replacing the old
and dying member of the forest;
The circle of life, never ending.

After a period of reflection I decided to continue my hike and not return the way I came. Besides, I didn't want to risk crossing the river again. I made my way along the bank of the river, encountering one more river crossing, this time much easier. At 1.3 miles I reached the junction with the Old Dicey Road. Once on the Old Dicey Road I found myself walking leisurely along, taking in the warming rays of the sun. Stone walls lined the road indicating that at one time this was a main road to somewhere, but where? There are no indications of a settlement in the area. Eventually after a mile walk I left the Old Dicey Road and began my circuitous route back to the Cardigan Lodge on the Back 80 Loop.

The Back 80 Loop Trail gradually climbed a ridge, reaching the junction with the Back 80 Trail. At the junction I found a good-size cellar hole, once the homestead of a pioneering family. I pondered the life of these early settlers who carved out an existence in the wilderness. I admired their fortitude and grit, their ability to build a substantial home in this desolate wilderness. Now I was returning to the comfortable accommodations of a

Twenty-First Century lodge. The hike from the cellar hole back to the lodge was a quick mile, mostly downhill. I made it back just in time for the start of our next session with no river crossing to impede my hike.

This hike can be done as an out and back to Welton Falls (two miles) or continue as I did. I would not recommend this trail during times of high water. Wait until the Fowler River is frozen or better yet, during the summer when the water crossing is an easy rock hop across and you can jump in the river for a quick dip.

There are a number of options you can choose as there is a vast array of over 50 miles of trails within the AMC Cardigan Reservation and the Cardigan Mountain State Forest. The AMC Cardigan Lodge can be reached by taking Rt. 3A out of Bristol, then turning right onto West Shore Road. Continue to Alexandria and then onto Cardigan Mountain Road. Stay on this road, it will turn into Shem Valley Road and you'll arrive at the lodge and trailheads. If you would like more information about the lodge and accommodations call (603) 744-8011.

Chapter 3 - Conservation Lands of the Lakes Region

Those who dwell among the beauties and mysteries of the earth are never alone or weary of life. Those who contemplate the beauty of the earth find reserves of strength that will endure as long as life lasts. The more clearly we can focus our attention on the wonders and realities of the universe, the less taste we shall have for destruction.

Rachel Carson

Today there are 216 town and municipal conservation commissions spread across New Hampshire, as well as several regional and state wide organizations, like the Lakes Region Conservation Trust and the Society for the Protection of New Hampshire Forests. All are committed to protecting the state's most valuable landscapes and are dedicated to conserving , protecting, stewarding and promoting the respectful use of our natural resources such as forests, lakes, streams, wetlands, meadows, and scenic visitas. Conserved lands provide opportunities for individuals and families to hunt, fish, hike, snowshoe, ski or just enjoy a scenic vista. This chapter takes you on adventures to just a few of the conserved lands in the Lakes Region.

Castle in the Clouds Conservation Area

Whose woods these are I think I know.
His house is in the Village though;
He will not see me stopping here
To watch his woods fill up with snow.

Robert Frost

View from the parking lot at Castle in the Clouds Conservation Area

It started snowing early in the morning. Light flakes were floating down from the overcast skies; a picture-perfect day for a woodland hike with Reuben. I thought of all the possibilities for a day hike in the Lakes Region: Page Pond in Meredith, Kelley-Drake in New Hampton, Piper Mountain in Gilford, Red Hill in Moultonborough, Pine Mountain, Alton and others. The opportunities were limitless. After much thought and consulting with Reuben (he's a very wise companion) I decided to return to the Castle in the Clouds Conservation Area in Ossipee. This magnificent conserved land sits on the side of the Ossipee Mountain Range and provides extraordinary hiking, snowshoeing and cross country skiing on 19 trails, totaling over 30 miles. The views from several of the peaks (Roberts, Shaw, Black Snout, Turtleback and Bald Knob) are some of the best in the area. This felt like the right decision for me and Reuben.

I thought about bringing my back country skis and giving them a try on the numerous carriage roads that crisscross the mountains. On second thought I decided on snowshoes and to climb Mount Roberts as I needed to ready my body for forthcoming hikes in the western Maine Mountains and the Adirondack Mountains in upstate New York. When we arrived at the trailhead parking lot it was snowing hard and we were the only car in sight, perfect! Reuben and I would have the entire mountain range to ourselves. Could this be possible? Quickly we hustled to the trail that would take us to Mount Roberts. I cherish the opportunities when Reuben and I can be alone and descend into the solitude of the mountains with only the occasional call of a raven disrupting the silence. Snow was falling silently, wafting around my feet, adding to the mythic setting. Reuben darted around in the fresh fallen snow, throwing it into the air with his snout. Glancing up at me he seemed to ask, "Is it time for a treat?"   Life is so simple for a dog. Why does it seem to be so complicated and confusing for us humans?

We climbed gradually through a hardwood forest, eventually claiming the ridge at about 2,000 ft. There were several viewpoints along the way but on this day the only vistas were a thick cloud cover and a sheet of snow. This was one of those climbs with several false summits. When you think you've achieved the apex of the mountain, you look up. The trail continues and you say, "Oh no, I have to keep climbing upward!" We hiked along in silence passing through a forest of scrub hardwood that seemed to have spent many years battling wind, ice, drought, possibly even fire. When we were finally nearing the true summit we entered a stunning spruce woodland. Fresh snow graced the boughs and icicles dangled downward, the perfect holiday scene. What changed in the ecology of the mountain, mangy hardwoods to beautifully groomed spruce? A question for the ecologist.

At 2.5 miles, after a two hour leisurely climb, we reached the summit of Mount Roberts. On a clear day we would have glorious views of the Ossipee Range, but today the mountains were draped in a blanket of clouds and snow. Not needing to linger, we continued our ramble on the High Ridge Trail. This trail could take us all the way to Mount Shaw, 5.3 miles away. With the unbroken trail I knew it would be risky to attempt to reach Mount Shaw and then have to hike another 7 miles back to the car. I pulled out the map and decided to take the Faraway Mountain trail. It would lead Reuben and me to the Cold Spring Trail and eventually the parking lot.

The High Ridge Trail is aptly named as it traverses the upper reaches of the conservation area. It follows the crest of the mountain range, which is actually the remains of a now extinct volcano, called a ring dike. If you were to view the Ossipee Range from above it would look like a giant circle, 40 miles around. What exists today is what's left of the now extinct volcano. The mountain range is the subsurface remains of the magma chamber and the center of the mountain range is the bottom of the caldera, the volcanic cone that collapsed. The Ossipee Range is one of the best known and most studied ring dike volcanic formations in the east.

With this geological history in mind I continued to break trail, along the High Ridge Trail, which at one time carried visitors to the summit of Mount Rodgers via horse and carriage. This wide trail is one of many old carriage roads winding through the property. Reuben trailed behind me, taking the easy way, while I broke trail. He occasionally scampered off into the woods to chase a ruffed grouse that was lying peacefully in the snow or following the scent of some critter whose prints left a clear path through the woods: deer, fox, coyote, squirrels, and turkeys. As I watched him follow the tracks, his nose plowing through the snow, I mused about all the paths traced in the snow. What a wonderful time to be outdoors in this beautiful setting.

When we reached the trail junction with the Faraway Mountain Trail, another carriage road, we began the long decent to Shannon Pond and the parking lot. The trail made long, sweeping switchbacks, as we cruised downward, occasionally bushwhacking through the open woods, making the descent shorter. If you are interested in bushwhacking and learning how to use a map and compass, this is the place: open woods, plenty of trails and maps are available at the Lakes Region Conservation Trust office in Center Harbor. Our bushwhack brought us to the Cold Spring Trail, which led out to the parking area, passing the Copp cellar hole, the long-gone home of one of the first inhabitants in the area. We arrived at our truck in plenty of time to make it home before dark. We covered about 9 miles in 6 hours, a good day hike in winter conditions.

The Castle in the Clouds Conservation Area provides 30 miles of trails, many are carriage roads constructed in the early twentieth century by Thomas Gustave Plant, a wealthy businessman who built the castle mansion as his summer retreat. You can reach the Castle in the Clouds Conservation Area by driving north on Rt. 25 to Moultonborough, turning right onto Rt. 109. Follow Rt. 109 to the junction of Rt. 171. After driving a short distance on Rt. 171 look for Ossipee Park Rd. and turn left. This road will take you to the parking lot. A trail map is posted on a kiosk. Better yet, you can stop at the Lakes Region Conservation Trust offices on Rt. 25B in Center Harbor and pick up a map. They also have hiking maps available for their other properties. For anyone interested in hiking all five summits and 30 miles of designated trails the LRCT offers a Hiker Achievement patch. All trails are very well marked with plenty of signage to keep you on the trail. For more information you can always call LRCT at 603-253-3301 or email at *(lrct.org)*.

Evelyn H. & Albert D. Morse, Sr. Preserve

Nancy and Reuben on the summit of Pine Mountain
overlooking Lake Winnipesaukee

Nancy, Reuben and I were on our way to hike Pine Mountain, a small summit with great views, when we passed the Mount Major parking lot. It was packed with cars and busses. The shoulder of Rt. 11 was also jammed, bumper to bumper for several hundred yards in either direction. I'm sure the trails and the summit of Mount Major were loaded with hikers. I knew Pine Mountain has equally magnificent views, and I was happy we passed by Major, as we planned to spend the morning in quiet solitude, walking the paths on this old farmland.

We drove to Alton Bay and took a sharp right onto Alton Mountain Road, and then made a left onto Avery Hill Road where we found the trailhead and a parking lot for the Town of Alton's

Mike Burke Forest just across the road. The hike began near the former farmstead of the Morse Family, who farmed this land for many years. The trail winds along a farm road, passing foundations and stone walls that were once part of a working farm, producing dairy products, vegetables, and fruit, especially blueberries. Now the vestiges of the farm lie in silent seclusion, except for the occasional hiker like us trekking to the summit. After passing through the open fields, the trail moderately ascended this small mountain. We soon reached views across open blueberry barrens. We stared for several minutes at the amazing views of Lake Winnipesaukee and the Belknap Range. Within a few hundred yards we were at the summit, sitting on a rock bench, taking in an impressive vista of the Lakes Region. Nancy, Reuben and I sat alone for quite some time, with only the sound of an occasional breeze drifting through the trees.

This 1.7 mile round trip hike took us less than two hours to complete. It is an ideal hike for small children and families who are looking for a short hike with great rewards. The hike can also be used as a teachable moment on farm life as it was lived many years ago. This property is managed by the Society for the Protection of New Hampshire Forests. More information about this preserve and other preserves can be found on their website, (*forestsociety.org*).

Merriman Forest

Around 1960 Frederika and Roger Merriman sold several parcels of their farm, bordering on Squam Lake, to private buyers. However, due to their love of the forests and cliffs rising high above their farm, they gave the Society for the Protection of New Hampshire Forests (Forest Society) 103 acres, now known as The Merriman Forest. The rocky outcrops of Eagle Cliff sit high above Squam Lake and offer some of the best views of the lake and the surrounding mountains, including Mounts Morgan and

Percival. Looking eastward from these cliffs the high peaks of the Sandwich Range arise in the distance, including Whiteface with its gleaming granite face, Passaconaway, and the majestic alpine-like summit of Mount Chocorua. To the west Mount Cardigan can be seen along with its fire tower. In my humble opinion these impressive views represent some of the finest in all the Lakes Region.

I'd heard a great deal about Eagle Cliff and its fine views, but had never climbed the trail leading to the ledges above Squam Lake, ultimately ending at the summit of Red Hill and its beloved fire tower. On a clear summer day, Reuben and I drove to the trailhead located on Bean Road, just north of the Moultonborough/Sandwich town line. There is no parking area, but the shoulder of the road provides ample room to pull off. Within 0.3 miles after starting on the trail, which is maintained by the Squam Lakes Association, we began a

View of Squam Lake from Eagle Cliff

steep climb, using solid foot and hand holds to scramble to the top of the cliffs, an elevation gain of 600 ft. We found a side trail to the right that detours around the cliff, which is a much more moderate climb, but we elected to take the challenging ascent. Once above the rock face the trail gently rose over rock outcrops with fine views, finally reaching the main viewpoint of Eagle Cliff at about 0.5 miles. Reuben and I rested, ate our snacks (sometimes he eating mine) and took in the panorama before us. After a short rest we decided to continue for another two miles to the summit of Red Hill, passing the Teedie Trail junction at one mile. Upon reaching the summit of Red Hill I climbed the fire tower to look in all directions around the Lakes Region.

We then headed back to Bean Road, the way we came, taking the by-pass trail around the cliffs. This was an exhilarating hike I would recommend for anyone who would like the challenge of hand-over-hand rock climbing, combined with fantastic views of the area's lakes and mountains, and a fire tower ascent to culminate the hike. Go to (*forestsociety.org*) for more information on this trail. Thanks to the Squam Lake Association for maintaining the trails.

Cockermouth Forest

This gem of the Forest Society's Reservation properties lies just north of Newfound Lake on North Groton Road. The town of Groton was once named Cockermouth for the river that runs through it. The 1,002 acre parcel was given to the Forest Society in 1991 by William Wadsworth, who had a special appreciation for the area and its diverse wildlife habitat.

The entrance to the property on North Groton Road was difficult to locate as the sign is partially hidden by trees. At the Forest Society sign we found a narrow drive leading to a closed gate and

View from the summit of Bald Knob Mountain

a small parking area, large enough for about three cars. We began our hike passing through the gate and finding a kiosk with a container of trail maps. The map was essential in following the web of trails and wood roads that wind their way through the 1,000 acres of the preserve. The trail system, originally cut by Wadsworth, is blazed in yellow. We followed the Romley-Remick Forest Road, turned onto the Old North Groton Road and then began to climb Bald Knob (2,032 ft.), following the Bald Knob Trail, about 0.8 miles to the summit with views of Newfound Lake, Mount Cardigan and the wind turbines on Tenney Mountain.

The trail then took us over to Crosby Mountain (2,222 ft.) where I found the initials "J.R. Phelps, N.O. Phelps, 1853" carved into the granite of a hidden ledge. On the summit of Crosby more splendid views to the north and east awaited me. We descended from Mount Crosby via the Beeline Trail. This was a steady steep decent on a soft hemlock forest floor. From the Beeline Trail we hooked up with the High Pasture Trail, making our way past the cellar hole of the former Remick Farm, continuing to make our way to Little Pond. We then trekked through an Ecoreserve section where we found at the end of the trail a nine-acre bog and Little Pond. This was a perfect place to eat lunch, overlooking Little Pond, with the sun warming our faces. Not far from our lunch spot we found an unique area supporting a rare patch of red oak and pitch pine.

The entire Cockermouth Forest Reservation is a vast area waiting to be discovered by families, nature enthusiasts, historians, and educators. If you would like more information on the Cockermouth Forest Reservation or other Forest Society properties please go to their website, (*forestsociety.org/reservation-guide*).

Page Pond and Hamlin Woods

My wife Nancy and I decided to hike for a few hours in the Page Pond Forest off Rt. 25 in Meredith. By hiking there we could also stop at Moulton Farm and pick up a few fresh vegetables, as the farm is on the road into the Page Pond Conservation Area. It was a warm sunny day, so we dressed lightly, packed a couple bottles of water, some snacks, and off we went for our two hour jaunt in the woods. We drove to Moulton Farm, continuing past the farm stand, until we came to the Page Pond trailhead parking area and kiosk.

The Page Pond Forest is a 567 acre town forest under the stewardship of the Meredith Conservation Commission. The conservation property not only holds Page Pond, but also a number of other interesting features: Page Brook, a watershed that drains most of

Page Pond

the surrounding forest, significant wetlands, an abandoned quarry, an old mill dam, old farm cellar holes, a family cemetery and stone walls. The well-marked trail system provides visitors the opportunity to walk through a beautiful, well maintained forest, as well as visiting historic landmarks.

At the trailhead we checked out the map located at the kiosk. We decided to make our way to Page Pond and from there hike to the abandoned mill site. It was an easy walk to the pond, which offered views across the pond to the distant hills in the south. After spending a few minutes at the pond we continued hiking over the rolling forest trail until we came to a magnificent dam that had been beautifully restored. The dam was part of a lumber mill complex built by Dudley Leavitt, an early settler in the Meredith area in 1836. Leavitt later sold the mill to John Page and over the years other owners took possession of the land and mill. The mill was powered by an undershoot water wheel. The dam itself is an impressive structure standing 18-feet high at the spillway, 96-feet long and 5-feet wide.

After exploring the mill area we backtracked to the trail that would eventually lead us to the site of the granite quarry and "store". After a casual walk on an abandoned wagon road we found the quarry that at one time was a local resource for building roads and rail beds. The so-called trap rock, an igneous rock containing high levels of magnesium and iron, was ideal for this purpose. The quarry operated during the early part of the twentieth century and closed in 1945. Next to the abandoned quarry lies the remains of the "quarry store", a treasure trove of abandoned machinery, cables, and vehicles once used to quarry and crush the rock.

After poking around the quarry store we headed back to the car, but first we wanted to find the Leavitt Cemetery, located just offthe trail, a few yards from the parking lot. The cemetery was part of the Dudley and Judith Leavitt farm. The Leavitts moved there in 1806. Dudley was a very prominent citizen of Meredith and wrote the annual Leavitt's Old Farmer's Almanac from 1797 until his death in 1851. After spending some time viewing old head stones we walked back to the car and drove to Moulton Farm, stopping to pick up fresh veggies for supper.

After getting home I planned the next "walk in the woods": hiking the trail complex at Hamlin Woods, another Meredith Town Forest. On this escapade Reuben and I planned to meet up with Adam, a journalist for the Laconia Daily Sun, his wife Shannon and their son Otis, a delightful young adventurer. We met at the trailhead parking lot, located on Chemung Road. We began our hike by trying to decide which trails would suit all age groups, two years of age through senior citizen (me). It was a beautiful, brisk, late fall day and we decided to walk the Ponds Trail, a route that would take about two hours to complete, with Otis walking part of the way. The series of ponds host abundant wildlife including a resident beaver family. It was a joyous woodland amble, taking in the views of the ponds, running into an old friend, who was leading an AMC orienteering class, and watching Otis as he explored the trail, many times lying prone on the ground. The roots and rocks proved quite the challenge for Otis to maintain walking upright, but he was a determined trekker. We wandered along the trail and encountered many others who had also come to Hamlin to enjoy a day on the trail.

In addition to the natural beauty of the area, we also found an old homestead and cellar hole, once the home of an early settler. We considered continuing on our hike by taking the trail to the height of land, which provides nice views of Wicwas Lake, but decided to return to the trailhead and head home. It was another short day spent in the great outdoors of the Lakes Region with fellow trekkers.

Both Page Pond Forest and Hamlin Forest offer well maintained hiking trails that can easily be completed in a few hours. The trail systems are also suitable for snowshoeing and cross country skiing. So get out and enjoy these two great town forests in Meredith. Accolades must be given to the Town of Meredith and the Meredith Conservation Commission for their tireless work in preserving and maintaining these invaluable tracts of land.

Waukewan Highlands and Belknap Woods

Site of the picnic area adjacent to the old Meredith Town Reservoir

When the Winter Solstice arrives, it is usually time to get out the snowshoes and other paraphernalia one needs for safe and comfortable winter hiking. On a cold pre-winter day I was fortunate to get in one more hike before we got hammered with snow, cold and the biting winds that mark our winter season. Reuben and I set out to hike the trails of the Waukewan Highlands Community Park in Meredith (Meredith Conservation Commission) and Belknap Woods in Center Harbor (Squam Lakes Association). Both areas offer moderate to easy hiking on well designed and maintained trails for all ages and abilities.

First on our agenda was Waukewan Highlands. Located off Rt. 106, this 190-acre forest is managed by the Meredith Conservation Commission. The area has three miles of trails maintained for hiking, jogging, mountain biking, snowshoeing, cross country skiing and horseback riding. There is a large parking lot that's plowed in winter. After parking our car in the empty lot we spotted a kiosk at the trailhead with a large map showing a trail system of over three miles. I decided to take the White Trail leading to Hart's Pond. This is the centerpiece of the park and once served as the reservoir for Meredith. We sat on the picnic bench while Reuben tested the water. The pond was beginning to freeze over and Reuben knew enough to stay off the ice rimming the shoreline. During the summer this would make an excellent spot for a snack or picnic lunch, but with a chilling wind blowing across the water, our respite didn't last long. We were tempted to follow the Yellow Trail, about a mile in length, but time was running short and we opted to follow the Blue Trail. The blue blazes took us away from the pond and down an old road where we found a swampy wet area. We looked around for a blaze and found none. Backtracking, I noticed a faint blaze to the right and headed into the woods. The moderately difficult trail climbed steadily for about a half-mile until we reached a ridge and began to swing back to the parking lot.

After reaching the parking lot we again headed down to Hart's Pond to the red blazed trail and began to circle the pond. This shorter trail of 0.6 miles was less challenging and it was a good thing, because it was getting late and we had one more area to visit, Belknap Woods. We reached the parking lot in short order, jumped into the truck and sped away to Center Harbor.

When we arrived in Center Harbor I turned onto Rt. 25B. After driving about three miles we arrived at the trailhead across from Dog Cove, a small bay of Squam Lake. The parking area can accommodate only two or three cars, and I was fortunate that there was only one other car parked in the lot. This 90-acre forest was donated to the Squam Lakes Association in 1986 and the trails are maintained by the Association. At the trailhead we found a sign indicating two trails, the Beaver Pond Loop, one mile in length and the Outer Loop, a two-mile trail. I looked at my watch, only 30 minutes until sunset at 4:15. I knew the two-mile trail would leave me hiking out in darkness with no headlamp. It was an easy choice, the Beaver Loop Trail. The entire forest is intertwined with wetlands and creeks. It's a prime habitat for amphibians such as salamanders, toads, frogs and newts. However, I knew that the time to find these creatures of the wetlands had long since passed. They were burrowed in the mud of the wetlands, ponds and streams until spring. It is interesting to note that amphibians are indicators of a healthy ecosystem and there are over one dozen different species in the immediate area. The importance of this ecosystem is underscored by the writing of Frederic Clements, an American plant ecologist who argued, *"Any given ecosystem must be understood as a living organism in which every component, from the soil to the animals to the trees form an interconnected superstructure."* (*American Canopy,* Eric Rutkow, p. 303).

The focal point of this forest is the beaver pond. The trail is dominated by mature hemlock and white pine, with a few hardwoods, such as red oak and beech scattered in the mix. The trail provided little challenge as I raced along, trying to beat twilight and hoping to get a photo of the beaver pond before darkness set in. Reuben romped ahead of me dashing off the trail at times, following a scent of some unknown critter. We reached the junction with the Outer Loop Trail and I was tempted to follow it, but common sense woke me to the fact that daylight was fading fast. When we reached the beaver pond I was astounded by its size, one of the largest I've seen. I lingered on the boardwalk spanning

Beaver Pond on the Inner Loop Trail
of Belknap Woods Conservation Area

the inlet to the pond and absorbed the splendor before me. Many dead and limbless trees stood upright in the water, straight and tall, like soldiers guarding the temple. I wanted to see beaver, but I knew they must be tucked away in their lodges, resting, eating and waiting for spring to arrive. It was time for Reuben and me to hustle back to the car.

When winter has fully engulfed the Lakes Region, these two trails offer a great opportunity to strap on snowshoes that have been stored away in the basement or garage, and get in shape for winter mountain travel. The trails are suitable for all ages and abilities, especially novices to the world of winter hiking. You can always wait until warmer weather arrives, and visit Waukewan Highlands and Belknap Woods to observe the unfurling of spring and be engulfed by the magic of the forest as it emerges from its four months of sleep. For more information and a map of the area go to, (*squamlakes.org/map*).

Ramblin' Vewe Farm and Lockes Hill

Reuben and I drove to Morrill Street, and when we saw the green, wide-open pastures of the farm we knew we were close. Sheep dotted the fields on both sides of the road and the trees lining the road were dazzling, with the colors of autumn: red, yellow, orange and brown.

We pulled into the hikers' parking lot and set out on the Farm View Hill Top Trail. The trail took us past fields and barns. We wound our way over old stone walls, past ancient, abandoned farm equipment, and even along the hillside that was once used for downhill skiing. The rope tow system made up of wheel hubs and an old car engine are still visible along the trail. There were also other old farm artifacts scattered along the trail that reminded me that this land was once cleared and farmed as pasture. From a high point we found a scenic view overlooking the farm and the hills beyond. It was a delightful start to the day, reacquainting myself with this wonderful recreational resource.

The 245-acres of the farm have been set aside for forestry and recreation and it has an extensive trail system that can be used for walking, skiing, snowshoeing and mountain biking. It is a non-profit 501(c)3 organization whose mission is to, "Protect and preserve Ramblin' Vewe Farm, conserve the heritage of working farms and rural landscapes, foster educational and recreational activities and create trails to connect people, communities and the land." It has been in operation since 1987 and maintains a flock of registered purebred sheep. There is even a store on the property to purchase meat, eggs, vegetables and other locally raised products. To find out more go to (*ramblinvewefarm.org*).

From Ramblin' Vewe Farm we drove over to Rt. 11, where we saw a sign for the Lockes Hill Trails. We pulled into the spacious parking lot and began our hike on the Lakeview Trail. There's a large kiosk at the head of the trail with maps to guide you on your sojourn up and over Lockes Hill. The trail system includes two trails, the Lakeview and Quarry Trails, which are marked with blue blazes. The two trails form a circuitous route which begin and end at the trailhead parking lot.

The property's 280 acres is a habitat demonstration area, maintained and managed by the Town of Gilford and the New Hampshire Cooperative Extension, "For the purpose of increasing public awareness, understanding and appreciation of the relationships between wildlife and their forested habitats". At one time the property was the estate of Benjamin Kimball, a Concord entrepreneur and President of the Boston and Maine Railroad. While traveling in Germany he became enraptured with castles built along the Rhine River. When he returned to New Hampshire he built his own castle on Lockes Hill, completing the structure in 1899. After Kimball's death his family continued to use the castle as a summer retreat. In 1960 Kimball's daughter Charlotte established a trust for the property and in 1980 the Town of Gilford was appointed trustee. The castle is now privately owned.

Reuben and I began our hike on the Lakeview Trail which took us up a number of switchbacks, through a combination of hardwood trees and towering hemlocks. At about the half-mile mark we reached "the glade" an opening in the forest that provided spectacular views of Lake Winnipesaukee and the Ossipee Mountains. Large telescopes were mounted on poles to get a closer look at the islands standing out in the glittering water. Nature guides posted on trees provided interesting information about the ecology found along the trail. Walking through the glade we found another view point and then reached a clearing referred to as an "oak savannah". This area is marked by low growing shrubs and blueberry bushes, with limited views from rock outcrops off the trail. Here Reuben and I rested, took in the views and watched chickadees dart in and out of the brush.

When Reuben and I returned to the trail we found ourselves on the start of the Quarry Trail and began our descent of Lockes Hill. The trail drops over ledges and rock outcrops, providing a very different hiking experience, than our ascent of Lockes Hill. Nearing the quarry site, I met three people vacationing from Boston. They just happened to see the Lockes Hill Trail sign while driving on Rt. 11 and decided to explore the trail. They were awestruck by the beauty of the forest, the fantastic views and were eager to find out more about this trail and others in the area. I began to pontificate on the astounding array of trails in the Lakes Region and the majesty of the mountains and hills found within a few miles. They seemed overwhelmed by my dissertation, so I let them be, to find their own calling to the trails.

As I neared the end of my hike I came to the quarry site where granite stones were cut to build Kimball's Castle. Reuben saw the opportunity to cool down and get a mud bath as he lunged into the quarry pool. From the small quarry we followed the old tote road that at one time was used to haul quarry stone to the castle site. We completed the 1.8 mile round trip hike in about two hours. This hike is ideal for a family, but is moderately difficult in some steep sections. The views and nature lessons posted along the trail are well worth the effort.

Slim Baker Area for Outdoor Living and Sugarloaf Ridge - Goose Pond Conservation Area

There are several Sugarloaf Mountains in New Hampshire: North, Middle and South Sugarloaf in the Twin Mountain area, trail-less Sugarloaf in Benton, Sugarloaf in the Nash Stream Forest near Groveton, and Little and Big Sugarloaf Mountains in Alexandria, located on the western shore of Newfound Lake. I wanted to complete my goal of summiting all the Sugarloaf Mountains in New Hampshire and I had summited them all except the Sugarloafs in Alexandria. Therefore, I planned a day to hike the trails in the Sugarloaf Ridge-Goose Pond Conservation Area. Before I began this quest, I explored the trails of the Slim Baker Area in Bristol. This would make for a full day of hiking close to home in two areas with fantastic trail systems, topped off with outstanding views. Both properties, Slim Baker Area for Outdoor Living and Sugarloaf Ridge - Goose Pond Conservation Area are only minutes apart; what a treasure for outdoor oriented

Signage at trail junction, Sugarloaf and
Goose Pond Conservation Area

families looking for a day of hiking.

Reuben and I began the day by driving to Bristol, turning onto South Main Street, bearing right onto High Street, and taking a right onto New Chester Road that led to the Slim Baker Area. This 135 acre property encompasses Little Round Top Mountain and is dedicated to the memory of Everett "Slim" Baker (1910-1953), a well-known, respected and much-loved New Hampshire Fish and Game Conservation Officer. With Slim's passing at forty three due to cancer, a dedicated group of Newfound area residents organized to establish a memorial in his name.. The area includes a newly designed and constructed network of trails, a rustic lodge, picnic areas, camp sites and a lean-to nestled in seclusion. The facilities are used by a number of community groups including a pre-school nature education program.

We first hiked to the summit of Little Round Top and Inspiration Point. The view from Inspiration Point overlooks Bristol and the surrounding hills of New Hampton. While taking in the view Reuben suddenly romped over to greet a couple taking pictures. After our introductions they told me they were celebrating their anniversary at Inspiration Point, where they were married ten years earlier. They went on to say that they fell in love thirty years earlier as children enrolled in the camping program here. Now they were returning to the place that brought them together. After our short encounter I moved along down the well maintained trails, hiking to the lodge where we were greeted by the happy voices of preschoolers. While Reuben was making friends with all the children, I learned about the outdoor education component of the Slim Baker Area, dedicated to, *"Provide programs of outdoor recreation, nature study and practical conservation for residents of the Newfound area and visitors."* (S.B.A. Master Plan).

Following our visit with the children, Reuben and I wandered down the path to an abandoned wagon road, the New Chester Mountain Road, which was cut though the wilderness in 1762. The wilderness road was used by stagecoaches to shuttle passengers between Concord and Haverhill until 1838. By 1878 this portion of the road was discontinued. It now serves foot traffic of hikers and campers. Reuben and I followed the abandoned road until it turned onto a trail that took us back to the lodge and the parking lot.

Next on our agenda was the Sugarloaf-Goose Pond Conservation Area on the western shore of Newfound Lake. This Conservation area is owned by the Lakes Region Conservation Trust and maintained by the Newfound Lakes Region Association. We drove to Wellington State Park, where we found the parking lot just north of the entrance to the park on West Shore Road. We began our hike following the Elwell Trail. The trail is named for Colonel

Alcott Farrar Elwell, long-time director of Camp Mowglis in Hebron. Within a short distance from the trailhead we reached a myriad of signs stuck to a post. I looked at the directional signs and gasped. From this point the possibilities for hikes of varying distance and degree of difficulty are abundant: Goose Pond 0.6 miles, Big Sugarloaf 1.8 miles, Bear Mountain 3.5 miles, Oregon Mountain 7 miles, Mount Cardigan and Cardigan State Park 12.5 miles. Take your choice. Since Reuben and I had only half a day, Big Sugarloaf and Goose Pond would be our destination. Reuben bounded off, down the trail, while I trotted behind, following the signs and yellow blazes that would take us to Little Sugarloaf (1,000 ft.) and Big Sugarloaf (1,307 ft.).

The trail wound through wetlands and a mix of hardwood-softwood forest, until we found ourselves beginning to climb steeply to the summit of Little Sugarloaf. At the summit we looked down on Newfound Lake. We could hear the buzzing of motor boats and the shrieks of swimmers at Wellington State Park. Most of the trekkers I met along the way were content to end their hike on Little Sugarloaf with outstanding views of Newfound Lake. However, the larger "Loaf" waited farther up the trail, another mile. Following the well-marked trail, we dipped into a col and up a small rock outcrop. Within a quarter mile of the summit, the trail climbed steeply to rock ledges and a viewpoint. It was well worth the effort to get to "Big Loaf". The views over the lake were outstanding as well as views to the south. Belknap and Gunstock Mountains were clearly seen in the distance. When I arrived at the summit of Big Sugarloaf I completed the "New Hampshire Sugarloaf quest".

Our next destination was Goose Pond, where Reuben could take a swim, get a drink and cool off. We backtracked down the mountain, coming to the intersection with the orange blazed trail that would lead us to the mountain pond. Upon reaching the pond Reuben hurtled into the water. After his dip into the crystal, blue waters on the pond we followed the shoreline trail circling around the pond. All along the way we were greeted with beautiful views of the pond and surrounding forest. Signs of beaver activity were everywhere, but we saw none. After finishing our hike around the pond we began our trek back to the parking lot.

Hiking the trails of the Slim Baker Area for Outdoor Living and Sugarloaf Ridge-Goose Pond Conservation area would make a fine summer outing for the whole family. Both areas can be hiked in one day or done as two separate escapades. At the end of the day your family could visit Wellington State Park, have a picnic and enjoy a swim in the spring-fed waters of Newfound Lake.

Whitten Woods and Kelley-Drake Conservation Areas

Trail sign at Kelley-Drake Conservation Area, New Hampton

In Ashland, NH lies a jewel of a conservation area, Whitten Woods. I was referred to this 414 acre property, located off Highland Street in Ashland, by a reader of my column in the *Laconia Daily Sun,* and after receiving his email I acted on the suggestion.

The property was named for the former owner and farmer, Reuben Whitten. In 1816 the Northeastern United States fell under a thick cloud of volcanic ash from a volcano eruption in Indonesia, causing the "the year without summer". In other parts of North America and Europe it was known as the "Starvation Year". Killing frosts and snow in summer resulted in lost crops and little food to get people through the winter. Reuben's farm was located high above Ashland on a south-facing slope called Indian Hill. Due to the location of his farm, he was one of a few farmers able to raise crops including more than 40 bushels of wheat which he and his wife Sally shared with their neighbors, saving them from starvation.

Reuben (not to be confused with Reuben Whitten) and I started our hike from the parking area on Highland Street. Most of the property is woven with old woods roads and skidder paths, making the trails desirable for hiking and cross country skiing. Trails are well-marked with blazes and signage. We followed a wide road to the beginning of a climb to North Peak. From a clearing, not far from the summit, we found a wide open vista of Squam Lake and the Squam Mountain Range. Following the climb to the summit we bushwhacked around the slope for other views. Deer tracks blanketed the woods, along with tracks of coyotes that I think were tracking prey.

Back on the trail I eventually came to the south summit trailhead. When I reached the summit I found a picnic table and a register, along with another outstanding view. The register had only a few names and dates which led me to believe not many people know about Whitten Woods and the spectacular summit views, or else the register would be crowded with names. I was the only person on the trail during this sun-filled day. I would guess that few people know or use this wonderful recreational resource sitting high above Ashland and Squam Lake. I would like to thank the reader of my column for suggesting this hike in Whitten Woods. The property is a collaborative effort by Ashland residents, the Ashland Conservation Commission, New England Forestry Foundation, the Squam Lakes Conservation Society and the Squam Lakes Association. Thanks to these organizations and individuals for preserving this property and making it accessible for the public to enjoy, learn about Reuben Whitten and the year without summer.

Following the Whitten Woods adventure I still had plenty of time to consider another short hike. This time closer to home, the Kelley-Drake Conservation Area in New Hampton. A network of trails had just been completed. Being a member of the New Hampton Conservation Commission and ushering the construction of the trails, it was important to check on their condition.

In 1775 Samuel Kelley (1733-1813) brought his wife and two young sons from Exeter, NH to New Hampton and built a log cabin adjacent to Kelley Pond (now known as Pemigewasset Lake). Over time he acquired large tracts of land in and around New Hampton. He moved his family to the summit of "the Pinnacle" and gave his sons William and Nathan land at the base of the hill, a part of which is now the 240 acre Kelley-Drake Conservation Area. Samuel soon became one of the guiding forces in the settlement of New Hampton. He built the Town House (1792) and a number of other buildings in the town. Around 1820 the original Kelley homestead was sold to Abraham and Nathanial Drake. The Luther Drake family farmed the land until 1950 when the house and barn were destroyed by fire on Christmas Day.

In 1966 the land was purchased by J. Willcox Brown from the estate of Luther Drake. Willcox Brown, a graduate of Yale School of Forestry, purchased other properties in the state for preservation and wrote a fascinating book, *Forest History of Mount Moosilauke*. In 1978 New Hampton bought the property through funds made available by the federal government's Land and Water Conservation Fund. The property has undergone various phases of reclamation. Most recently, the New Hampton Conservation Commission cleared the cellar hole complex, mowed the fields and meadows, reclaimed the apple orchard, and built hiking, skiing and biking trails.

I arrived with Reuben at the parking lot off of Kelley Pond Road, a short distance from the entry into the property. I began my mission by hiking up the old farm road. Moseying along the road I soon came to a trail sign marking the trailhead for the Valley and Ridge Trails. The Valley Trail, blazed in blue, follows the course of a small stream, while the Ridge Trail (red) climbs steeply, then follows the ridgeline with views to Dana Hill. Massive hemlock and white pine trees dominate the terrain. Both trails junction with the Farm Road Trail and return to the Kelley-Drake cellar holes. A kiosk has been placed adjacent to the cellar holes by the New Hampton Historical Society and describes the history of the property. I cruised the trails checking for blowdowns and doing some brushing along the way. We then took the Farm Road Trail to Pemigewasset Lake, where Reuben enjoyed his last swim of the day.

The conservation area is open year-round and is not only ideal for hiking and biking, but also snowshoeing, cross-country skiing, hunting or just enjoying a walk along the old stone walls and open meadow. To get to the Kelley-Drake Conservation Area take Rt.104 from Meredith and in New Hampton turn left onto Sinclair Hill Rd. Take the next left onto Kelley Pond Road and drive to the designated parking area. Walk around the gate and onto the Farm Road. Watch for the trailhead on the right. Farther along you'll find the cellar hole complex and large open meadows. If you continue following the road you will eventually end up on the shores of Pemigewasset Lake.

Red Hill River and Homestead Forest

Reuben peering into Devil's Den

I thought I had run out of trails to hike in the Lakes Region. I have lived in the area for more than forty years and have hiked all the trails in the Ossipee, Belknap and Squam Range, and many others throughout the area. I also have looked northward to the White Mountains, summiting all the peaks above 3,000 feet and trekked hundreds of miles of trails. Always looking for new trails to hike and areas to explore, I wandered to the mountains of Maine, Vermont, and New York. I even traveled westward, hiking in the Rockies of Montana and the Sierras of California, south to the Appalachians. For some of us I think it's in our DNA to look beyond our own shores, to lands yet to be discovered. There is a strange longing to search for new and far-off domains. Emily Bronte wrote: *"I'll walk where my own nature would be leading, where the wild wind blows on the mountainside."*

Yet, if I look closely in my own "backyard", I can find those unique and beautiful places, *"Where the wild wind blows on the mountainside."* I don't need to travel far and wide. John Muir wrote, *"In every walk with nature, one receives far more than he seeks."* Looking for trails closer to home, I discovered a number of areas, conserved by local, regional and state-wide conservation organizations. Two properties recommended by the Lakes Region Conservation Trust (LRCT) were the Red Hill River Conservation Area in Sandwich and the Homestead Forest Conservation Area in Ashland, two amazingly unique and stunning properties.

The Red Hill River Conservation Area is located between Range Road and Great Rock Road, not far from Center Sandwich. It not only provides a scenic woodland and wetland complex, but also contributes significantly to the area's wildlife communities and water quality. The Red Hill River and its tributaries flow from and through areas such as: Red Hill Pond, Red Hill, and Garland Pond, where significant land has been conserved by the town of Sandwich, LRCT, and The Nature Conservancy. The original parcel of 372 acres was purchased from Denley Emerson, a Sandwich resident, who sold five properties to the LRCT, including the magnificent Dinsmore Mountain Preserve. Another parcel, sold to the LRCT by the David Leach Family, was added later to the Red Hill River property, bringing the total area to 416 acres of conserved land. In addition the Red Hill River Preserve abuts the 176 acre Myers-Schneider Property on which the town of Sandwich holds a conservation easement, totaling 592 acres of unfragmented forest The conserved land provides habitat for bear, bobcat, beaver, fox, moose, and many other animals and plants. The conserved land also helps to maintain water quality in the Red Hill River watershed for the benefit of Sandwich and nearby towns.

Reuben and I began our hike through Red Hill River Conservation Area on the Jocelyn Fleming Gutchess Trail starting from the parking lot on Range Road. The trail took us through open woodland, bounded by stone walls. We eventually reached the Red Hill River and discovered a large complex of stone walls, a barn foundation and a cellar hole. After exploring the abandoned farm complex Reuben and I journeyed along the entire length of the trail, as it runs along the bank of the river. We encountered massive white pine trees, gnarly hemlocks overhanging the river bank and a large beaver flowage. Gnawed tree trunks and beaver lodges indicated an active colony living in the area. Our hike came to a halt when we reached an abandoned bridge abutment. We turned around and headed back toward Great Rock Road, passing through wetlands, cedar groves, huge ash and towering white pine trees. We ended our hike on Great Rock Road, then ambled back to the parking lot, bushwhacking through the forested landscape.

A few days later Reuben and I drove a short distance from our home to the Homestead Forest Conservation Area in Ashland. The conserved property is literally 10 minutes from my home, located at the end of Lambert Road. Some locals know it as Devil's Den, because of a rock slide and the numerous "caves" created by the fallen boulders. These 604 acres of conserved land contain a collection of cellar holes, barn foundations and rusted wire that indicate it was once home to at least five farms, and an agricultural community that existed here in the mid-1800s. Now the pastures and fields have grown back into forests, leaving little evidence that this area had a rich agricultural tradition. Property to the north and west is conserved by the New England Forestry Foundation, a private landowner and the Squam Lakes Conservation Society via ownership or a conservation easement, creating contiguous parcels of land totaling 1,128 acres.

From the end of Lambert Road Reuben and I began another exploratory adventure into New Hampshire's past, as well as discovering beautiful woodlands, steams, rock formations, caves, wetlands, and viewpoints. We first climbed the Winona Ledge Trail (blazed yellow) which led us to a series of cliffs overlooking Winona and Waukewan Lakes. At the end of the trail we found a rock cairn marking the height of land. We continued to follow the cliff edge, hoping for a better viewpoint. As we bushwhacked along the ledges I found trees stripped of their bark, signs of porcupines living in the crevices and openings in the ledges. I quickly summoned Reuben to my side (he's been quilled before) and hustled back to Lambert Road to continue our mission of discovery.

There are red, white and blue blazes throughout the property that identify the internal and outer boundary lines of the property. Don't mistake these for trail blazes as I did. They will take you into areas where you may get lost. Stay with the yellow blazes. We returned to the Lambert Road Trail, which at one time served as an important thoroughfare for the families who lived in the area, connecting Holderness and Ashland. Staying on the road, after walking a mile, we found the trail sign for the Gobban Trail. Adjacent to the trailhead is the largest stone foundation I have ever seen, a fantastic structure. When viewing these old cellar holes I'm always amazed by the immense granite boulders that had to be lifted and fitted into place.

After a thorough inspection of the foundation, we began a 600 foot climb to a rock outcrop with a remarkable view of Winona Lake and the Belknap Range. We then continued on the Gobban Trail, climbing over ledges and through stands of white pine, red oak, sugar maple and ash. We then came to the junction with the Devil's Den Trail and began the last leg of our journey to a series of rock outcrops and the infamous Devil's Den. We found the "cave" where the legendary devilish phantom lies in waiting for an innocent hiker to plummet into his hole. Reuben looked into the den and cocked his head, as if hearing the scream of an ancient wild beast. He turned with his tail between his legs and scampered down the rocky path. I quickly followed after

Reuben, thinking I heard footsteps behind me, and we were soon back to the parking lot.

Maps of trailed properties of the LRCT can be obtained from the LRCT office, Dane Hill Road, Center Harbor or on-line at *lrc-t.org*.

Chapter 4 - Leaving the Crowds Behind

Nature has become a passion and a tonic for me, so finding a way to keep it close is a priority. It satisfies what I call my appetite for solitude.

Helen Mirren

Driving north through Franconia Notch, heading to a remote peak north of the notches, I was amazed at the number of vehicles parked along I-93. The trailhead parking lots were clogged with cars and hikers and the pull- off lane was now the new parking lot. Each weekend and even during the week, the endless lines of hikers march up and down the trails leading to Franconia Ridge, Mts. Lincoln, Liberty, Flume and Lafayette. The same holds true for other destinations in the White Mountains. The parking lots at Pinkham Notch, Appalachia, Crawford Notch, and others are crammed with vehicles, crowded beyond capacity with hikers donning packs to reach the high summits of the White Mountains. The trails are loaded with marching hordes. I wonder, how can these lovers of the mountains have a quality experience? I also beg the question, can these mountain trails withstand the throngs of hikers marching up and down their well-worn pathways every day? At what point will these beautiful, rugged mountain trails become another sidewalk, like those found in the city. When I occasionally hike these trails, which I now try to avoid, it is common to find litter, clothing, even human waste and used toilet paper lying along the path.

This trampling of the trails has had a devastating effect not only on the wilderness experience we all long for, but also on fragile alpine vegetation. Peak bagging junkies, cackling on their phones and hooked on their social media devices further erode what John Muir called, *"The grandest temple of nature I was ever permitted to enter."* The natural beauty of the White Mountains is being consumed and eroded by those who crave to find inspiration and solace. I totally understand the attraction and pull of hiking in the Presidential Range: the vistas, the challenge, the exertion of a long hard day of hiking and earning the distinction of summiting the forty-eight. I have also pursued that goal, and I may sound like an old curmudgeon. However, I've come to understand that these renowned mountains cannot continue to withstand the pressure of endless lines of hikers. There is a price to pay. The natural beauty that draws us to the mountains is being diminished by the sheer number of hikers who are on the trails every day.

In the past few years I have taken the paths less traveled and find them to be as rewarding as a climb to the summit of Mount Madison or Adams. There are many gems waiting to be explored, offering solitude, natural beauty and a wilderness experience many of us cherish. There are hundreds of trails outside of those leading to the highest peaks that provide spectacular views, natural beauty, challenging hikes and the serenity that only nature can provide. Below are several of my favorite trails where you will find, in the words of Gary Snyder, *"The fertility of the soul, the magic of animals, the power vision of solitude."*

Walking into Color

Because in the end, you won't remember the time you spent working in an office or mowing the lawn. Climb that goddamn mountain.

Jack Kerouac

I was transfixed by the colors before me as I stood on the Z-Bridge which crosses a massive beaver flowage along the Zealand Trail. The mountainside was filled with the textures and hues of the northern forest as the autumn season approached. The green

Fran and Reuben hiking on the Ethan Pond Trail located on the side of Whitewall Mountain

of the spruce and balsam fir contrasted with the red and yellow of the maple, beech and birch. This is a time of transition: the hummingbirds have left our feeders at home to begin their journey to South America, our flower gardens are turning brown, our window boxes have been dumped into the compost bin, the woods are silent as the chickadees, warblers and finches seem to have disappeared and hawks circle overhead getting ready to exit New Hampshire. The "snow birds" are making plans for their migration to warmer climes, just like the birds around our home. The days are getting shorter. These signs are signaling the beginning of autumn and serve as a signpost that winter is not far off.

Fran, Reuben and I were heading into the Pemigewasset Wilderness immersed in this period of transition, with the reminder that summer is behind us and winter is waiting in the wings, ready to spring into action. Hiking the Zealand Trail on this warm fall day was like returning to visit an old friend. I've hiked this trail many times, going back to the early 1990s. The trail, which for the most part is the rail bed of the long abandoned Zealand Valley Railroad, meanders along the Zealand River eventually ending at a junction with the Ethan Pond Trail and the Appalachian Mountain Club's Zealand Falls Hut. Today we weren't hiking to the hut, but on a mission to climb an obscure mountain, Shoal Pond Peak (3,051 ft.) which stands alone between the Shoal Pond Trail and the Thoreau Falls Trail.

Following the Ethan Pond Trail we traversed the shoulder of Whitewall Mountain on an old railroad grade which serves as a footpath. The steep talus cliffs rose high above. In the early 1900s, immense forest fires swept through the mountains and valleys of this area, due to the masses of slash left by the loggers of the J.E. Henry Company, as they cleared entire mountainsides. The fire's intense heat caused the mountain's steep cliffs to crack and crumble, wiping out sections of the roadbed. Over time erosion has taken its toll on the trail and numerous rock slides have rumbled down the mountain and onto the trail. Still, even with a few rock scrambles, the trail is a pleasure to hike and offers some of the best views in the White Mountains. We continued on the trail until we reached the short spur to Thoreau Falls and the junction with the Thoreau Falls Trail. In his mountain guide, *The White Mountains: a Handbook for Travellers* (1881) Moses F. Sweetser (1848-1897) named these falls on the North Fork of the Pemigewasset River for the writer and naturalist Henry David Thoreau. Thoreau hiked in the White Mountains, climbed Mount Washington twice, but never saw the falls named in his honor. A hike to Thoreau Falls from the Zealand Road parking lot, via Zealand Trail and the Ethan Pond Trail is a very achievable 4.5 miles over relatively easy trails following logging railroad beds of the now defunct Zealand Valley Railroad. The trail offers spectacular views all along the way. Birds such as boreal chickadee, white-winged crossbill, spruce grouse, black-backed woodpecker and gray jay are commonly found in the area along with moose, American martin, snowshoe hare and Canada Lynx. This makes a great day hike, especially during the changing colors of autumn. If you choose to hike in autumn beware of moose. This is rutting season, when bull moose are looking for a mate. If you hear thrashing in the woods, groaning and grunting, you may be entering into a "no fly zone." Be on the lookout.

Reuben, Fran and I decided not to take the time to view Thoreau Falls and we continued on our way, following the Ethan Pond Trail to the junction of Shoal Pond Trail, which would lead us to the base of Shoal Pond Mountain, where we would begin our bushwhack to the summit. After hiking a short distance to Shoal Pond, we found two campsites that would make a perfect spot to pitch a tent for an overnight backpacking trip. Shoal Pond, the name refers to its shallowness, is one of the few backcountry ponds in New Hampshire that provides opportunities to fish for wild trout. A sign posted on a tree adjacent to the trail states, "*The trout population is not supplemented or maintained by stocking. These waters are subject to catch and release only, fishing tackle is restricted (artificial lures and flies), and the open season is shorter to protect spawning trout in the fall.*" If you do decide to make an overnight backpacking trip to Shoal Pond, be sure to bring your fly rod. The season is only open from the fourth Saturday of April until Labor Day. The area around the pond would make a great place to view wildlife and you have a good chance of seeing a moose feasting on plant life in the pond so don't forget your camera.

Fran, Reuben and I continued along the pond, following the trail through wet, boggy areas over rotting and broken bog bridges. It was evident that this section of the trail is not well used and is probably not a high priority for maintenance, since it is within the boundaries of the Pemigewasset Wilderness. The bogs and small streams offered Reuben many opportunities to cool off and take a

Beaver Pond on the Zealand Trail

mud bath. After crossing the boggy areas we began our whack up Shoal Pond Mountain, following old skid roads and herd paths, made by moose. Reaching the ridge of the mountain we plowed our way through tightly packed spruce and fir. As we struggled through this thick growth, Reuben found the easy routes under branches and blow-downs blocking our path to the summit. After much pushing and plowing we found the summit canister, signed in and quickly made our way back down the mountain.

On our way back along the Shoal Pond Trail, I noticed many wild-flowers growing in abundance and turning brown with the advance of autumn: goldenrod, aster, Indian poke, clintonia and marsh marigold. We also ran into two Appalachian Trail thru hikers, "Willy Nelson" and "Penguin" (trail names) rushing to get to Mt. Katahdin, before October 13th when Baxter State Park closes. Just another indication of transition, telling me winter is not far off.

Use Extreme Caution

Jumping from boulder to boulder and never falling, with a heavy pack, is easier than it sounds; you just can't fall when you get into the rhythm of the dance.

Jack Kerouac

Sandy leading the way up the Huntington Ravine Trail

The Appalachian Mountain Club's *White Mountain Guide* states, *"The Huntington Ravine Trail is the most difficult regular hiking trail in the White Mountains"*. I would go one step further and say that along with the trail from Basin Mountain to Saddleback Mountain in the Adirondacks, the Huntington Ravine Trail is one of the two most challenging in the Northeast. The Guidebook continues, *"Many ledges demand proper use of handholds for safe passage and extreme caution must be exercised at all times."*

About 20 years ago I hiked the Huntington Ravine trail with Peggy, a fellow AMC Volunteer. We were working at the AMC Lakes of the Clouds Hut for the weekend. We decided to take the Huntington Ravine Trail and continue on over a series of other trails to "Lakes". As we approached a steep and narrow section of the trail with a shear drop-off to the side, Peggy began to freeze. She couldn't continue to climb and anxiety took control of her thinking. I instructed her to drop her heavy pack down the side of the cliff and I would assist her in continuing the climb to the top of the ravine. Once she felt secure and safe on the level section of trail I returned to retrieve her pack. We then continued our journey to the hut, arriving well after supper, and late for our assigned duties that evening, but at least we were at Lakes of the Clouds Hut, safe and sound.

Huntington Ravine is one of four cirques on Mount Washington. A cirque is a deep-sided glacial valley usually formed on the south side of a mountain carved out by glacial activity thousands of years ago. Of the four major cirques on Mount Washington, Tuckerman Ravine, Oakes Gulf and Great Gulf, Huntington Ravine has the steepest and highest headwall. It was named for Joshua H. Huntington, principle assistant to New Hampshire State Geologist Charles Hitchcock. In 1870-71 Huntington spent a winter on Mount Washington to study weather patterns. Because of the success of this winter project the U.S. Signal Service, a precursor to the U. S. Weather Service, set up a weather observatory on the summit. The Mount Washington Observatory followed and began keeping records in 1932.

I returned to Huntington Ravine to climb the trail up the headwall, and onto Mount Washington via the Nelson Crag Trail, a total of about four miles with an elevation gain of slightly over 4,000 ft. I was joined by Sandy, Gail and Marion who were"redlining" (hiking all the trails described in the AMC *White Mountain Guide)*. Fran and Dick, both experienced climbers, also joined us. We met at the AMC Visitor Center in Pinkham Notch and began our hike on the Tuckerman Ravine Trail. At 1.3 miles we veered onto the Huntington Ravine Trail and began our entry into the base of the ravine. Here the trail began to climb sharply as we wound our way along the ridge, crossing the Cutler River and the fire road.

Reaching the floor of the headwall we found the first-aid cache, a small enclosed shelter housing equipment needed for rescues. The shelter is named for Albert Dow. The memorial plaque reads, "Climber, rescuer, friend, killed in an avalanche while on a search for a fellow climber". Dow was a member of the Mountain Rescue Service and was part of a search party looking for two missing climbers when he was caught in an avalanche on Jan. 25, 1982. This incident is described in Nicolas Howe's best selling book, *Not Without Peril: 150 Years of Misadventure on the Presiden-tial Range of New Hampshire* (AMC Books, 2001).

From the shelter we crossed a boulder field and shortly after be-gan to climb the talus slope named the Fan. Above the Fan we found outstanding views of Pinkham Notch, Wildcat Ski Resort and the Carter ridge. After taking a short break to regroup and grab a bite to eat, we began climbing through scrub and small patches of late-blooming wildflowers in the seeps coming off the headwall. Climbing the headwall, we ran headlong into the first and most difficult scramble, a steeply sloping smooth ledge. We carefully placed our feet in rock crevices and found secure hand holds. This particular section of the trail can be dangerous to climb in wet or icy weather. It winds steeply up the center of the headwall, requiring several tricky scrambling moves that are in-timidating to less-experienced and sometimes acrophobic hikers. We were thankful that the weather was with us and the rock face was dry. Several times we had to coach each other on the best route up the rock face. We came prepared with climbing rope just in case we needed it, while climbing this class 3 section of the trail.

It's here where many hikers who are not prepared for a challenging and technical climb have to be rescued. These rescues usually take place because people are not properly prepared to hike this trail or have mistakenly taken this trail in the attempt to climb or descend Mount Washington. It should not be attempted with a dog or small children. It is strongly recommended that this trail not be used for a descent off Mount Washington. A few years ago a solo hiker, after summiting Mount Washington late in the day, looked at his map he recently purchased at the Pinkham Notch Visitor Center and decided to take the Huntington Ravine Trail for the return to Pinkham. He had neither guidebook nor knowledge of the trail. Shortly after beginning to descend he found himself unable to continue. He began to experience leg cramps and could not ascend back to the rim of the headwall. He had to call 911 and after rescuers arrived they roped him up and led him back, up the rock face and to the Auto Road. (*Appalachia, Winter/Spring 2017*).These situations happen far too often, not just on the Huntington Ravine Trail, but on many other less challenging trails. Rescues by the New Hampshire Fish & Game Department and other search and rescue organizations usually occur due to hikers being ill prepared: no map, compass, or headlamp, improper footwear, limited physical condition and lack of experience and knowledge of hiking in the Presidential Range.

After slowly climbing the rock slab we continued along the route marked with yellow blazes through short sections of the rock face. Our scrambling continued over and around rock ledges and boulders. Fran ran into one particularly difficult scramble up a rock referred to as the Chimney. The rest of the party avoided the Chimney by finding a less-used segment of trail that led to a talus slope. We then climbed with confidence to the top of the headwall, where we hooked up with Fran who made it up the Chimney. We stopped to look into the ravine below and congratulated ourselves for a successful climb without incident.

After a photo-op we continued onto the Alpine Garden Trail where Marion headed down the Nelson Crag Trail and Gail returned to Pinkham via the Tuckerman Ravine Trail. Sandy, Dick, Fran and I continued on to the summit of Mount Washington, where we mingled with the Auto Road tourists and took a long break before beginning our hike back to Pinkham via the Tuckerman Ravine Trail.

The Huntington Ravine Trail is one of several challenging trails that climb to the summit of Mount Washington. Others are the Six Husbands Trail, Sphinx Trail, Great Gulf Trail and the Tuckerman Ravine Trail. You must use extreme caution when hiking these trails. They are exceptionally steep and may prove to be beyond the capabilities of even experienced hikers. They should not be attempted when wet or icy. If conditions deteriorate while climbing, retreat is the rule. Remember, the mountain will always be there, so stay safe.

The Blueberry Mountain with a Big View

I found my thrill on Blueberry Hill

Fats Domino

Maybe you have never heard of Foss Mountain. It lies close to the New Hampshire border with Maine in the town of Eaton. It stands at only 1,647 ft. in elevation, yet has a magnificent view for over 90 miles in all directions and has 30 acres of wild blue berries. It's one of the best kept secrets of eastern New Hampshire.

I hiked Cragged Mountain previously with several friends, one of whom is on a mission to hike the highest point of every town in New Hampshire (over 230). While driving to the Cragged Mountain Farm, located on the side of Cragged Mountain, I noticed a band of cliffs to the north that looked intriguing. Not being familiar with the area, I had little idea what I was eyeing. In hindsight,

Gordon and Reuben at the summit of Foss Mountain,
Mount Washington and Presidential Range in the background

I was viewing Foss Mountain, famous for its views and low bush blue berries. On that day in December we drove to East Madison, past King Pine ski area and Purity Spring Resort to Towle Hill Road and Cold Brook Road. We then came to several pigsties along the road. At this point we knew we were nearing the Farm on Cragged Mountain. This is a working farm and summer camp owned by the Utter Family and has a captivating history.

The camp was established in 1927 when Dr. Henry Utter, a Boston Pediatrician envisioned a wilderness camp where children and young adults could, "learn responsibility, self-care, teamwork, camping skills and leadership in a wilderness setting". Unlike other summer camps, which have extensive amenities and facilities, the Farm on Cragged Mountain provides a rustic and wilderness experience, free from phones, computers and TV. It sounds like the ideal summer camp for my grandchildren.

We stopped at the farm and met Nick Utter who manages the farm operations. The farm raises pastured pigs, selling cuts of pork, sausage, bacon and ham. In addition the farm produces maple syrup from over 1,000 taps. Nick kindly gave us directions to the summit of Cragged Mountain and also encouraged us to stop back after our hike to check out their pork sale. This we did following our short hike through pastures and woods to the rounded summit of Cragged Mountain.

Since that initial hike to Cragged Mountain I often thought about those bare cliffs rising in the distance. I decided to return to the area to climb those cliffs. My friend Steve agreed to accompany me on this foray. We drove to Ben Road in Freedom, NH, and followed it a short distance, until it was no longer plowed. From here, with Reuben and Skipper, Steve's dog, we began our walk on an abandoned class-6 woods road. The snow was soft enough to require snowshoes. We broke through the snow about three inches, so it was relatively easy walking. In addition, it was a beautifully warm, sunny spring day. The snow and ice were melting from the small streams we crossed giving Skipper and Reuben plenty of opportunities to drink. We hiked along Ben Road for a short distance, passing by a large cellar hole, before turning on to a logging road.

We then began to climb the side of a ridge that represented a series of hills leading to Foss. At the summit of the first rise we came to a large clearing that was obviously a commercial blue berry flat. Harvesting equipment sat in the large expanse of field which overlook the mountains of Maine and the Presidential Range of New Hampshire. This was a spectacular view and represented only a glimpse of what lay ahead, the jaw-dropping views from Foss summit. We continued climbing the ridge, eventually coming to the open summit of Foss Mountain. Before us were expansive views that made us feel like we were on top of the world. Below the knob, Ossipee Lake and King Pine ski area were clearly visible. Mount Chocorua in the Sandwich Range, Mt. Washington in the Presidential Range and Mt. Shaw in the Ossipee Range, along with the western Maine mountains sparkled in the bright sun. For such a small mountain it provides some of the best views in New Hampshire, without having to climb several thousand feet. After spending about a half hour exploring the summit in a stiff wind, taking photos, having a bite to eat and trying to find the snow-obscured path to Foss Mountain Road we decided to bushwhack back to Ben Road, following the ridgeline of Foss Mountain and the ledges that approach Foss. We wandered through beautiful hardwood forests, finally ending our trek on Ben Road and following it back to the car.

This would make the perfect family hike, especially for toddlers, during summer and fall months. The mountain is easily accessed from Foss Mountain Road (not plowed in winter). There is a parking area on the road, opposite the trailhead. Directions to the mountain are available on several Foss Mountain web sites. Do not drive from Ben Road, you'll be in for a rough and risky ride. From the Foss Road parking lot hike through a wooded area, along a commercial blueberry field and you'll emerge on the open summit. There will be plenty of blue berries to pick during the month of July. It was a great day spent hiking in an area I knew little about and I would like to return with my granddaughter Maggie in tow, to pick those sumptuous blueberries. We may be reminded of one of Maggie's favorite books, *Blueberries for Sal*, by Robert McCloskey. I just hope we won't run into a mother bear and her cub as Sal did.

An easier route (not bushwhacking) is Route 25 east to Route 153 for 10 miles. Take Brownfield Rd. east for 1.6 miles to Bull Pasture Road south for 1.2 miles and then turn onto Stewart Road west, and you're almost there. Another 0.3 miles you'll find yourself on Foss Mountain Road. Drive 1.9 miles to a small parking area. The trail is across from the parking lot. Walk a few hundred yards through commercial blueberry fields (no picking) to the summit of the mountain where you can pick berries "to your heart's content".

Following Moose to the Goose

In every walk with nature, one receives far more than he seeks.
John Muir

*Summit of Goose Eye Mountain, looking east
along the Appalachian Trail*

The wind was howling as I approached the summit cone of Goose Eye Mountain. Fran had already reached the summit with Reuben and was returning to below tree line when he spotted me precariously maneuvering up the wall of ice directly ahead. I should have put on my crampons, but thought I could get up the shelf of ice with my mountaineering snowshoes. After a gargantuan struggle I successfully reached the ledge above, but knew I would need crampons for the return trip down the ice covered rock face. Fran shouted through the wind-whipped snow, "It's only another few hundred yards to the summit." He turned back towards the peak of Goose Eye with me trailing behind. I was trying to stay upright as the velocity of the wind increased with each step. I lost my footing when a strong gust pushed me into the krumholtz lining the trail. I fell, losing my poles. I struggled to return to an upright position, and finally was able to stand, with the wind pushing me from side to side. I found my poles and continued forward, trying to stay erect as the fierce wind assaulted me.

I finally made it to the summit. Fran and Reuben were waiting for me. Reuben was hunkered down in a hole he dug in the snow to protect himself from the pounding winds. We quickly celebrated our summit conquest, took a few pictures, donned our crampons, extra layers of clothing and headed back down the mountain. If we could have lingered longer I would have spent more time taking in the 360 degree view of the Mahoosuc Mountain Range and the western Maine mountains, but it was a quick retreat. Reuben, with his built-in crampons (claws), cautiously crawled along the ice covered ridge. We finally reached tree line, where we took a deep breath, happy to be out of the gale force winds. Fran had another New England Hundred Highest under his belt.

We began our hike at the Goose Eye Mountain trailhead, eight miles east of Berlin on the Success Pond Road, a logging road of 14 miles that connects Berlin to Grafton Notch, Maine. Goose Eye

Mountain at 3,870 ft. lies in the Mahoosuc Range. Mahoosuc is obviously of Indian origin and can be translated into several meanings. The first in Abenaki means "abode of hungry animals". Another possible origin of the word is derived from the Natick Indian language meaning "pinnacle or mountain peak". This meaning fittingly describes the mountain range as it is a rugged and isolated mountainous area lying in both New Hampshire and Maine.

Other major peaks in the range are Mount Success (3,565 ft.), Mount Carlo (3,565 ft.) Mahoosuc Mountain (3,470 ft.) Mahoosuc Arm (3,765 ft.) and Old Speck (4,170 ft.). The Mahoosuc Trail/ Appalachian Trail traverses the entire range from Shelburne, NH to Grafton Notch, ME. This is one of the most rugged sections of trails in the White Mountains and some say it's the most challenging section of the entire Appalachian Trail. Legend has it that Goose Eye Mountain derives its name from viewing Canadian geese migrating from Rangeley Lake in Maine over the peak of Goose Eye, almost grazing the summit. I was also told that the summit cone of the mountain resembles a goose eye. Either way, Goose Eye is a unique name that conjures up the wild nature of the Mahoosuc Mountain Range.

Two weeks prior to our Goose Eye trek, the temperatures had warmed and it seemed as though spring had arrived early. Snow melt had begun and the rivers and streams were running high. We should have anticipated these changes, but as they say, "Hindsight is always better than foresight." Within a half mile from the trailhead we came to a stream that normally could be crossed with little effort. Today the stream was a raging torrent of melt water from the peaks above. Fran made an attempt to jump the fast running water, only to find himself sinking though the soft ice. He quickly pulled his leg up through the slush and scrambled up the stream bank to safety. Reuben had no trouble jumping the brook. But I was left on the other side to find another way across. We wandered downstream, Fran on one side of the stream and me on the other. I finally came across a large spruce tree spread across the stream. I easily traversed across the log with Fran and Reuben cheering me on. At Last Fran, Reuben, and I were reunited.

We returned to the trail by bushwhacking back upstream. Our next challenge was plowing through the wet, soft snow that was up to four feet deep. The above-freezing temperatures had softened the snow to the point that it wouldn't support our weight, even with snowshoes. We wallowed along the trail, sinking to our knees at times in wet snow and slush following a set of deep moose tracks. Moose have the innate intelligence to usually follow a cleared path through the woods. It makes their journey much less troublesome when they can meander through the forest without ramming their racks or antlers into trees. I find it truly amazing how moose can wind their way through a thick stand of trees and not get hung up. They have a method of tilting their heads to one side or the other in order to fit their massive racks through the closely knit trees. It is also a wonder these huge beasts, weighing over 1,500 pounds, can walk through four to five feet of snow, sinking up to their bellies. They are extremely powerful and it's an incredible experience to witness a moose as it glides gracefully through the snow-covered woodland.

Sadly, the moose population is being devastated by the parasitic winter tick. Studies by the N. H. Fish and Game Department have concluded that the population of this iconic north woods animal is declining significantly. This is happening all across the southern range of the animal's habitat, from Minnesota to New Brunswick. The ticks latch onto the moose during the summer and live off its blood for months. By spring the animal is totally emaciated and death is imminent. Ticks are not new to moose, but this explosive growth in the tick population is a relatively new phenomenon. Researchers believe that climate change and global warming account heavily for the current situation. Eric Orff of the National Wildlife Federation stated, *"The warming of winter means less snow and warmer temperatures, which means more ticks, and fewer moose."*

We continued on the trail, following the moose tracks off and on, through logged out areas and wet seeps until we reached the state line, crossing into Maine. We continued angling up the summit cone of Goose Eye until we reached the steep ascent that leads to the peak. Reuben and Fran raced ahead of me, while I lumbered along sinking through the soft snow and ice. When I reached the ice covered ledges I struggled to reach the rock outcrop above. It was here where Fran and Reuben met me and we fought through the wind to finish my climb to the summit. We made our quick turn around and began our trek back to Success Pond Rd. and our waiting vehicle. This hike proved to be a lesson in late winter/early spring hiking, and preparing for soft, deep snow, monorail, open water crossings, and ice covered ledges. With the approach of the shoulder season hikers should be prepared for the change in snow and weather conditions. It may be 60 degrees and grass showing around your home, but winter lingers well into May at higher elevations. For any spring hike, carefully study maps and trail descriptions. Research trail conditions by planning your hikes carefully, talking to other hikers and checking trail condition reports on (*TrailNH.com*) or (*NewEnglandTrailConditions.com*).

Ancient Pines of Hemenway State Forest

God has cared for these trees, saved them from drought, disease, avalanches, and a thousand tempests and floods. But he cannot save them from fools.

John Muir

Throughout the world ancient forests, such as the Amazon Rain Forest, are disappearing, being devastated by man, for economic gain. These age-old forests are being destroyed every day to supply cheap lumber, paper, pulp and palm oil to the world. Thousands of

*Steve, Karen, Tom, Beth and Karen in the
old growth forest of ancient pines*

acres are cut daily, extinguishing the last remnants of woodlands that in some cases are over 1,000 years old. However, some pockets of ancient forests have been protected from the modern industrial machine. They have been preserved in our national parks and monuments as well as state forests and parks. Private individuals, conservation groups, and nonprofit organizations such as the Nature Conservancy have played a major role in the preservation of our forests and woodlands. These protected forests can be found throughout the United States: the giant sequoia in California, the redwoods in Oregon, the bristle cone pine in California, and the cypress in Florida.

Here in New Hampshire we have our own protected ancient forests, small but worthy of protection: the red spruce in Nancy Pond Natural Area, pitch pine-scrub oak in the Ossipee Pine

Barrens, hemlock in Chesterfield Gorge and Pisgah State Park and black gum in Rockingham County. The black gum tree is the longest-lived broadleaf deciduous tree in North America. Six sites have been documented in New Hampshire that have black gum trees older than 500 years of age, with the oldest found in Rockingham County, exceeding 679 years.

Close to the Lakes Region is the Big Pines Natural Area of the Hemenway State Forest. This 108 acres of protected forest represents one of the last vestiges of the old growth forests of white pine that at one time blanketed the northeastern United States. Within the past 200 years, most of the forestland has been cut over for farming and logging. For some unknown reason this stand and other stands in the northeast escaped the woodsman's ax. These behemoths have not only withstood the colonial mast trade, but the great lumbering era, survived the great hurricane of 1938, disease, rot, and invasive pests.

For many years I drove past the Hemenway State Forest and it had always intrigued me. Then a friend suggested a hike through the woodland and I accepted. I started the hike with several other hiking companions at the Big Pines Trailhead, off Route 113A in Tamworth. When we entered the State Forest we were struck by the towering and immense stand of white pines that have been around for more than 200 years. Hemlocks 250 to 300 years also grow here. The snow on the trail was well-packed and it was an easy stroll, stopping to admire the many gigantic pines, some over 150 ft. tall. We craned our necks looking upward, toward the sky, trying to see the upper reaches of these trees. We stopped in front of one monstrous white pine and were awestruck by the circumference of the trunk. We then made a chain of human hands around the tree and it took five of us to totally encircle the tree, amazing!

We continued our walk through the ancient forest and then began the ascent of Great Hill, a steep climb to a height of land with views of the surrounding terrain. A fire tower graces the summit, still maintained by the Tamworth Conservation Commission. We climbed to the top of the tower and entered the fire warden's cabin to find spectacular views of the Ossipee and Sandwich Mountain Ranges. In the distance Whiteface, Passaconaway, Square Ledge and Chocorua gleamed in the bright sun.

As I gazed at Chocorua, with its distinctive summit, I thought of the Native American legend, "The Curse of Chocorua". As legend has it, in 1720 Chocorua, a native chief, was on friendly terms with settlers and in particular the Campbell family, who had a home in the village, now called Tamworth. Chocorua was called away and left his son in the care of the Campbell family, early settlers in the village. Chocorua's son found and drank a poison that Mr. Campbell had made to eliminate troublesome foxes. When Chocorua returned he found his son had died of the poison. Chocorua, distraught with grief, pledged revenge on the Campbell family. Shortly thereafter, Mr. Campbell returned home one afternoon to find his wife and children had been slain. Campbell suspected Chocorua and pursued him up the mountain that today bears his name. Chocorua was wounded by a shot from Campbell's rifle. Before Campbell could reach Chocorua, he uttered a curse upon the white settlers and their homes, livestock, and crops, and leapt from the summit to his death, screaming these words, "*May the Great Spirit curse you when he speaks in the clouds and his words are fire! Lightning blast your crops! Wind and fire destroy your homes! The Evil One breathe death on your cattle! Panthers howl and wolves fatten on your bones!*" Perhaps Chocorua's curse did ring true as many early settlers, tired of trying to farm the rock-laden soil, left New Hampshire to find more fertile land farther west. Most certainly they sensed the curse of Chocorua whenever a storm hit, or they lost livestock to bears or wolves. (*Place Names of the White Mountains, Revised Edition*, Robert and Mary Julyan).

With Chocorua's curse in mind I hustled down the tower and began the trek back to the highway. The total distance of this abbreviated hike was two miles.

This would make a terrific outing for a family. The trail is easy to follow as it winds its way through the Big Pines Natural Area, and eventually ends up on Great Hill with the iconic fire tower. Following our exit from the forest preserve we made our way back to Tamworth for a respite at the Other Store on Main Street. This general store is very welcoming and sells everything from ice cream to snow shovels, from nails to post cards. We stopped in the store and were greeted warmly by the counter person, who offered us hot soup and sandwiches. We had lunch, chatted briefly with town folk, learning more about the store and the history of the town. This is one of those quintessential New England towns that appear on the Currier and Ives pictures we see in *Yankee Magazine*.

Following our lunch, we made our way over to the Remick Country Doctor Museum and Farm. We found the farm museum closed, but took advantage of a trail that encircles the property. While walking this trail we found striking views of the farm and Tamworth Village along with Mount Chocorua in the far distance. Located on Cleveland Hill Road in the center of Tamworth village, this working farm was the home of the Remick family since 1790. Dr. Edwin Remick and his son Dr. Edwin "Doc" Crafts Remick, lived and practiced medicine on the farm for a combined 99 years, serving the rural population of Tamworth and the surrounding area. The museum and farm are open year-round, but the best time to visit is during the summer when the livestock: goats, pigs, chickens, sheep, and dairy cows are grazing in the pastures, willing to greet visitors, especially children. Special programs are offered year-round. If you are interested in learning more about this unique New Hampshire institution check out their web site, (*www.remickmuseum.org*).

Crescent Range and Beyond

Hiking is a bit like life: The journey only requires you to put one foot in front of the other...again and again and again. And if you allow yourself opportunity to be present throughout the entirety on the trek, you will witness beauty every step of the way, not just at the summit.

Unknown

The Northern Presidential Range
as seen from Lookout Ledge in Randolph, NH

It was an overcast, dreary day when Reuben and I drove past the Appalachia Parking lot on Rt. 2 in Jefferson. Countless cars were parked in the large lot, but I continued on my way. I was heading toward Randolph Hill Road to begin a hike of Crescent, Randolph and North Randolph Mountains. It was another warm day in November with little snow on the ground. Most hikers give little consideration to a series of mountains north of the Presidential

Range, called the Crescent Range. They are generally thinking about the higher summits, Madison, Adams, Jefferson and the many trails that interlace the northern Presidential summits. Today I was only thinking about exploring a series of trails in the Crescent Range maintained by the Randolph Mountain Club. The Crescent Range lies in an area north of Rt. 2 and west of Rt. 16 in the towns of Jefferson, Berlin and Randolph. The primary summits are Crescent, Randolph, North Black Crescent, South Black Crescent, Jericho Mountain and Mount Forest.

I first learned of this mountain range when sitting in a pub on Main Street in Gorham. I was having a beer and burger after completing a long day of hiking the Carter Range. A couple of guys were sitting next me talking about their trail duties with the Randolph Mountain Club. I was eavesdropping into their conversation about their trail work and overhead the words, "trails in the Crescent Range". Having never hiked there, I wanted to learn more and was emboldened to jump into their conversation with several questions. They took me into their banter and I quickly became enthralled with their descriptions of the many trails in the southern end of the Crescent Range. They also introduced me to the Randolph Mountain Club, the volunteer organization that maintains these trails.

The Randolph Mountain Club was founded in 1910, following the destruction of established trails when the lumber barons came to the northern slopes of the Presidential Range in the early 1900s. They obliterated not only the forests, but miles of trails established earlier by the Appalachian Mountain Club. Lovers of the mountains and avid hikers alike, many of them AMC members and summer residents, came together to begin reopening the trails and restoring the paths that once climbed to the higher summits. They organized themselves as the Randolph Mountain Club and took responsibility for reopening trails destroyed by logging. Today the RMC maintains 102 miles of hiking trails, principally on the northern slopes of Mount Madison, Mount Adams, and Mount Jefferson, but also in the Crescent Range in the town of Randolph, NH. They maintain two cabins, Gray Knob and Crag Camp, along with the Perch and the Log Cabin shelters. RMC's trails are maintained through the joint efforts of volunteers and a seasonal, paid professional trail crew, as well as a part time fall trail crew. It's an amazing grassroots organization that does remarkable work in, *"Building and maintaining paths, and building, maintaining, and controlling camps, in and among the White Mountains, in New Hampshire so that the public can continue to enjoy the splendor of the northern peaks. While this goal has remained constant, the RMC has responded to changing conditions and expanded its mission to play a broader role in the stewardship of the northern peaks and their fragile environment."*(randolphmountainclub.org).

After learning about the RMC and the trails maintained in the Crescent Range, I decided to explore this area and in so doing, I came to experience a spectacular mountain range with a myriad of trails. Now Reuben and I were at the trailhead of the Mount Crescent Trail. We checked out the trail map at the kiosk recently built at a large parking lot at the end of Randolph Hill Road. Since this trail system was new to us, we carefully studied the map. We found that we could make an eight-mile loop going up and over Mount Crescent and then taking the Crescent Ridge Trail to Mount Randolph. Along this ridge trail was the obscure summit of North Randolph. Knowing this was on the New Hampshire 200 Highest Mountain List, I decided to bushwhack over to that summit, via map and compass.

Reuben and I began our journey, taking a long steady climb to Mount Crescent. We found an outstanding view near the summit, looking to the north. We continued on the Crescent Ridge Trail to where the trail dipped into a clearing laced with thickets of hobble bush that had been heavily browsed by moose and deer. The trail, marked with faint blazes, was difficult to follow in some sections but Reuben, with his nose close to the ground and eyes glancing upward, led me along the path. I crossed the shoulder of North Randolph. After briefly wandering around the height of land I found a jar dangling from a small tree. This marked the summit. I opened the rusty lid and signed the register. Only a few other hikers had been to this obscure summit in the past two years. After reading through the names and returning the register to the jar, I returned to the trail.

Once again on the trail I checked my map and trail guide. I noticed a prominent rock cliff called Lookout Ledge, noted for its outstanding views of the Northern Presidential Range, especially King Ravine. I decided to have lunch there and hustled onward. I found the ledge and rested for a short time with Reuben by my side. Just as we were about to depart the veil of clouds that had been hanging low the entire day lifted and King Ravine emerged with its shear walls of granite looming ominously across the valley. After taking in the view for several minutes, I descended off the mountain, returning to the parking lot via the Pasture Path. This last section of trail was a pleasant walk through an old pasture and new growth forest. I met several local residents on their way to take in the views from Lookout Ledge.

This challenging but tranquil hike whetted my appetite for other treks in this section of the White Mountains. I plan to return to bushwhack to Black Crescent and its related peaks, North and South Black Crescent. I also want to visit the Pond of Safety, a small but stunning pond lying just west of the Crescent Range. It can be reached via the Four Soldiers Trail. The name is derived from an incident that occurred during the Revolutionary War. Four North Country men from Jefferson who were in the Continental Army were captured by the British. The British turned them loose with the agreement that they wouldn't bear arms against the British. Being true to their word, they refused to take up arms against their former captures. Branded as traitors and threatened with imprisonment they fled into the mountains, finding the Pond of Safety as a refuge. Here they lived for three years until the war ended. They returned to their homes in Jefferson and became prominent and respected citizens. In 1826 they were exonerated from all charges. (Place Names of the White Mountains, Revised Edition, Robert and Mary Julyan).

I look forward in continuing my explorations of this section of the White Mountains and suggest that you check out this trail system. Easy to moderate trails are linked together to provide a variety of experiences, from snowshoeing to Lookout Ledge, or hiking into history by visiting the Pond of Safety. In thewinter you may want to avoid the challenging trails of the northern slopes and discover the beauty of Crescent Range and beyond.

A Wild and Beautiful Ravine

May your trails be crooked, winding, lonesome, dangerous, leading to the most amazing view.

Edward Abbey

Dave and Sandy climbing through the rock pile of Ice Gulch

Ice Gulch, located in Randolph, NH, is a rare and spectacular ravine filled with huge boulders, alpine flora, matts of moss and lichen. It's one of the most ecologically unique and diverse areas in the White Mountains. The technical term for the ravine is sub-alpine cold-air talus shrub land, a narrow gorge that holds a reverse alpine zone. The environment is similar to that found in alpine regions above 4,000 ft., yet its base lies at only 1,780 ft. *"Because of the steepness of its walls and its east-west orientation, the north-facing slope of the gulch is in almost permanent shade, allowing ice to persist beneath and between some of the boulders well into summer. This extreme microclimate creates very difficult growing conditions for most plants, and some black spruce trees in the ravine, while little more than inch in diameter, are over 100 years old"* (NH Division of Forest and Land). Plants such as black spruce, alpine bilberry, mountain cranberry, and mats of Labrador tea cover many of the boulders. Because the ravine is very narrow and the walls are vertical it receives little sunlight. Ice can be found lingering into mid-summer beneath the jumble of boulders on the ravine floor.

I wanted to hike the ravine for quite some time and the opportunity came knocking when my friend Sandy invited me and others to hike the Ice Gulch Path with her. The day before I climbed to the summit of Mount John Quincy Adams via the King Ravine Trail. The King Ravine Trail is rough and difficult, winding up the sheer headwall. It provides significant challenges, especially non-technical rock climbing skills. To say the least, I wasn't enthused to trek through a boulder strewn ravine trail the following day, rated as one of the most difficult in the White Mountains. The AMC White Mountain Guide states, *"The trip through the gulch itself is one of the most difficult and strenuous trail segments in the White Mountains."* However, even with these trepidations it was an opportunity I couldn't pass up.

On a bright, sunny day Sandy, Dave and I drove to Randolph Hill Road, which runs off Rt. 2 in Randolph, where we found the trailhead. The trail system into Ice Gulch, as well as many others in the area, is maintained by the Randolph Mountain Club. We parked the car in a small turnoff located across from the Ice Gulch Path. We hiked through a managed forest and came to a sign that read, "The Marked Birch". From here the trail split. We took the left fork which headed down to the lower end of the ravine. After a steep descent into the ravine we trekked eastward toward the Peboamauk Fall, which means "winter's home". At this point Moose Brook leaves Ice Gulch on its way to the Androscoggin River. The falls were impressive, even though the water flow was reduced due to a lingering drought. The trail to the falls was rugged and difficult to follow in some places, climbing over downed trees and rock ledges. This was a foreshadowing of things to come.

We then backtracked up the gulch to Fairy Spring, the beginning of Moose Brook, and began our 0.8-mile trek through the gulch. The AMC White Mountain Guide "book time" estimates the hike should take 1.5 hours. This is one time the book was way off the mark. Due to the incredibly difficult rock scrambles, jumping over gigantic slabs of rock and climbing through tunnels of boulders, it took us well over three hours to complete our journey through the ravine. Of course we spent considerable time marveling at the rock formations, the cliffs above our heads and the diversity of plant life. It was a photographer's paradise.

We began our nearly constant struggle over wet rocks and boulders, with deep, dark holes between them. I knew from others that this was not a hike for dogs. I heeded their advice and left Reuben at home. We made our way slowly and carefully and knew we couldn't afford to misstep and break an ankle or leg. The fissures between the rocks seemed bottomless and signaled disaster if we lost our balance or slipped on the moss-covered rock slabs. We were amazed at the dense cover of small spruce growing over the boulders covered with lush layers of moss and liverworts, plants that thrive in moist, wet environments.

As we made our way deeper into the ravine, the trail became more challenging. We struggled over boulders that were wet, slick and slippery. We carefully worked our way along, often searching for the best way over and around the boulder field. We felt cold air as it rose from the deep, dark crevices in the rock-strewn trail. The cold air rising up through the rock creates a microclimate similar to that found at higher elevations. We peered into the deep holes between the boulders, looking for ice left from the last winter. We found none. If we were hiking earlier in the summer I'm sure we would have discovered blocks of ice, deep inside the rock openings. This persistent accumulation of ice supports the unique growing conditions and gives the ravine its name.

Sandy, Dave and I trudged on, wondering when the trail would start its climb out of the ravine. The continued rock-hopping, ducking under angular boulders and climbing over slippery rocks seemed never-ending. But even with our grumbling about the challenges of the hike we were continually fascinated and in awe of the hue in the granite walls, the beautiful carpets of moss and piles of gigantic boulders that had fallen from heights above. This had to be not only one of the most challenging hikes I've been on, but also one of the most rewarding. At 0.7 miles we entered the Vestibule, the portal out of the ravine. Climbing the rock-strewn trail we followed a stream and a series of cascades that took us out of the dark, cool environment of the ravine and into the bright, warm sunlight above. We were relieved to be out of Ice Gulch with no broken bones, torn muscles or bruised ribs. At the terminus of Ice Gulch Path the trail turned left in a southerly direction and onto the Cook Path. We hiked another 2.6 miles back to Randolph Hill Road, where we started our hike.

It was a hike I looked forward to with great anticipation and I'm elated that I did it. Would I do it again? I'm not so sure. Perhaps I would go back if I could again photograph the incredible scenery found in the ravine. It is a rare, unique and beautiful environment.

Hedgehog, A Challenging Mountain for All Ages

Walker, it is in your footsteps that are the road, the road is made by walking.

Antonio Machado

Mount Passaconaway as seen from the ledges on Hedgehog Mountain

I awoke to find the skies overcast and a steady drizzle predicted to fall all morning. I was planning to hike King Ravine and summit J.Q. Adams, an "unofficial" 4,000 footer on the side of Mount Adams. The weather forecast did not sound promising, consequently I needed to change my plans. I studied the AMC White Mountain Guide and map, looking for an interesting hike I could do with Reuben, and not deal with inclement weather I would most likely find in the Presidential Range.

I remembered years ago I had hiked a small knob, off the Kancamagus Highway, Rt. 112, called Hedgehog Mountain (2,532 ft.). This Hedgehog is not be confused with Hedgehog Mountain in Wonalancet. Hedgehog is a strange name for a mountain since hedgehogs are not native to New Hampshire or even North America. They are found in Europe, Asia and Africa, but not here. So how did this mountain get its name? The mountain summit is accessed via the UNH Trail, so-named because at one time the University of New Hampshire Forestry Camp was located in the vicinity of the mountain. Perhaps some inventive forestry student thought the mountain looked like this ancient spiny animal that's related to the porcupine and has been around for thousands of years.

After waiting a couple of hours for the weather to clear, I headed up I-93 to the Kancamagus Highway, also referred to as the "Kanc". Lincoln was abuzz with leaf peepers, out and about, walking the streets, wandering in and out of the many shops and restaurants lining Main Street. My drive took me over Kancamagus Pass, past turn-offs and parking lots filled with tourists admiring the mountain vistas beginning their multi-colored show of autumn. The skies had cleared and a brilliant sun was warming the air. Reuben and I arrived at the trailhead parking lot located opposite the White Mountain National Forest, Passaconaway Campground. When we pulled into the lot, we strangely found only two other cars. I assumed that with the many tourists who flock to this area in autumn the lot would be filled with autos and the trail busy with hikers.

I began my hike with Reuben running ahead as usual. He was happy to be hiking again, after a long lay-off. We followed the Downes Brook Trail for a short distance and then began our trek along an old railroad bed. We soon came to the junction with the UNH Trail. This is where confusion set in. One trail sign read "UNH Ski Trail" the other "UNH Trail". I was curious to find out where the UNH Ski Trail would take me, so I decided to begin my hike on this trail, thinking it might take me to Hedgehog, wrong! The ski trail led me into a large wetland. After hiking for some time I realized the ski trail was steering me away from the mountain, so I turned around and returned to the trailhead, where I began. This was an interesting exploratory tramp, but not one I had planned.

After returning to the UNH Trail I began an easy climb, following yellow blazes to the beginning of the trail junction and had to make a decision. The trail begins a circuitous route over and around the mountain. By taking the loop to the left I would head in a clockwise direction, gaining elevation to the East Ledges. I chose to go right, hiking in a counter-clockwise direction. This path led to Allen's Ledge and the summit of Hedgehog. The trail began to climb steeply over rocks and roots that proved to be slippery after the rainfall. Reuben scampered along, while I carefully plodded up the trail, trying to avoid the many wet roots and rocks lining the trail. As the trail gained elevation and continued its way up the mountain, I began to notice the yellow blazes on trees became barely visible and even nonexistent. The path was well-worn, so I knew I was on the trail, but I checked my map just to be sure.

When I reached the summit the skies had cleared and the views were astounding. Mount Passaconaway, at 4,043 ft., dominated the skyline to the south. It loomed over me like a giant, watching as I ate my lunch. I shared my sandwich with Reuben and a visiting chipmunk, who rested at my feet waiting for a snack. The chipmunk scurried back and forth with my discarded peanuts, disappearing and then emerging from the woods looking for more. I wondered if he was storing his food cache for the winter. It was only 70 days before the Winter Solstice. I was reluctant to leave the rock summit, with its magnificent views, but I realized I needed to move on if I was going to make it home for supper.

I continued my trek, by heading down the mountain, continuing in a counter-clockwise direction toward the East Ledges. The trail dropped steeply off the rock face of the summit. The blazes were faint and I was cautious to stay on the trail. There were several side paths that may have led to other sections of the mountain. The trail descended into the forest below the summit and then began to climb moderately via switchbacks to the east- facing cliffs. Again, spectacular views to the south and east awaited me. The trail followed the edge of the cliffs. There were no cairns and blazes were very faint on the rocks, so I had to be cautious along this section. The trail then dipped into the woods, continuing its circuitous route back to the loop junction, where Reuben and I turned right and made our way back to the parking lot.

This was a great half-day hike of 4.8 miles. It presented a stimulating climb through rich spruce forests and along rock ledges that offer outstanding views of the Sandwich and Presidential Ranges. It is a moderately difficult hike and can be combined with a climb to the summit of Potash Mountain (2,700 ft.) for a full day of hiking. Potash lies adjacent to Hedgehog and is climbed via the Downes Brook Trail to the Mount Potash Trail. With the magnificent colors of our northern forest on full display in autumn, it makes an ideal hike for the entire family during the shoulder season.

The Alpine Zone in Bloom

What's in a name? That which we call a rose
By any other name would smell as sweet.

William Shakespeare

Lapland Rosebay on the Boott Spur Link Trail

When I reached the alpine region on the Boott Spur Link Trail I was greeted by a beautiful display of alpine flowers: diapensia and Lapland rosebay. While Reuben led the way, I scrambled to the high reaches of the trail. I had forgotten that the alpine zone of the Presidential Range would be ablaze with a flower show in early June and I was overtaken by the brilliant display of these early alpine flowers. It is truly amazing that these flora can thrive, let alone even exist, in this harsh, extreme environment. Yet, throughout the alpine zone in the Presidential and Franco-nia Ranges of the White Mountains, alpine plants are in full bloom: diapensia, lapland rosebay, mountain avens, cinquefoil, harebell, mountain aster, bog bilberry, and others. During this period one can witness a marvelous display of flowers that defies the extreme conditions where these plants flourish. A sign at an AMC hut reads, *"Welcome to the Alpine Zone. Enjoy the fragile beauty. Be a caring steward. Stay on the trail or walk on rocks. Help preserve the delicate balance of the Alpine Zone. It's a tough place to grow."*

With this in mind, Reuben and I cautiously stayed on the worn path with the goal to summit Boott Spur. All along the trail, above tree line, we were accompanied by the flowering diapensia, which resembles a large pin cushion, and the pink flowers of Lapland rosebay. Lapland rosebay is considered an imperiled alpine plant. This miniature version of common rhododendron grows in small populations and only found in a few alpine regions of the world. This expanse of alpine flora reminded me of a domestic rock garden. However, this garden was not made by man, but by the hand of Mother Nature. We were careful to stay on the trail and not trample the delicate plant life around us. Even Reuben was careful where he placed his paws. I always knew he was a smart dog.

We started our day at the Pinkham Notch AMC Visitor Center, hiking the Tuckerman Ravine Trail for 2.4 miles. I met a few other hikers heading into the ravine to begin their climb of Mount Washington. At the Hermit Lake Shelter I began my climb to Boott Spur Ridge via the Boott Spur Link Trail. With Reuben in the lead, we climbed the steep ascent to Boott Spur Trail which would lead us to the peak of Boott Spur (5,500 ft.) The trail follows a prominent ridge running south from Mount Washington, located on the east side of Tuckerman Ravine. The ridge was named for Dr. Francis Boott, who was a member of the Bigelow scientific expedition to the White Mountains in 1816. Some speculate that this ridge was the route of the first ascent of Mount Washington by Darby Field in 1642.

As we made our way along the trail, dark storm clouds gathered in the south. I grew anxious about continuing on my route, knowing I would be in danger if a storm hit when I was above tree line. I continued on, rushing to make my goal. The weather can turn quickly in the mountains, but to my good fortune the thick bank of clouds began to break up as they blew into Tuckerman and Huntington Ravines and Mount Washington to the north. I was in luck, no storm today, just a minor weather system pulling through. I made the summit of Boott Spur and then turned onto the Davis Path which would lead me to the Tuckerman Ravine Trail and back to the Hermit Lake Shelters.

The Davis Path is a 15 mile trail running from Crawford Notch and Rt. 302 to the summit of Mount Washington. It was built by Nathaniel T.P. Davis, manager of the Crawford House, and son-in-law to Abel Crawford, patriarch of the region and premier trail builder. The Davis Path, built as a bridle path to Mount Washington, was completed in 1845. In the years following the trail was used less frequently due to the popularity of the Mount Washington Carriage Road (now the Auto Road) and the Cog Railroad, and was reclaimed by the forest. In 1910 the trail was reopened by the AMC as a foot path to the summit of Mount Washington and now closely follows the route of the original bridle trail.

When I arrived at the junction of the Tuckerman Ravine Trail I considered continuing to the summit of Mount Washington, but thought better of it, as I have been on the summit many times and it wasn't worth climbing another mile, over 600 feet in elevation, and being inundated with crowds of sightseers. I began my descent into Tuckerman Ravine, excited to view the massive walls of the ravine and the spring runoff, tumbling down over the headwall, 1,000 feet to the valley below. The ravine is a classic glacial cirque carved out of the southeast slope of Mount Washington during the ice age. It was named for distinguished botanist Edward Tuckerman who taught at Amherst College and studied alpine plants and lichens in the White Mountains during the 1830s and 40s. He is best known for categorizing botanical life zones in the Presidential Range. Tuckerman Ravine is renowned for the massive amounts of snow that blow off Mount Washington into the bowl-shaped cirque, providing challenging and unique opportunities for climbers and extreme skiers. In 1939, at the Third American Inferno Ski Race, 19 year old Austrian Toni Matt became a ski legend. Starting from the summit of Mount Washington, he hit the Tuckerman headwall and schussed (skied in a straight line) down the headwall at close to 85 mph, finishing at the Pinkham Notch Visitor Center in just six minutes and 29 seconds.

Unlike Toni Matt, Reuben and I carefully made our way down the Tuckerman Ravine Trail. We could see massive ice sheets still hanging on the cliffs. Snow fields lingered in the recesses of the ravine. Indian poke was beginning to unfurl its large, deeply veined leaves from the side of trail. Soon they would be in full bloom. The famous snow arch created by water flowing under many feet of snow had collapsed and was now just a gigantic mass of ice laying at the bottom of the ravine. I spent a good deal of time gazing at the raw beauty of this magnificent cirque, reluctant to leave, but I must, as darkness was setting in. I slowly hiked out of the ravine, occasionally looking back at the beauty behind me. I paused to eat a snack at the ranger station before beginning my final leg of the hike down to the AMC Pinkham Notch Visitor Center. As I was getting up to leave, I met a couple from Norway who shared with me that they had returned to Tuckerman Ravine, drawn back to this very special place, to celebrate their wedding anniversary, where they were married 40 years ago. Tuckerman Ravine and the alpine gardens have a magnetism that draws people from around the world to experience their majestic beauty.

Confronting a Forest Blockade

Keep close to nature's heart, yourself; and break away, once and a while, climb a mountain or spend a week in the woods. Wash your spirit clean.

John Muir

Mud Pond, headwaters of Tunnel Brook

The footpath was obliterated by downed trees, spread asunder by powerful winter storms that swept through Tunnel Brook Ravine, which is nestled between Mount Clough and Mount Moosilauke. Spruce, fir, maple and birch lay like match sticks spilled from a matchbox. The Tunnel Brook Trail that Dave and I were following suddenly disappeared under this mass of timber. We were having a pleasant amble, wending our way along the trail when we reached the blockade. We had to continue following the footpath, obliterated by winter storms, if we were going to continue our trek to the Benton Trail and on to the summit of Mount Moosilauke.

We started our 14-mile circuitous trek from High Street in Glen-cliff, following Long Pond Road a short distance before beginning our trek on the Tunnel Brook Trail. The trail follows Slide Brook where Reuben found several swimming holes to bathe in the crystalline waters. It was a pleasant walk on an old logging road, climbing gradually to Mud Pond and the headwaters of Tunnel Brook. The trail slabbed along the side of the pond, where beavers had taken up residence. The slides on Mount Clough stood above and presented an interesting test for climbers in their quest to summit the mountain via this challenging route. The hike to Mud Pond was, in itself, a rewarding ramble. The views of the cliffs, the ponds, the beaver dams, and the active bird life offered us a chance to experience the wilderness that awaits those who are fortunate enough to live so close to the wonders of the natural world.

However, this wasn't our goal, climbing to the summit of Mount Moosilauke was, and as we approached a camp site at the northern end of the ponds we encountered the barricade. The trail was recently blazed, but finding openings through the downed trees was nearly impossible. Fortunately for Reuben, he was able to creep under many of the fallen trees, but not me. Dave and I continually lost the trail in the tangle of tree trunks, limbs, branches, hobblebush and wild raspberries. Up until this point we were making good time, but now our trek came to a slow crawl. To our advantage we had the walls of the ravine to keep us on track and after several misguided attempts to stay on the trail we reached the upper reaches of the pond and found ourselves free from the maze of fallen trees.

Proceeding along the Tunnel Brook Trail, now free from blow-downs, we were confronted with the work of beavers. In building their dams they had flooded the trail under several feet of water. Dave and I looked for passages around the flooded trail, but to no avail. However, Reuben, by instinct, seemed to know the best way forward, so it was a matter of following Reuben until we were once again on a dry trail. Leaving the beavers behind, we marched to the terminus of the Tunnel Brook Trail. We then continued along Tunnel Brook Road until we reached the trailhead for the Benton Trail, where we began the long gradual climb of 3.6 miles to the summit of Mount Moosilauke (4802 ft.).

The trail follows the route of an old bridle path. The path was built during the great mountain hotel era, when tourists rode horseback or in a carriage to the summit of the mountain and stayed at the Prospect House. Built in 1860, known later as the Tip Top House of Mount Moosilauke, (not to be confused with the Tip Top House on the summit of Mount Washington), it was destroyed by fire in 1942. The foundation walls of the inn are still evident today and used as shelter by hikers during windy or inclement weather.

Mount Moosilauke is a massif, meaning it is a large mountain mass with several dominant peaks that form an independent range. Over the years it has had other names including Moose-hillock, Mooshelock, and Mooselock. The Abenaki name means "bald place", derived from the fact that much of the upper reaches of the mountain are above tree line. It was not named for the many moose that live on and near the mountain. Other summits on the massif are Mount Blue, Mount Jim, and South Peak. All of these are connected by a system of trails that cover much of the mountain. These trails offer a variety of options for not only hiking but cross country skiing, snow shoeing, rock and ice climbing in the remote Jobildunc Ravine, the head waters of the Baker River. One can even sled or toboggan on the Carriage Road Trail. The recreational opportunities on the mountain are limitless.

Much of the mountain is owned by Dartmouth College and the trails, not only on the mountain, but many in the area are maintained by the Dartmouth Outing Club. The college also owns and maintains the Ravine Lodge and cabins. The lodge, which was recently rebuilt, sits on the southeast side of the mountain off Rt. 118. It was built in the 1930's and once served as the base lodge for some of the earliest competitive skiing in the country. In the summer it is open to the general public for meals, overnight accommodations and special events. From the lodge there are numerous trails perfect for cross country skiing and snow shoeing for a wide variety of ages and ability levels. For more information on Ravine Lodge check out their website *(outdoors.dartmouth.edu)*.

The Benton Trail was a moderate climb along the north ridge of Little Tunnel Ravine, with good footing along the way. At 1.3 miles a spur trail led us out to an overlook to a magnificent view of Little Tunnel Ravine. I rested here while Dave and Reuben trudged on, waiting for me periodically to catch up. Occasionally Reuben would jog back looking for me, just to satisfy his curiosity. We continued climbing the ridge through beautiful stands of spruce and fir, the trees getting smaller as we climbed. Reaching the trail junction with the Beaver Brook Trail we soon entered the alpine zone. The bare summit lay ahead. When we emerged from treeline we were hit with blasts of wind. It was time to put on an extra layer of clothing. This .4 mile section of trail to the summit is exposed to the elements and can be extremely dangerous in deteriorating weather conditions. This wasn't the case today and we scurried along the trail anxious to reach the walls of the old hotel foundation so we could hunker down and eat our lunch without being blown over.

Rounding the stone wall we found two AT thru hikers eating their lunch. Moosilauke is the first mountain northbound AT thru hikers climb that's totally above treeline. We learned their trail names were Caboose and Thrill Seeker. Both women were northbound, planning to reach Katahdin by October. Having hiked the trail myself in 2007 and 2011, we exchanged AT trail stories while drinking a cold brew offered by Thrill Seeker. It was a great way to celebrate the summit finish, before we headed back to our car via the Glencliff Trail. Dave, Reuben and I bid farewell to our lunch mates and began the last leg of our hike on the Glencliff Trail.

The descent of Moosiluake on the Glencliff Trail had its challenges with the wet rocks and steep declines impinging on a quick hike out. We again met several AT thru hikers making their way both up and down the mountain. Finally reaching the parking lot, legs feeling heavy and worn out, we checked the total mileage for the day: 13.8 miles with a total elevation gain of 4,050 ft. No wonder I felt spent when I returned home. I have hiked every trail on the Moosiluake Massif and I'm never disappointed. It's a great climb to the summit whichever trail you choose to take. Just be sure you're prepared for a "slugfest" if you choose the Tunnel Brook Trail.

A Hike to the Unknowns

One touch of nature makes the whole world kin.
William Shakespeare

The April day started cold and clear, wind gusting to 30 MPH and wind chills near zero. According to the calendar, spring arrived a month ago, but in northern New Hampshire we were still in the grips of winter. As T.S. Elliot wrote in the Wasteland, *"April is the cruelest month, breeding lilacs out of the dead land..." We've been run over by a last minute blast from "Old Man Winter."* I thought the "Old Man" had left our domain, but He always returns this time of year, so we don't forget his phantom embrace and eventual return in December. At home the daffodils were shooting up through the bare ground, red buds were appearing on the maples, phoebes had returned to claim their territory and

Unknown Pond

bears were emerging from their sleeping quarters to ravage bird feeders. All signs pointed to spring, yet we were in the throes of an unrelenting winter. We were expecting to be hiking in a warming sun, with the smells of spring filling the air, not this throw-back day to winter. We know so little about what to expect when we head to the northern mountains to tackle a summit. Today is not what we hoped for, but we gritted our teeth and pushed ahead into the biting winter wind.

Fran, Sandy, Reuben and I drove to Berlin, NH to hike to the summit of Unknown Pond Peak. The car temperature gauge registered 23 degrees and we knew it would be colder at higher elevations. We drove to York Pond Road, passed the New Hampshire Fish Hatchery and parked at the trailhead for the Unknown Pond Trail. This area of the White Mountains is rugged and wild. Unknown Pond, a mountain tarn, lies at 3,190 ft. It was created by glacial action and filled with melt water as the ice sheet retreated northward. Just hiking to the pond is rewarding enough, but we wanted to summit the peak sitting to the north of the pond, appropriately called Unknown Pond Peak. During the late 1800s, the forests in the area were obliterated by logging operations. The Brown Company, located in Berlin, needed pulp wood to keep the mill in Berlin churning out paper and other wood products.

At one time, the Brown Company was one of the largest paper manufacturers in the world, producing newsprint, tissue and hand towels as well as other products associated with paper production. The Brown Company was also on the cutting edge in the advancement of paper production with the infusion of chemists working alongside the production crew to improve the quality of paper. At one time, the Brown Company's Research and Development Department employed over 100 scientists and eventually received 600 U.S. patents. Brown also created and produced other products such as peanut oil used for cooking, Peanut Flakes breakfast cereal, Nibroc Paper Towels, Onco, an artificial leather used for making shoes, and Kream Krisp, a product similar to Crisco. It owned 4,250,000 acres of woodland in Maine, New Hampshire and Quebec, Canada, which it needed to feed the mills for the manufacture of its many products. By 1917 it was the largest single producer of pulp and paper in the world. This was truly a diversified company.

But diversification couldn't stave off the eventual outcome of the company. With the Great Depression of the 1930s and the changing economics of the paper industry, the company went through bankruptcy in 1935. The company reorganized several times, but could never recover. In 1968 the Brown Company was bought by the Gulf and Western Company. In the 1980s other companies, such as James River and Frasier Paper purchased the mills. Reinvestment and new ownership couldn't turn the tide. Its assets were sold off in the face of foreign competition, high energy and transportation costs. The mills finally shuttered their doors in 2006. In its place now stands a $275 million, 75 megawatt biomass power plant, owned by Burgess BioPower, which started generating power in 2013.

Sandy, Fran, Reuben and I began our hike on the Unknown Pond Trail, which is an abandoned railroad grade. Logging trains used to haul timber from the upper reaches of Kilkenny Ridge to feed the paper machines of the now defunct Brown Paper Company. We were hiking through history, when logging was king and most people residing in the area made their living from the mills in Berlin. The trail was not well marked and it appeared to be no longer maintained. We lost the trail and began bushwhacking along the stream that drains Unknown Pond. We crossed the stream several times and were fortunate that winter was prolonged, because if the weather had warmed we may not have been able to cross the swollen stream.

Leaving the stream we headed into a beautiful birch glade where the sun was warming the snow to such a degree that our light traction footwear was being sucked off our feet by the sticky snow. We then stashed our Microspikes in our packs and barebooted to a steep grade and into the depression of the pond. At times we sunk up to our hips in deep snow drifts lingering from winter. When we emerged from a thick stand of trees, a stunning view of the mountain pond greeted us. It was well worth the 3.3 mile hike and bushwhack. The pond was still frozen solid and it would probably be weeks before the ice began to recede from the shoreline.

After admiring the views from the pond, we found the Kilkenny Ridge Trail and strapped on our snowshoes. If we turned south, the trail would take us to the Horn (3,905 ft.), Mount Cabot (4,170 ft.), over several other mountains and eventually to Mount

Waumbek (4,006 ft.), 14 miles away. However, we headed north on the Kilkenny Ridge Trail, about 0.5 miles to the height of land, where we turned east, bushwhacking to the summit of Unknown Pond Peak (3,501 ft.). We arrived at our destination after a pleasant walk through open woods with little snow cover and found the canister on a downed spruce tree. Sandy signed the register, making it number 90 on her list of hiking to the highest 100 peaks in New Hampshire. Ten more to go. After signing in, we turned and reversed our track, returning to the parking area on York Pond Road.

During the summer and autumn, the hike to Unknown Pond is a pleasant amble along a mountain stream and you'll be wrapped in the solitude of a pristine spruce-fir forest. Just under two miles south from Unknown Pond lies the Horn, a rock outcrop at 3,905 ft. This lesser known mountain offers spectacular views of the Presidential Range and the Pilot Range. You can also hike north on the Kilkenny Ridge Trail, two miles, to Rogers Ledge, another rock outcrop offering views of the Bulge, the Horn and Hutchins Mountain. The rock outcrop was named in honor of Robert Rogers, who led the famous militia Rogers Rangers during the French and Indian Wars. The area is remote and has few visitors as compared to the neighboring mountains to the south. At the far end of the Unknown Pond are five secluded campsites. These are ideal for a family with children encamped in a wilderness paradise. I'm sure that in the summer the pathway is well worn and easy to follow. I can't think of a more picturesque place for a family backpacking trip in the wilds of the North Woods.

A Commemorative Hike to Remember
The Search and Recovery
of Kate Matrosova

We have not, of course, beaten the storm or conquered the mountain. Nature has convincingly shown who's boss.

Guy and Laura Waterman

Clearing Skies over Mount J.Q. Adams and Mount Adams

On February 15, 2015, in the darkness of early morning, Kate Matrosova left her husband, Charlie Farhoodi, at the Appalachia parking lot on Route 2. Kate disappeared into the predawn hours as she made her way to the Valley Way Trail. That morning would be the last time Charlie would see Kate alive. She hiked into a tempest that would take her life on the side of Mount Adams. This was one of many tragedies that occur in the White Mountains almost annually, but Kate's death is beyond understanding. Just below tree line a sign along the Valley Way Trail reads, *"STOP, The area ahead has the worst weather in America. Many have died there from exposure, even in the summer. Turn back now if the weather is bad."* Kate most likely read this sign, and continued on. She believed that the uninhabitable weather system that was racing toward the White Mountains would arrive later in the day, when she would be safely below tree line on the Ammonoosuc Ravine Trail. She was prepared physically to hike fast and she carried only the most essential items for a rapid pace over mountainous terrain.

Kate was an accomplished climber and had summited some of the highest mountains in the world, Kilimanjaro, Elbrus, Aconcagua and Denali. She was also a very successful stock trader and had an insatiable appetite for challenges, both in the business world and the arena of mountaineering. She was a strong hiker and her plan to hike the Northern Presidential Range in one day during winter was not beyond her ability. What she didn't plan for was the extreme weather that was about to hit while she was making her way up the Valley Way Trail. On the higher summits temperatures would be falling to -35 degrees F., winds would soar to over 80 MPH, with wind chills of -88 degrees F. Anyone caught in these conditions would have little chance for survival.

Kate's attempt to complete the Northern Presidential Traverse ended on the side of Mount Adams, where her body was found the next day by search and rescue teams from Androscoggin Valley Search & Rescue, New Hampshire Department of Fish and Game and Mountain Rescue Service. They began the search on the evening of February 15, when Farhoodi notified authorities that Kate hadn't returned. Rescue teams began the search in the full force of the storm, risking their lives, hoping to find Kate and bring her down off the mountain. Unable to continue the search that evening, they resumed the following day in the face of continuing high wind and extreme cold. After hours of searching, getting blown around, sinking into chest-deep snow, and facing frostbite, they found Kate's body. The rescue turned into a recovery.

I too was planning to hike in the mountains the same day Kate started up Valley Way Trail. I heard the weather forecast and abandoned my plans. A few days later I learned of the search and recovery efforts. I read accounts of the events and watched a video of rescuers. There have been numerous interpretations of those two days written in journals, the Internet and print publications. Sandy Stott wrote two excellent articles in *Appalachia* (Winter/Spring, 2016 and Summer/Fall, 2016) and Ty Gagne wrote an in-depth account, *Where You'll Find Me, Risks, Decisions, and the Last Climb of Kate Matrosova*.

After reading Mr. Gagne's book, I wanted to honor the search and rescue teams who cast aside their own welfare and put their lives at risk in hopes to save a life. I also had an inherent need to relive Kate Matrosova's trek that took her to the summits of Mount Madison and Adams. I wanted to understand what drove her in her attempt to cross the Northern Presidential Range in the face of a furious storm. Her decision-making was foolhardy. Her determination and fortitude remarkable.

I asked several friends to join me, but for various reasons the only hiking partner I could muster was my faithful companion Reuben. He never refuses to hike with me or anyone else for that matter. Reuben and I arrived at the Valley Way Trailhead early on the morning of February 14, the date before Kate began her trek in 2015. Clouds hung low over the mountains and there was an eeriness to the day. The Mount Washington Observatory was predicting a cloud cover over higher elevations and winds up to 55 mph with gusts hitting 70 mph. With this forecast in mind, my plan was altered to hike only to tree line, have lunch at Madison

Hut and return. I wasn't about to repeat mistakes made by others, trying to summit in severe wind and fog. Nevertheless, I wanted to experience, to some degree, the conditions that Kate, as well as the rescue teams faced. In order to commemorate those fateful days on the mountains I needed to put myself in their place, without taking any undue risks.

Reuben and I began the gentle grade of the Valley Way Trail as it gradually climbed 3.8 miles to the AMC Madison Springs Hut. The trail was packed down. No snowshoes needed, just trail crampons. While I stomped along, crunching the snow beneath my boots, I heard the wind roaring above. The tree tops were swaying wildly. This was an indication that the fierce winds forecast for the day would only get stronger the higher I climbed. When I reached tree line I was confronted by the sign warning me to turn back if the weather was bad. I considered turning back, but knew the Madison Springs Hut, although closed for the winter, would offer protection against the howling winds. Reuben and I found shelter close to a wall of the hut, protecting us against the gale force winds. Fortunately the temperatures were mild, in the twenties, making the wild chill less severe than expected. I settled in to quickly eat my lunch and afterward planned to head back down the trail.

After Kate had summited Mount Madison she returned to the shelter of the hut, maybe where I was eating my lunch. Here she hesitated, probably reevaluating her attempt at the traverse. For some reason she chose to forge ahead in the face of hurricane force winds and sub-zero temperatures to begin the climb of Mount Adams, where she eventually died of hypothermia. As Ty Gagne surmised in his book, *Where You'll Find Me,* had hypothermia already begun to alter her thinking? The wind and temperature I was experiencing were nowhere near those that Kate was battling in 2015, but I felt somewhat allied with her endeavor to push on, that inner force challenging me to my limits.

I wanted to climb Mount Madison and continue on to Mount Adams, but my rational side said no. Kate's inner call pulled her onward, in opposition to her rational, calculating side. Isn't this a conundrum for many of us?

As I was packing up and getting ready to leave my haven, I gazed upward. The clouds were breaking up and the winds were lessening. The White Mountains are noted for sudden changes in weather conditions, this time to my advantage. I reconsidered my options. I wasn't sure if it was totally safe to climb, but Reuben looked at me and his eyes said, "Let's go!" We began to climb, and as we did, the overhanging clouds continued to break apart. Then the skies suddenly cleared and the sun burst forth. We continued to climb upward, scrambling over and around massive boulders under bright, cloudless skies. I peered toward Mount Adams and billowing clouds were rolling over the summit. The entire Presidential Range was clearing. It seemed mystical. Why did the skies clear just as I was considering abandoning my plan to climb Madison? As Reuben and I battled 50 mph winds, we crawled the last 50 yards to the Mount Madison summit. I kept thinking of Kate and what she must have endured on this mountain. I thought of the rescue teams and their resolve to rescue Kate, before she perished; their hope that somehow she would still be alive, however unlikely. For some strange reason I felt their presence as I began my retreat back to the hut.

When I reached the hut I thought about climbing Adams. I found the Star Lake Trail and continued on. When I reached Star Lake, a small alpine pond, I realized I didn't have enough time to summit Adams and return safely. I retreated back to the Valley Way Trail and descended the mountain, returning to the Appalachia Parking Lot just as darkness was falling. Driving home, I continued to mull over in my mind Kate's attempt at the Northern Presidential traverse in the face of killing wind and cold. I kept returning to the question, why? My thoughts also turned to the bravery and courage of the rescuers. I recalled a Buddhist saying that courage is, *"Not the absence of fear or despair, but the strength to conquer them."* Their commitment and resolve to rescue Kate and many other hikers is a testament to their mission. We are fortunate to have such people willing to put their lives on the line without fanfare or accolades.

Chapter 4 - Whacky Bushwhacks

Sometimes, you find yourself in the middle of nowhere, and sometimes, in the middle of nowhere, you find yourself.

Unknown

A Word About Bushwhacking

The following essays are about off-trail hikes that involve trekking through the forest without the aid of a distinct path, blazes or signage with trail names and mileage. Bushwhacking involves using a map and compass, GPS, an ability to read the terrain, a good deal of common sense and knowledge of woodland signs (herd paths, old wood roads, moose browse, animal tracks.) Quite simply, bushwhacking can be defined as, "Forcing one's way through a forested or overgrown area where no path exists" (*Definitions.net*). People often ask me, "Why bushwhack, when you can tramp along a nicely maintained trail?" For me, the primary reason is the passion to go to places where few people go; to find a view from a remote mountain top or camp along a wilderness stream. It's also the peace and solitude I experience when hiking off-trail. Rarely have I encountered other people while bushwhacking, just the cries of ravens, the groans of a bull moose during rutting season, the call of a Canada jay, the wail of bear cubs, the howls of coyotes or simply silence. The appeal for me is the challenge of finding one's way to a destination, a mountain summit, a wilderness pond, or a spectacular waterfall without following an established trail and being immersed in solitude and beauty that only nature can provide.

Another Day in Paradise

Do not follow where the path may lead. Go instead where there is no path and leave a trail.

Ralph Waldo Emerson

A birch glade on a mountainside in the North Country

The hiking trails in the New Hampshire wilderness, north of the notches of the White Mountains, are often overlooked by most hikers. On a beautiful, warm late autumn day, Fran and I were driving to the North Country of New Hampshire, better known as "North of the Notches," to hike another trailless peak. As we approached Franconia Notch on I-93, we came to an abrupt stop. Cars were darting in and out of the lanes of traffic, drivers trying to find a parking spot. The shoulders of the road were packed tightly with cars, SUVs, and trucks, a mile-long on both sides of the highway. People were dashing across the roadway carrying packs, children hanging from arms and in one case a family pushing a baby stroller, what madness. After our stop-and-go experience we breathed a sigh of relief when we cleared out of the hub-bub of the Notch and continued on our way to Lancaster.(Since I wrote this essay the shoulders of I-93 through Franconia Notch are now closed to parking.)

Our plan was to hike to South Baldhead Mountain using the Cohos Trail as an approach to our predetermined bushwhack to the summit. When we stepped onto the Cohos Trail it was still as I remembered it, wild and remote, providing a true wilderness experience.

Earlier in the month we hiked the Cohos Trail to summit Sugar Hill and Tumbledick Mountains. Now we were walking the same trail to capture another peak on the New Hampshire 200 Highest list, South Baldhead. As we followed the Cohos Trail, it brought back many memories, when I sectioned hiked the trail: reaching the summit of North Percy Peak with my daughter Meghan on our first long distance hike together; sitting in Baldhead shelter with my step-grandson Austin sharing stories; wading through head-high ferns after a soaking rain; watching the rain drip through my ancient L.L. Bean tent, feeling the water soak through my sleeping bag. These and many more memories jumped out of the storage cells in my noggin as we marched silently along the path.

The Cohos is a 170 mile trail from the Canadian border to Crawford Notch, staying within the bounds of Coos County. Kim Nilsen was the founding father of the trail. In 1978 he envisioned a trail running through Coos County, north to south. By the year 2000 he and a small group of dedicated volunteers, The Cohos Trail Association, had mapped and cut portions of the trail, utilizing herd paths, logging roads and ATV trails. Now the trail is blazed, with signage and several shelters placed in strategic places. The southern section of the Cohos Trail takes advantage of existing trails in the White Mountains, maintained by the Appalachian Mountain Club and the U.S. Forest Service. The true wilderness of New Hampshire awaits as you hike north from Stark, NH. From Stark the trail gradually begins to climb the distinctive North Percy Peak and then plunges into the Nash Stream Forest. Following the Nash Stream, a stunning wild river, the trail climbs out of the river valley, passing through Kelsey Notch, into Dixville Notch, over Sanguinary Ridge, through Coleman State Park, and into the Connecticut Lakes Region, eventually terminating at the Canadian border. If you want to continue your journey north you can cross over into Canada (bring your passport) and continue on the Sentier Frontalier's Trail to Lake Megantic or Mount Gosford in the Eastern Townships of Quebec. When I hiked the Cohos, several years ago, I chose to do it in sections. There are few places to resupply on the entire route of the 170 mile trail. When planning to do a thru hike you need to prepare carefully. If a thru hike is not in your cards, then sectioning the trail is a reasonable and fulfilling experience. The real charm of the trail is its remoteness and absence of other hikers. In the words of Kim Nilsen, *"That's its appeal. People want to be in a woods and wild areas that are not frequented by much of anything (except wildlife). Where people don't reign. Where the wild things reign."* Guidebooks and maps of the trail are available at the Mountain Wanderer Bookstore in Lincoln or through the Cohos Trail website, (*www.cohostrail.org*).

Snapping back to attention after seeing Fran drop his bushwhacking goggles, I regained consciousness from my lapse into the past. Reuben, Fran and I had started our hike on the Cohos Trail from Kelsey Notch Road (a logging road) and continued our trek for two miles when we reached the Baldhead Mountain Shelter. This was the first shelter built on the trail and is still in excellent condition. Here we dropped our packs, made our way through the woods, finding the summit of Baldhead only a few hundred yards from the trail. We returned to the shelter, had a leisurely lunch while admiring the views to the east. On the return to our parked vehicle we laid out plans for several more hikes to the remote mountains of the North Country. Whenever we pass through Franconia Notch and see the masses of hikers climbing up Franconia Ridge, we will be thankful we are heading to the land north of the notches, where wild things reign and people don't.

Borderlands

Not all those who wander are lost.

J.R.R. Tolkien

*Fran following border swath to Mount D'Urban
on the Canadian-U.S. Border*

In the far north of New Hampshire, along the border with Canada, lie a number of mountains that are rarely climbed: D'Urban, Snag Pond Peak, Kent, West Prospect Hill, and Perry Pond Peak, Deer Mountain South, Salmon and Scott Bog Mountain. Fran and

I set out to summit these eight peaks in three days. The northern reaches of New Hampshire, north of Pittsburg, are resplendent with natural beauty. Here is a wilderness that holds rugged mountains, wilderness ponds and fast flowing streams filled with brook trout. The forest floor is carpeted with deep growing moss and lichen. Angel hair and old-man's-beard lichen hang from spruce boughs and wild flowers bloom abundantly along roadsides and meadows. It's a land of untold beauty. Cutting across this vast wilderness are numerous gravel logging roads that were once used to haul timber from the forest to lumber and paper mills. Now these roads are used by fishermen, hunters and snowmobile enthusiasts to access the deep recesses of these forested lands.

The region is best known as the headwaters of the Connecticut River. The 406-mile river is the longest river in New England, starting at the Fourth Connecticut Lake, a small pond on the Quebec border, flowing south to Long Island Sound. Its watershed encompasses five states and the province of Quebec. In the late nineteenth and early twentieth centuries the river was used for massive log drives. Now the river offers first-class fishing waters and serene canoeing as it runs through the Upper Connecticut River Valley.

The region is also known for its historical roots, the Indian Stream Republic. In the early nineteenth century the area was settled by woodsmen from both the U.S. and Canada, then a colony of Great Britain. Following the Revolutionary War and War of 1812 the ambiguous boundary between the two nations was not settled. Therefore, settlers of this region lived in limbo with both Canada and the U.S. claiming this as sovereign territory. In 1829 the settlers of the territory took matters into their own hands and formed an independent republic, declaring their independence from both Great Britain and the United States. They wrote their own constitution, created a judiciary, legislature, issued their own stamps, collected taxes and established a 41-man militia. After continued squabbling between the two great nations, the U.S. took control of the territory in 1835 and the dispute ended with the Indian Stream Republic being dissolved. The Webster-Ashburton Treaty of 1842 formally settled the boundary dispute along with other boundary discrepancies. It's interesting to note that New Hampshire native Daniel Webster signed the treaty as the U.S. Secretary of State.

I have always loved and appreciated the culture and natural beauty of the North Country and I looked forward to returning to this majestic land. We drove Rt. 3 to East Inlet Road, following the rough and tumble logging road for 11 miles to Boundary Pond. We started our trek by tracking along an old corduroy road that was most likely the "smugglers' road" we had heard about. This abandoned road is said to have been used to smuggle whiskey into the U.S. during prohibition. The pathway led us directly to Mount D'Urban, which is just off the border swath, inside the U.S. Border. After signing the register located in a canister nailed to a tree, we hiked the border swath to Snag Pond Peak. The swath, about 50-feet wide, cuts through the wilderness and small obelisks are located along the swath marking the boundary. It was easy hiking along the lengthy opening in the forest, reaching Snag Pond Peak in about an hour. We then retreated back to Boundary Pond, bushwhacking through thick woods and bogs, until we reached our parked truck.

We still had Mount Kent on our agenda, so we hopped into our vehicle and drove on another logging road to the base of the mountain. Mount Kent lies farther south of the border, therefore we didn't have the luxury of hiking the swath. We entered the woods and quickly found old skidder roads and moose runs to guide us through the thick forest. There are advantages to bushwhacking in this area, which include hiking vast numbers of old skidder roads and herd paths that wind around and up the mountains. We discovered numerous paths that moose had created and many signs (poop, chewed-off twigs, hoof prints) of these natives of the north woods, but strangely enough we never spotted one.

After finding the recognized summit and signing the register, we wound our way through blow-downs and hobblebush, again picking up herd paths along the way. After reaching the truck, we made the long drive over well-worn logging roads to our cabin on Back Lake. Here we could rest, have dinner and lay out plans for our climbs the next day of Prospect Hill Peak, Perry Pond Peak and Deer Mountain South.

The next day we began whacking to the border swath again, where we encountered a number of four-sided tree stands on the Canadian side of the border swath. They looked like small cabins mounted on tree legs, 10-15 ft. high. Near the tree stands were numerous salt licks to entice the deer and moose into the open. Some of these stands were furnished with comfortable seating, heating devices and toilet facilities. Located on the swath, the stands gave hunters a clear shot at any wildlife wandering along the open meadow. After finding the summit of Prospect Hill, we returned along the swath and began our next climb to Perry Pond Peak. Again we hiked through thick forest, interspersed with log landings, herd paths and skidder roads, until we reached the summit.

Our last climb of the day took us to Deer Mountain, South Peak, not to be confused with Deer Mountain a few miles to the north. Deer Mountain is trailed and has an abandoned fire tower at the summit. South Deer Mountain is trailless. The thick woods and cliffs posed a challenging climb and proved to be the most difficult climb of our North County adventure. Scrambling through blowdowns, scaling moss covered cliffs and fighting our way through thick fir and spruce presented us with an extremely difficult and challenging climb. As we struggled up the mountain, the skies darkened and we began to hear the rumble of thunder. When we reached the obscure summit the heavens opened up. Lightning flashed around us, followed by tremendous booms of thunder and torrential rain. It was time to find our way back down the mountain as fast as we could. Heading in a more northerly direction took us away from the scrub spruce and cliffs that blocked our way earlier. Using the map and compass we returned to the truck, soaked to the bone and ready for the dry confines of our cabin. That evening we laid out plans to climb Salmon and Scott Bog Mountains.

Our last day of climbing was a gift. Salmon Mountain was a beautiful climb through open woods, along herd paths, plucking ripe raspberries along the way. From the summit we checked the register, reading the names of others who had signed in before us: the regular band of brothers and sisters we see in all the registers. We all have a passion for hiking to these remote peaks, using only a map, compass and in some cases a GPS. After signing in, we found an obvious trail leading to the border swath and views to the east into Maine and Canada. Scott Bog, the last climb of our three-day excursion was another ramble through a wide-open hardwood forest, until we began a steep climb to the ridgeline, through bogs and a push into tightly packed spruce. Upon reaching the summit we felt elated, because we had accomplished our goal of eight peaks in three days, all bushwhacks. Now it was time to head back to the cabin, pack up and drive to the nearest pub for burgers and beer.

Following the Rocky Branch Railroad

Thousands of tired, nerve-shaken, over-civilized people are beginning to find out that going to the mountains is going home; that wildness is a necessity.

John Muir

Abandoned logging railroad beds are found throughout the White Mountains and offer walkers and hikers of all ages and degrees of fitness a romp through the woods on open level pathways. The railroad beds were built to haul timber out of the mountainous forests to sawmills, where the logs would be cut into millions of board feet of lumber. Reuben, Fran and I found ourselves hiking on one of these rail beds of the now defunct Rocky Branch Railroad. We were making our way up the Rocky Branch Trail, to begin a climb of East Stairs Mountain. This was my second attempt to climb East Stairs Mountain (2,967 ft.) a craggy peak, noted for the steep cliffs and thick woods that lie below the summit. My first attempt was in early spring when snow slowed the approach from the Davis Path and I had to turn back. This new route off the Rocky Branch Trail would prove to be a significant challenge also, but for different reasons. Following the Rocky Branch Trail seemed a good idea, as it would get us to within 1.5 miles of the summit and this route would avoid the band of cliffs that surround the mountain on three sides. Little did we know what was in store for us.

We began our hike by driving to the trailhead via Jericho Road or U.S. Forest Service Rd. #27. This road begins in Glen off of Rt. 302, traveling along an old railroad grade. For several years, following the infamous tropical storm Irene, the road and the trail were closed. The Rocky Branch River had spilled over its banks and washed out portions of the trail and Jericho Road. The road was rebuilt and the trail re-opened a few years later. However, the devastation caused by Irene was still evident while we hiked along the trail.

We drove to the end of Jericho Road, parked the truck and when we opened the doors we were greeted by hordes of mosquitos and black flies, waiting for fresh blood. We quickly donned our packs and head nets and dashed down the trail. The trail began by taking us across the Rocky Branch River on a newly constructed bridge. It was then an easy stroll through the woods, following the railbed. As we made our way on this easy amble, we encountered several views of the river, as well as the scars of Irene along the river bank. Monstrous dead trees and massive boulders were piled up by the inundating waters created by the storm. It was a stunning sight and a testament to the power of the river as it blasted away trees, rocks and soil. Within an hour we had hiked two miles to the 3-sided shelter, known as Shelter #1. Scattered about were vestiges of the logging era, a broken cast iron shard, most likely from a wood stove and pieces of iron. This was the site of a large complex of railroad tracks and buildings called the "The Store". It served as the headquarters for the Conway Lumber Company's logging operations along the Rocky Branch River.

The lumber company's mill was located in Conway and was one of the largest in New England. It cut upwards of 30 million board feet annually and obviously needed vast amounts of timber to keep the operation in business. In 1907 the Conway Company and the Central Maine and Boston & Maine railroads entered into an agreement to begin harvesting the untapped forests of the Rocky Branch drainage system. The rail line was laid that same year, but logging operations didn't begin until a year later, due to financial difficulties. Two large Climax engines hauled massive pine and spruce from high up on the slopes of Resolution, Stairs, Isolation, and Davis Mountains. Due to the extreme grade of the tracks into the mountainous areas, these powerful engines would often run out of control, careening down the mountain, crashing with a thunderous blast.

Logging operations continued in the Rocky Branch drainage system until 1914. During this time, as the forested mountainsides were being stripped clean of trees, the area was also plagued by a series of forest fires that further shortened lumbering operations. With the mountainsides exhausted of wood, and increasing pressure from environmentalists, the Conway Company pulled the rails and terminated operations. Now the only apparent sign of the massive logging operations is the Rocky Branch Trail.

After a short break at Shelter #1, battling mosquitoes, we resumed our walk up the trail. Within a few 100 yards we came to an opening that led down to the river. Along the river we found a small, sandy beach and deep pools of water. This would make a great destination for a family picnic and a swim in the crystal clear waters (minus the bugs). It was an easy walk of two miles to a newly renovated shelter for camping and a mountain stream for fishing and swimming. This hike would make a great outing for a family on a hot summer day.

Shortly after admiring the "picnic site" we found ourselves back on the trail and soon started our off-trail hike to the slopes of East Stairs Mountain. The first mile was through open woods, but soon we were hampered by innumerable hobblebush (viburnum lantanoides). This is a member of the honeysuckle family. It sprouts beautiful white flowers in the spring and red berries in the fall. Also known as witch-hobble and moosewood, it's found in rich, moist woods throughout the White Mountains. The name hobblebush is well deserved, since when it grows in thick patches it literally cripples anyone trying to hike through it. Fran and I found ourselves having to push through this thick scrub stumbling as we continued our climb.

Making our way up the mountain, after having to shove our way through the thick hobblebush and avoiding insurmountable cliffs, we were met with thickening woods. It was evident that the woods on this side of the mountain have been slow to recover from the fires and logging that plagued the forest 100 years ago. The spruce and fir were only six to ten feet high. We were continually fighting branches and getting poked in the face. We had difficulty even seeing the ground below. We finally made it to the summit, found the canister and signed in. Feeling exhausted and spent, we sat down to eat our lunch, battling black flies the entire time. The climax to the ordeal occurred when I laid my roast pork sandwich next to me, Reuben assumed it was his meal and my long-awaited lunch ended in Reuben's belly.

Now it was time to move off the mountain. However, we knew we didn't want to hike back the way we came, battling tree branches and hobblebush, so we decided to hike out along the base of the cliffs of Stairs Mountain, and find the Stairs Col Trail, which would lead us back to the Rocky Branch trail. The route turned out to be the way we should have climbed the mountain: open woods, no hobblebush and beautiful views of the cliffs above. We ambled down the western slope of East Stairs Mountain and within an hour we were on the Stairs Col Trail, an old logging roadbed which at one time was part of the Rocky Branch logging operations. This trail took us out to the Rocky Branch trail. On our way back to the trailhead we met a couple who were out for an easy stroll. They noticed our battered legs and wondered where we had been. We described our ordeal. They just shook their heads and probably asked themselves, "Why do that?" This was a very reasonable question and I asked myself this same question. Fran and I learned, as we have many times before, a map may show you trails and elevation gain, but it can't show you the obstacles like hobblebush, mosquitoes and "pencil woods." Bushwhacking is always an adventure and a challenge into the unknown.

Mount Bemis Fire Tower

Mountain solitude: is it lost and gone forever?

Laura and Guy Waterman

*Sandy, Tom, Karen and Reuben
bushwhacking through mountain meadow*

This was my third climb of Mount Bemis. Why hike this un-trailed mountain three times? A good question to ask. In short, it's a majestic mountain named for an iconic figure of the White Mountains, Dr. Samuel Bemis. The climb offers the trekker a hike along an abandoned jeep road, through an open forest meadow filled with lush vegetation, a challenging bushwhack through "pencil" spruce and blowdowns, fantastic views and a wrecked fire tower close to the summit. What more could one ask for?

I first climbed Mount Bemis several years ago with a few close friends. We were on a mission to climb the 100 highest mountains in New Hampshire, of which Bemis is #67 at 3,725 ft. Later I hiked the mountain in winter with my friend Sandy, but we didn't reach the summit due to the unforgiving snow depths. As darkness fell we had to turn back just before the final push to the summit. This time Sandy and I were determined to reach the summit in her quest to hike all NH 100 Highest peaks. We were accompanied on our outing by hiking friends Tom and Karen. This time I was sure we would make the summit of Bemis Mountain. It was a gorgeous spring day, unlike most days that spring, which had been cold, damp and rainy. It felt good to be out hiking again after several days trying to get the garden planted in between downpours.

We started our hike on the Nancy Pond Trail, just south of the Notchland Inn on Rt. 302. This distinctive granite mansion was originally built by Dr. Samuel Bemis as his summer residence, and he lived there until his death in 1881. He was born in Putney, VT in 1793, moved to Boston in 1812 and became a renowned dentist. He began visiting the White Mountains in 1833 and befriended Abel Crawford and his son-in-law Nathaniel Davis, while staying at their Mount Crawford House Tavern. Samuel Bemis had many interests including horticulture, surveying, watchmaking, and geology. He was one of the original White Mountain landscape photographers. Bemis purchased a daguerreotype camera in 1840 and immediately began to take photographs of the White Mountains. Many of his images are on display at the George Eastman House in Rochester, NY.

We began our trek by climbing the Nancy Pond Trail. We crossed three small streams with easy rock hops until we reached the fourth and largest crossing of Nancy Brook. After searching for a safe crossing, we made it to the other side without incident, where we found the abandoned jeep road, which at one time served to take forest rangers to the fire tower on Mount Bemis. The old road, which has been in disuse since the fire tower closed in 1948, was still very distinguishable from the surrounding forest, even though it has been abandoned for almost 70 years. At the start of the pathway a sign was posted on a tree, warning hikers that this route is an unauthorized hiking trail and should not be maintained in any way. To do so is, "punishable by a $5,000 fine and/or six months in prison". Apparently there have been "outlaws" cutting and slashing trees trying to keep the old road open, which is illegal in the White Mountain National Forest.

As we hiked along the abandoned road we climbed higher on the ridge leading to Mount Bemis. Blowdowns began to obstruct our leisurely pace. The trail soon became obscured by thick growth. The forest had reclaimed the land and this reclamation represented a major challenge. We carefully wove our way through, under, over and around the maze of downed trees and thick brush. With some luck and skill we were able to continue on the abandoned roadbed, finally emerging from the dense cover to find a meadow of Labrador tea, scrub spruce and shadbush or service berry. The service berry was in full bloom, with striking white rose-like flowers filling the meadow. Its name comes from the time of year when the shad are running. The flowers were also used in funeral services in the spring, hence the common name, service berry.

We stopped here to take in the views and the warmth of the sun on this chilly day before we continued our trek to the summit. We then entered back into the woods, found the well-worn "herd" path to the remains of the fire tower. Many bushwhackers, upon gaining this height of land, think they've reached the summit. However, the official high point lies another 300 feet to the west. We explored the shambles of the fire tower, found a few artifacts and admired the views to the east. While we lounged, discussing the fate of the fire tower, a flood of questions rushed into my head: When were these fire towers built, why were they taken down and how many others existed? I remembered climbing several other mountains where I found the remains of towers: Carr, Cherry, Iron, Hale, and closer to home, Mount Major. I also knew there are fire towers still standing: Belknap, Red Hill, Carrigain, Cardigan, and Smarts Mountain. This brief respite stirred up my interest, not only in this tower, but the others that had blanketed the state.

There were a total of 85 towers in New Hampshire, built between 1909 and 1940. Sixteen of these towers are still standing and some are still periodically active. The network of fire towers came about in the early twentieth century, because of a series of dry summers, when sparks from wood-burning, logging locomotives set off huge fires destroying thousands of acres of forest. The New Hampshire Forestry Commission, established in 1881, combined forces with the Timberlands Owners Association, the Appalachian Mountain Club, U.S. Forest Service and the Society for the Protection of New Hampshire Forests, to build and staff these fire lookout stations. Some of these early towers were built by woodsmen employed by the timber operators during the winter. They constructed their own cabins and towers, mostly of local materials. By 1929 the state was operating 29 stations. Many of the original structures were made of wood but in the 1920s the state began to replace these with steel structures which we know today. The Hurricane of 1938 blew many of the towers into oblivion, but these were replaced and the state continued to use the tower system to control the potential of forest fires. During WW II, some of these towers were used for spotting enemy aircraft.

By 1948, with the decline of fire danger and the use of aircraft, a number of stations were closed. By the end of 1960 the National Forest Service closed all of its stations, with only the state retaining a few. There are now 16 stations still in service, 15 funded by the state and one on Red Hill operated by the Town of

Moultonborough. Locally, one can have a "lookout" experience by hiking Red Hill or Belknap Mountain, which are periodically manned by a volunteer. If you want to paddle your canoe across Lake Winnipesaukee you can visit the tower on Bear Island. You can also hike to other locations and find the remains of towers that were taken down. A complete list of the towers can be found on the New Hampshire Dept. of Forest and Lands web site (*nhd-fl.org.*).

After an extended lunch break, exploring the remains of the tower and looking for artifacts, we began the final stretch to the summit of Bemis. It was a short distance to the peak, through scrub spruce, where we found the jar hanging from a tree, along with an old canteen. Sandy got her peak. We celebrated, signed the registered and headed back the way we came. I don't plan to return any time soon, as three times to Mount Bemis is more than enough for me.

East Spruce and Greens Cliff

In the mountains, there you feel free.

T.S. Elliot

When spring arrives it comes with opportunities to discard the winter hiking garb and all the paraphernalia that winter hiking requires: snowshoes, crampons, extra clothing, winter shell, insulated water carrier, and more. This adds an additional 15 lbs. to the pack. Thank goodness for spring. We have left winter behind and with it, snow, ice, bitter winds and freezing temperatures. If you are one of those shuttered, winter hibernators, spring is the time to emerge from your cave and begin to move about in the warming sun, greening forest and melting slushy snow. It's the season to hit the trail and take advantage of the bright sunshine and warming temperatures.

Dick crossing the Sawyer River on the Sawyer Pond Trail

With my hiking partner Mike, along with our dogs Lyla and Reuben, we decided to take advantage of a beautiful spring day and tackle East Spruce Mountain, continuing on our quest to summit the highest 200 peaks in New Hampshire. This list includes not only the well-known New Hampshire 48, but 152 other lesser-known peaks, some located in remote areas of the state. We were fortunate that the day was filled with deep blue sky and a blazing sun reflecting off the snow, making sun glasses necessary. The mountain showed signs of a fading winter: snow turning to slush or in hiking terms, "mashed potatoes," bare rocks, snow bridges over streams breaking apart, buds beginning to show on the red maples and hobblebush and lots of animal tracks in the soft snow signaling the romantic frenzy of the woodland wildlife. Poet E. E. Cummings wrote, *"I thank you God for this most amazing day, for the leaping greenly spirits of trees, and for the blue dream of sky and for everything which is natural, which is infinite, which is yes"*.

East Spruce Mountain lies in an arch formed by several other mountains including Spruce, Teapot, Savage, Goback and Lightning Mountains. It lies directly east of the town of North Stratford, NH. We began our hike to East Spruce Mountain (3,010 ft.) by driving to an unplowed road off Rt. 3 in North Stratford, better known as Lamm's Trail. We followed this road for a mile before coming to a set of remote cabins and began to follow a series of logging roads, passing through log yards and skid paths that disappeared up the side of the mountain. We were able to walk the road without snowshoes, but as we gained elevation on the logging road, we found ourselves post-holing in one to two feet of snow. The snow was a reminder that winter may have ended on the calendar, but it kept a grip on April in the mountains of northern New Hampshire, so we reluctantly strapped on our snowshoes. We continued on our trajectory toward the summit of East Spruce following skid paths, some relatively new and others disappearing with disuse. These wide pathways through the wilderness serve as a testimony of the logging industry that once ruled this part of the state and in some respects still plays an important role in the economy of Coos County.

After a short bushwhack through a heavily forested area we reached the summit, found the canister and signed in. The sun was at its peak and we bathed in its warmth, while we downed our lunch. However, a cool breeze suddenly sprang up and my perspiration-soaked shirt sent a chill running down my spine. At this point I was reminded of the Robert Frost poem, *Two Tramps in Mudtime.*
The Sun was warm but the wind was chill
You know how it is with an April Day
When the sun is out and the wind is still,
You're one month on in the middle of May.
But if you so much as dare to speak,
A cloud comes over the sunlit arch,
A wind comes off a frozen peak,
And you're two months back in the middle of March.

Following our respite on the summit we started back the way we came, but soon found ourselves exploring a new skid road descending the mountain. The entire side of the mountain was a complex of skid roads and log landings. On our way down the mountain we chatted about our next climb, leaving the decision with Mike.

After considering a number of options, Mike decided on a climb to Greens Cliff. A few days later we met at the Sawyer River Road parking lot, off Rt. 302 in Crawford Notch. Dick and Fran decided to join us. For several years Mike had thought about hiking these cliffs that rise above Sawyer Pond and the Sawyer Pond Scenic Area. The easterly facing side of Greens Cliff is breathtaking: a solid granite wall rising 250 feet above the forest floor. It is well-known in the rock climbing community as one of the finest cliffs in the state for climbing. There are numerous routes up the sheer walls, but it wasn't until 1975 that rock climbers made a full ascent of the cliffs. Rock climbing wasn't in our plan for our day, we had a different approach in mind.

Our hike began on Sawyer River Road. This U.S. Forest Service Road, gated during winter, was at one time the roadbed of the Sawyer River Railroad, hauling loads of logs out of the wilderness for the Grafton County Lumber Company. We followed this well-maintained roadway, which is also part of an extensive network of snowmobile trails in the White Mountain National Forest. We passed the abandoned village of Livermore, once a logging community of about 150 residents. Since a good deal of snow had melted we could make out the foundations of the store, lumber mill, log pond, school house and homes. The only sign that this was once a thriving community were the skeletal remains of the buildings and structures built by these hardy people of the North Country.

After a four-mile hike on Sawyer River Road, we reached the summer parking lot and a kiosk with a trail map of the area. As the sun rose higher in the sky, the air warmed quickly and with it the snow was turning to "mashed potatoes." We relaxed for a few minutes, put on our snowshoes and watched Lyla and Reuben frolic in the snow. Reuben had found a good hiking companion, plus he's attracted to her beautiful curly red fur. Reuben reminds me of Charlie Brown from the Peanuts cartoon and the his infatuation with, "The girl with the curly red hair."

After crossing a bridge over the engorged Sawyer River, running high due to the rapid snow melt, we began the bushwhack through open stands of hardwood. We aimed for the summit, veering slightly east to avoid cliff bands which rise sharply to the peak. As the climb became steeper and more difficult in the soft-deep snow we began to perspire. We peeled away the outer layers of clothing, and we were now hiking in our shirtsleeves. Sunscreen was the order of the day. Signs of spring were all about us, most notably the streams had opened up, their snow cover was quickly disappearing. Reaching the ridge of Greens Cliff we now had views to the east: Chocorua, the Three Sisters, and Passaconaway lay in the distance. As we moved up the ridge to the summit, the cliffs became more pronounced, dropping several hundred feet to the valley floor. We had to keep Reuben and Lyla close-by as we worried they would stray over the edge and meet their demise in a long fall.

We finally found what we thought was the recognized summit canister jar, but Mike found another farther along the ridge. Which spot represented the official summit? Not knowing, we signed both registers. Following the summit ceremony with photo-ops, we headed back to a view point for a leisurely lunch, basking in the sun, taking in the views of the valley below and the mountains rising on all sides. We eyed Owls Cliff, with its sheer ledges and considered this mountain as next on our NH 200 list. With the day closing out, we reluctantly began our trek back to the Sawyer River Forest Road and the four-mile road walk in soft, slushy snow. This walk back to our cars closed out another day of spring in the mountains. Soon the snow would be gone from many of the trails in the higher elevations, no more snowshoes, trail crampons and layers of clothing. Spring also signals the blooming of hepatica, spring beauties, trout lilies and trillium. Wild leeks start to peek out of the ground. Wood frogs begin calling from trees, spring peepers can be heard chanting in the evening hours. Spotted salamanders make their way into vernal pools. The warblers can be seen hopping from branch to branch. New life would be popping up throughout the forest and with it a new hiking season.

The Hog and the Loaf

To find the air and the water exhilarating; to be refreshed by a morning walk or an evening saunter... to be thrilled by the stars at night; to be elated over a bird's nest or a wildflower in spring - these are some of the rewards.

John Burroughs

The following column has nothing to do with eating pulled pork on a loaf of bread. It has everything to do with a bushwhack hike to the summits of two little known mountains: Hogsback and Sugarloaf Mountains. A few summers ago I hiked the Chippewa Trail to the summit of Black Mountain in Benton, NH and I spied another mountain just to the south of Black Mountain, with a long ridge running toward Mount Moosilauke. After looking at my map, I deduced that the mountain was Sugarloaf and the ridge was Hogsback. However, according to the map there are no trails to the summit. That would mean doing some research and planning to reach my goal via a bushwhack. I put the plan on hold, and then a year later invited my friend Steve to join me on my quest to hike another Sugarloaf Mountain, as there are several others in New Hampshire.

Looking east at Hogsback Mountain from Sugarloaf Mountain

In researching the hike, I found that at one time there was a trail to the summit as described in an earlier edition of the AMC White Mountain Guide. However, the trail, which starts in close proximity to Lime Kiln Road, has been closed for many years and according to trip reports, it is difficult to find. Steve Smith, Co-Author of the AMC White Mountain Guide and owner of the Mountain Wanderer Book Store in Lincoln, NH cites the classic 1876 guidebook by Moses Sweetser, *The White Mountains: A Handbook for Travelers.* "*Sugarloaf ...is a sharp and conspicuous peak of light colored rock, alpine in appearance, and easily recognized from a great distance. Although its height is but 2,565 ft., it will probably be a favorite point of attack when alpine exercise becomes popular in New England, on account of the fascination of its defiant cliffs, the exciting perils of the ascent, and the beautiful view from the summit.*" Upon reading this post from Steve Smith I became even more intrigued with this rather unknown and obscure peak.

On a warm spring day, Steve and I headed to western New Hampshire on Route 25. When we arrived in the village of Glencliff, we turned onto High Street (formerly Sanatorium Road) and then onto Long Pond Road, a Forest Service Road that is sometimes gated. The gate was fortunately open and we drove to a point almost directly east of Mount Jeffers, where we began the bushwhack, setting the compass at 266 degrees. Steve and I, along with our dogs Skipper and Reuben, who have been hiking buddies for years, set off into the thick forested mountainside.

On our way through the woods, we found beautiful wildflowers as well as numerous ramps. Ramps, *Allium tricoccum*, also known as wild leeks, are native to the eastern North American mountains. They can be found growing in patches in rich, moist, deciduous forests. They are in the Allium family, related to garlic and onions. They have a smooth, pleasant taste of young spring onions with an aroma similar to garlic. They are sought after by many natural food gurus and make a wonderful addition to a salad. In the south, especially in Tennessee and North Carolina, ramp festivals are quite popular.

After pausing to contemplate pulling some ramps to take home for a salad, we moved on, leaving these delicious woodland plants to grow and multiply. Within two hours we reached the summit of Jeffers Mountain (2,994 ft.), marked by a canister mounted on a tree. We sat for a while and watched several ruffed grouse fledglings and the mother hen scurry around in the brush. The youngsters were learning to fly by fluttering from tree branch to tree branch above our heads, with mother looking on. I'm sure she was hoping we would let her children be and we would move on quickly.

After signing our names in the register, we set out for Hogsback Ridge. We found several old trail markers, which were no more than slash marks on a tree, but these markers disappeared well along the ridge. Our track took us along the ridgeline to several viewpoints, and we could see the long, rocky ridge summit of Hogsback just ahead. When we climbed to the pinnacle of Hogback, the views were unexpectedly remarkable. We could see well into Vermont and over to Mount Moosiluake and Clough Mountain to the east. Since few people climb Hogsback we may have been one of the few trekkers in the past several years to hike this long narrow ridge.

From Hogsback we continued our climb to Sugarloaf. As we made our approach, we viewed Black Mountain with its rock cliffs, and scanned the area around the mountain for any sign of the limestone quarries, located at the base of Black Mountain. In the mid-1800s limestone kilns were built to turn the rock into a powdered form that was used for building construction, sculptures, mortar, glass making, fertilizer, and even toothpaste. The two Haverhill lime kilns were built in 1838 and 1842 and operated profitably until 1888. The woodland surrounding the kilns provided the wood needed to fire the kilns to high temperatures.

When Steve and I reached the summit we explored the open rock face, finding a trail that led down the mountain toward Black Mountain and another trail that seemed to be the remnants of the old abandoned trail leading out to Lime Kiln Road. After eating our lunch, we packed up and began the bushwhack back to our car. Our route took us through open woods, log clearings and overgrown logging roads. It was clear that this side of the ridge was heavily logged over the past several years and offered browse for moose, deer and bear. We eventually found a more recent forest road that led us directly back to our cars. The bushwhack took us about seven hours, walking a total of 6.5 miles, a long slow slog, but well worth the effort.

Visiting a Scene of Devastation

Still round the corner there may wait
A new road or a secret gate,
And though I've often passed them by,
A day will come at last when I
Shall take the hidden paths that run
West of the Moon, East of the Sun.

J. R. R. Tolkien

Fran and Dave with Reuben hiking
down the rock slide on Northwest Hancock

On August 15, 2011 a tropical depression exited off the North African coast. Over several days it gained strength, nearing the North American coastline as a tropical depression and was later upgraded to a hurricane named Irene. Irene approached the Outer Banks of North Carolina and slowly progressed up the eastern seaboard, moving into Vermont and New Hampshire on August 29, when it was downgraded to an extra tropical depression. However, even though Irene's intensity weakened, it remained a powerful storm with sustained winds of up to 50 mph and dumping more than 11 inches of rain in the White Mountains. This massive amount of rain caused tremendous damage to roads and bridges throughout the state, especially in the White Mountain National Forest, where many trails and roads were obliterated. Governor Lynch declared a state of emergency. The storm caused more than ten million dollars in damage to the White Mountain National Forest. The aftermath of Irene is legendary and the scars caused by this storm can still be seen today.

Dave, Fran and I, with Reuben accompanying us, visited one of the vestiges of Irene, a freshly-scoured slide on the west-facing slope of the ridge running between North Hancock Mountain and its trailless neighbor Northwest Hancock. I have climbed North Hancock several times, but the main goal this time was to summit Northwest Hancock, a seldom climbed peak that can only be reached by bushwhacking a mile, along the ridge connecting the two mountains. Our hiked started by following the Hancock Notch Trail to the Cedar Brook Trail and then to the Hancock Loop Trail, which would bring us to the summit of Mount Hancock. From here we would bushwhack, following a north-westerly track, along the ridge to the summit of Northwest Hancock. We then planned to hike down the western side of the ridge, following the slide that originally fell in 1927. It was deeply gullied and enlarged by the rains of Irene. This track would take us back to the Cedar Brook Trail.

We began our hike soon after sunrise, knowing we would most likely be hiking out of the woods well past nightfall. We followed our planned route, arrived at the summit of Hancock, North Peak, stopping to grab a snack and admiring the limited view. We changed into our shells, knowing that the bushwhack would be wet with melting snow falling from fir and spruce boughs, as we had to plow through scrub conifers. After our short break, we dove into the woods following a herd path a short distance, but it disappeared after only a few minutes of hiking. We broke out the compasses and pushed on toward our mountain destination. It took us almost two hours to cross the one mile ridge, where we found the canister that marks the summit of Northwest Hancock. We lingered for a while, signing the register, eating lunch and discussing our climb down the ridge, to the infamous slide.

Fran, Dave and I followed our track back along the ridge to where we thought the slide would be found below. We made our way through thick woods and blowdowns, until we reached the top of the slide. It appeared to us as a clearing, until Fran took one too many steps and found himself falling into the ravine, which marked the uppermost part of the slide. This is where the deluge from Irene hit the side of the mountain, and the flooding rains ravaged the slide, created earlier in 1927, opening a new swath of rock and gravel. We were awestruck by the size of the gouge. The immense force of the wall of water rushing down the mountainside caused whole trees, boulders and gravel to wash down the old slide.

As we began our descent, sliding and slipping on the loose scree and gravel, we found ourselves in a canyon of destruction. A section of the mountain had been made anew in a matter of a few days by Irene's ferocity and the terrain was permanently altered. A new scar on the mountain had been created. We did notice that the woodland was attempting a comeback. Small trees and grasses were inching their way into the chasm of the slide. There's a saying: "Nature doesn't like a void," and we were witnesses to Nature's reclamation project. We stopped often to marvel at the destruction caused by Irene, amazed at the force of water as it charged down the mountain, permanently changing the topography. However, our gazing had to be limited as time was running short and sunset was approaching. We didn't want to be on the slide trying to scramble along in the darkness with only our headlamps to light the way.

We did succeed in making it to the Cedar Brook Trail, before total darkness enveloped us. Once on the trail we strapped on our headlamps and started our four-mile trek back to the car. It was another rewarding hike, finding the summit of Northwest Hancock, a seldom climbed summit, and then climbing down the slide of Northwest Hancock.

A Return Attempt at Southwest Twin

With beauty before me, may I walk

With beauty behind me, may I walk

With beauty above me, may I walk

With beauty below me, may I walk

With beauty all around me, may I walk
Wandering on the trail of beauty, may I walk.
Navajo: Walking Meditation

As we were nearing the summit of Southwest Twin (4,357 ft.), located in the Pemigewasset Wilderness, we hit a wall of scrub fir that was as dense as anything I had ever experienced. Fran and I were stopped cold in our tracks. We started our climb around 8:30 in the morning and had made relatively good time climbing the western slope of this rarely summited mountain. Temperatures were in the high 30s and a chill had penetrated our clothing, as we attempted to bust through the thick under-growth and blowdowns that resembled "pick–up-sticks". We only had a third of a mile left to reach the summit, after hiking from Thirteen Falls Campsite, via the Twin Brook Trail. We tried to punch through the firs, our clothing soaked from melting hoarfrost dripping from the trees, as the sun warmed the air. It

*Gordon, Beth, Dave and Reuben at the base of Southwest Twin,
Red Rock Pond in the background*

seemed almost impossible to continue as we struggled deeper into
the fir barrier. Should we turn back before we become hypother-
mic, or continue on through the maze to reach the summit? Fran
and I considered our options. I thought, "even if we make the
summit, we have to find our way back through this impossible
tangle of trees and blowdowns". My legs ached and my clothes
were sodden with icy water. I reached for my water bottle and it
was gone, the last of my water snatched from my pack by the
arms of balsam fir as I struggled to push through the maze of
head-high fir and spruce . Why go on? The answer came to me,
through words of George Mallory, the noted British mountaineer.
When asked why he persisted in trying to reach the summit of
Mount Everest he stated, "Because it's there."

Earlier in the year I joined Beth and Dave for an attempt at summiting the same mountain, Southwest Twin. The mountain is trailless, therefore you must bushwhack using a map, compass and/or GPS to navigate. The mountain is rarely climbed due to its isolated location, numerous cliff bands and a dense forest surrounding the summit. We planned to hike into Red Rock Pond via a series of abandoned logging railroad beds and tote roads that crisscross the area. Between 1880 and 1920, this area was heavily logged and there are many signs of the by-gone logging era: railbeds, clearings where logging camps once stood, cookware, bed springs, and parts of wood stoves. Numerous artifacts are scattered throughout this vast wilderness, left behind by the loggers of the J.E. Henry Company.

By following an abandoned railbed, we were able to reach an area near Red Rock Brook that looked to be the site of an old logging camp. After making camp we found a series of tote roads that led us to Red Rock Pond, a beautiful tarn that sits at the bottom of a glacial cirque. The trek to Red Rock Pond was certainly worth the effort. The view of the pond and the cliffs rising above were stunning. After scanning the walls of the cirque, we decided that a climb from this direction would be difficult and possibly dangerous due to the broken rock and scree covering the sides of the cirque. At this point we decided to hike back to camp, spend the night, and head home in the morning. We vowed to return, using a different approach to summit Southwest Twin.

Now I had returned with Fran for another crack at summiting Southwest Twin, this time from a different approach, the Twin Brook Trail. We hiked into Thirteen Falls Campsite and spent the evening. The summer had ended, and autumn was coming to a close. There was a distinct chill in the air and snow was predicted to fall that evening. When we awoke in the morning we joyfully found clearing skies and a warming sun, a great day for, "a walk in the woods." We began our journey by hiking a mile up the Twin Brook Trail and then heading into the woods, following a predetermined compass bearing that would lead up a steep section of the mountain. The woods were relatively open with few blowdowns, but several rock scrambles slowed our progress. We thought this new route was going to take us to the summit in record time. Little did we know what was waiting for us: a wall of scrub spruce and blowdowns.

When we reached the ridge, we stopped to take in the views of Mounts Garfield and Lafayette. We knew it was a short distance to the summit and were eager to celebrate our accomplishment when we reached the apex of our effort. However, much to our chagrin, we ambled into the dreaded fir wall that we had read about. We had planned our route with the intention of avoiding this solid mass of scrub spruce and fir. We learned quickly that we hadn't bypassed it at all and were literally neck-deep in tree limbs. Fran and I were determined to push through, no matter what. We had gone this far, we couldn't turn back now. It took us well over an hour to go one-third of a mile. When we eventually reached the summit we signed our names in a small notebook stored in a canister nailed to a tree. We ate a sandwich, took in a few limited views and began our trek down the mountain. Amazingly, this route was relatively free of the miserable scrub growth that hindered our route up the mountain, but was extremely steep in sections with loose rock and scree hampering our way down the mountain. We did make it back to the Twin Brook Trail in one piece, but I had to endure a huge thirst after losing my water bottle in the scrub.

When we returned to our base camp at 13 Falls Campsite, a heavy rain began to fall. We quickly packed up our gear and began our trek out of the wilderness and into civilization. We were elated that we had stood on the summit of Southwest Twin, a mountain that few people climb. For Fran and I this could have been the most difficult bushwhack we have ever done. Why put ourselves through this ordeal? "Because it's there."

On our trek out of the Pemigewasett wilderness, along the Franconia Brook Trail, we were met by several groups of N. H. Fish and Game officers and U.S. Forest Service staff. They were searching for a missing hiker named Claire, who disappeared in the area where we had been hiking. She was missing for several days and the outcome of the search seemed grim. We were questioned regarding the possibility that we may have seen her. We later learned that her body was found in the Gale River, where she most likely died trying to cross the stream swollen by heavy rains. This was a sobering moment for us. It reminded us of the fact that the wilderness can be a place of splendor and beauty, but it also holds risks and dangers.

Hunting for the Headwaters

As you sit on the hillside, or lie prone under the trees of the forest, or sprawl wet-legged by a mountain stream, the great door, which does not look like a door, opens.

Stephen Graham

Just as Henry Schoolcraft searched for the headwaters of the Mississippi River in 1832, Dick, Tom and I, along with Reuben, were on a mission to discover the source of Wonalancet River. Henry Schoolcraft found Lake Itasca in Minnesota, the source of the Mississippi River. We were unsuccessful in our hunt for the beginning of the Wonalancet River. Our mission was denied by the sheer walls of the Bowl Natural Area, a stunning glacial cirque carved out from the side of Mounts Whiteface, Passaconway, and Wonalancet during the Pleistocene epoch. Why search for the source of a little known stream in New Hampshire? Because it lies in a beautiful wilderness that contains one the few

Tom looking south into the basin of the Bowl Natural Area

remaining old growth forests in the White Mountains. Our search would take us through an area that is rarely traveled, where few have seen the cliffs of Mount Whiteface rising overhead or trekked the floor of a valley that has never been logged or trammeled by man. We had the opportunity to experience what the first settlers in New Hampshire saw when they entered the New Hampshire wilderness. For the hiker who is looking for solitude or a saunter in an old growth forest, the Bowl Natural Area should not be missed.

We began our mission of discovery by taking Dicey's Mill Trail from the Ferncroft parking lot off Rt. 113A in Wonalancet. The trails in this section of the Sandwich Range and the Sandwich Range Wilderness are maintained by the Wonalancet Out Door Club. We followed Dicey's Mill Trail for about two miles, before turning onto the Tom Wiggin Trail. The snow was crusted over from the recent warm weather and rains, so we didn't need snow-shoes, but preferred instead to wear light trail crampons. Within a few hundred yards we came to the Wonalancet River, beginning our wilderness meander to find its source. Staying on the east side of the brook, we entered an area that few elect to explore. Most hikers are not interested in old-growth forests or the flora and trees that exist in this type of woodland. As we strode along the frozen snow, we entered a northern hardwood forest of large sugar maples, American beech and yellow birch. The understory was dominated by young spindly beech and plenty of hobblebush that frequently slapped us in the face or tried to trip us up. We stopped frequently to admire the gigantic trees, their gnarled arms stretching resplendently skyward into the pale blue sky.

This spectacular treasure of the Northern Forest was made possi-ble by the dedicated work of innkeeper Kate Sleeper Walden and members of the Wonalancet Out Door Club. Kate, who owned a 600-acre farm and inn, was also married to Arthur Walden, who raised and trained sled dogs. He became well-known for his breeding of the Chinook, a powerful sled dog used by Admiral Perry in his quest to reach the South Pole. In 1914, fourteen members of the WODC met with members of the U. S. Forest Ser-vice. The WODC advocated strongly to have the "Bowl", as they called it, included in the creation of a section of the White Moun-tain National Forest. Their efforts were successful and in 1931 the Forest Service set aside 500 acres of the Bowl as a Natural Area. This was expanded in 1975 to 1,500 acres and designated as a Re-search Natural Area, set aside for research as it pertains to old growth forests. Studies indicate that some of the trees are 200-250 years old. In 1984 the U.S. Congress designated 25,000 acres of the Sandwich Range as a Wilderness Area, and this was later expanded by 10,000 acres in 2006, which included the Bowl Natural Area.

Ice flow on the ravine wall of the Bowl Natural Area

We continued to follow the stream through the glades of the old forest, continually moving higher up into the valley where we began to encounter fingers of smaller streams flowing into the main branch of the Wonalancet River. Climbing higher on the wall we found ourselves post-holing in more than a foot of snow, making our trek slow and exhausting. The snowpack at this higher elevation forced us to change over to snowshoes. With snowshoes now strapped to our feet and televators extended, we were able to easily glide over the snow. It was guesswork as to which stream would lead us to the source of the Wonalancet River. We came to a branch we thought was the main artery. Looking up, we viewed the cliffs and ledges high above. The forest canopy turned from hardwood to balsam fir and red spruce. The summit of Whiteface and its connecting ridge to Passaconway stood clearly in view. We began to gain elevation quickly as the trek turned into a stiff climb. The steep walls of the Bowl rose before us, exposing the ice-encrusted precipices above. Trudging upwards, we were suddenly confronted by a ledge blocking our track. The icy outcrop was impossible to climb without technical climbing gear. We carefully weighed our options and decided to traverse across the face of the bowl to find another route to the cliffs above.

The traverse was no easy matter with a pitch of about 25-35 degrees. Tom broke trail, Reuben found his own path and eventually we came to an open glade of beech and maple where we settled down for a relaxing lunch, the sun warming our hands and faces. We were high above the floor of the valley, looking across at Mounts Whiteface and Wonalancet. After lunch we began climbing through the glade, up to another rock shelf that blocked our ascent. We were beginning to doubt we'd find the source of the Wonalancet, when I heard Tom and Dick yell, "Come on down off the cliff and look at the frozen waterfall. We think the source is just above." I scurried down the cliffs, securing my steps against tree trunks and roots as I descended. Sure enough, a significant frozen waterfall lay just above Dick and Tom. I was tempted to climb the ice flow, but Tom reminded me that it was getting late in the afternoon and we still had a three hour hike out of the Bowl.

After viewing the frozen waterfall, we began out trek back into the base of the Bowl. As we made our way down and out we happened upon a small cave. Standing in front and listening carefully, we heard the cries of some newly born critters. Reuben became excited, sniffing around the opening and barking. I first thought of bear cubs which would have just been born. Dick suggested bobcat. Either way it was a rare event to stumble across this cave. In reviewing data from research done in the Bowl by the U.S. Forest Service, Northeastern Forest Experiment Station, signs of bear have been present but there were no sightings or signs of other animals that would bear their young in a small cave in late winter. It was most likely a bear's den, occupied by mama bear and her newly born cubs.

I'm counting the days to spring when I can return to the Bowl and again search for the source of the Wonalancet River, when there's no ice and snow to impede the journey. The spring flora will be in full bloom: Canada mayflower, wood sorrel, painted trillium, purple trillium, lady slipper, starflower, bluebead lily, hobblebush and yellow trout lily. I may also find a small patch of the rare and threatened plant squirrel corn. Even if I don't find the source, a trip into the Bowl Natural Area will be well worth the effort. If you are looking for solitude in the wilderness and a setting where few people have trodden, spend a day in this old growth forest. It's a marvelous resource that's been preserved through the diligent work of the U.S. Forest Service, Kate Sleeper Walden and the Wonalancet Out Door Club.

If you would like more information go to: (*mountainwandering.blogspot.com/2013/06/exploring-in-bowl-53013-i-chose-fine.html*, or *fs.fed.us/nrs/pubs/gtr/gtr_ne189.pdf*).

Jobildunk Ravine
A Walk Into Pristine Beauty

When snow accumulates week after week, month after month, it works curious miracles. Familiar objects simply disappear...and one tends to forget that they are there.

E.B. White

When I hike to the summit of Mount Moosilauke, via the Beaver Brook Trail, I always marvel at the deep ravine on the south side of the trail, just after passing the junction with the Asquam-Ridge Trail. A former hiking partner, who has gone missing, told me about an abandoned trail that he would use to descend into the

Fran crossing the Baker River on the Asquam-Ridge Trail

Jobildunk Ravine to climb the headwall. He explained that the water flowing down the cliffs of the headwall, coming off Mount Moosilauke, are the headwaters of the Baker River. The remoteness of the ravine, the spectacular headwall and the abandoned trail into the floor of the ravine have always intrigued me. I have wanted for years to experience the wildness of this place and view the headwall from its base. The image of the ravine has stayed with me for years.

The Jobildunk Ravine is a glacial cirque, one of several ravines on the Mount Moosilauke massif: Gorge Brook Ravine on the southeast, Slide Ravine on the southwest, Benton Ravine on the northwest and the Little Tunnel Ravine on the north. The strangely named Jobildunk Ravine, I would assume, is a Native American name, but others say that the ravine's name is an amalgam of the first three hikers to explore the ravine: Joe, Bill and

Duncan (*Place Names of the White Mountains*, Robert and Mary Julyan).

I decided to attempt a descent into the ravine by way of the Asquamchumauke Trail (Native American name for "Place of Mountain Waters") the abandoned trail my ex-hiking partner told me about. The trail was cut in 1949 by the Dartmouth Outing Club and abandoned around 1973. I hiked the Beaver Brook Trail to the junction with the Asquam-Ridge Trail. According to an old map, the abandoned trail starts near this trail junction. I found what I thought was the Asquamchumauke Trail and followed it for a mile before it began to peter out, climbing steeply the east face of Mount Moosilauke. I realized I wasn't heading into the ravine and turned back. I learned later that I was on an abandoned section of the Beaver Brook Trail. The current Beaver Brook Trail was rerouted years earlier. Having been foiled on this attempt, I was still determined to get into the ravine. I was advised by Steve Smith, Co-Editor of the AMC *White Mountain Guide* that the best time to hike into the ravine is winter when the Baker River is frozen and the ravine, *"Is in its midwinter garb, with the beaver ponds on its floor frozen and the ice cliffs fully formed on its headwall."*

On a cold midwinter day Fran and I began our search for the Asquamchumauke Trail that would take us into Jobildunk Ravine, the headwaters of the Baker River and the magnificent ice cliffs of the headwall. We parked at the beginning of Ravine Lodge Road, off of Route 118 and hiked 1.5 miles passing the rebuilt Dartmouth Ravine Lodge, an architecturally magnificent structure which is open to the public, (except during the winter season-darn!). After admiring the Lodge we set out on the Asquam-Ridge Trail, a logging road built by the Parker-Young Company in 1949. Fran and I admired the pristine beauty of this woodland trail. Snow balanced on the boughs of spruce and hemlock trees. Clouds had draped themselves over the Moosilauke massif, hiding the summit from sight. The air was crisp and cold. The only sound in this wooded wonderland was the crusty snow crunching beneath our snow-shoes as we trudged along the trail.

On the Asquam-Ridge Trail two narrow bridges cross the Baker River and were piled high with snow. The hand rail was knee lev-el, not much help in maintaining our balance. We looked like high wire acrobats as we slowly tightroped across the bridge on a nar-row band of snow high above the river. Having made another pre-carious crossing of the second bridge we began our search for the lost trail. Looking for a trail that has been abandoned for 45 years is not a simple task. It's like playing detective. What are the clues that would indicate a trail even existed: a bit of red tape on a branch, a pile of rocks, a fading ax blaze, a small opening in the trees lining the established trail, a few broken branches, animal tracks indicating a route used by woodland animals.

Our detective work paid off when we found some red tape and a slight opening in the copse. We found the Asquamchumauke Trail or what we thought was the trail. It was definitely a small narrow footpath through the woods, paralleling the Baker River. This had to be it. However, to be sure we needed to find an old blaze, or other indications that this was a trail, not an old woods road, skidder path or ski trail. The confirmation came when we found a metal pole sticking out of the snow, painted orange, the trail blazes of the Dartmouth Outing Club. Now we knew for sure we were on the "road to victory." We checked our watches and it was already approaching noon, our turnaround time was set at 2:30. Our trek through two feet of unbroken snow was taking longer that we had planned. We forgot that snow travel can double the time it takes to trek a mile in summer.

We labored on, following the obvious path through the woods and then we found another trail sign: a bucket sitting on a tree stump. I learned from Steve Smith that the bucket is a relic from the

Jobildunk Cabin, built near this spot in 1931. The cabin was most likely used by ice climbers, but was abandoned after the infamous hurricane of 1938. Soon after spotting the bucket we lost the trail and began a long and arduous bushwhack toward the floor of the ravine, looking for an opening that would indicate we were at the first beaver pond and could view the ice bound cliffs of the headwall. Climbing higher into the ravine the snow got deeper and we got slower, slogging through soft, deep snow.

At about 2:30 we came to the opening we thought was the first pond. Our hearts and hopes jumped with glee. We made it. Within a few minutes after walking through the opening in the forest, we realized this wasn't the beaver pond, but more likely a frozen bog. The pond was just beyond a thick wall of conifers that stood like a heavy curtain protecting the "Wizard of Oz" from discovery. Fran and I searched for an opening through the thick wall of trees and with time ticking away we knew turnaround time was closing in. Our search ended when we reached an impossible crossing of the headwaters of the Baker River, not far from the bog that was once Deer Lake. Our quest for the headwall of Jobildunk Ravine ended with the realization we had to turn around and begin our trek back to Ravine Lodge. Darkness was closing in soon and we didn't want to be searching for our path in the dark.

My long-held desire to stand at the headwall of Jobildunk Ravine was over for the moment. The good thing is the ravine will always be there, it's not going away. As the sun was slowly dropping behind the Moosilauke ridgeline, a red glow appeared above the darkening landscape. Donning headlamps to light our way, we began to plan for another attempt to reach the Jobildunk Ravine headwall later in the winter. The goal of reaching the headwall was only secondary to the walk in the woods and following an abandoned trail. Most people tramp along the same worn out paths over and over again. I prefer the solitude and the mystery that awaits me on these adventures. The beauty of the woods that engulfed us that day was the most important aspect of this hike. I look forward to returning to Jobildunk, it will always be there for another try.

The Final Push —
Hiking the Final Four Summits of New Hampshire's 200 Highest Peaks

The mountain-top became a ubiquitous symbol of emancipation for the city-bound spirit, a crystallization for the Romantic-pastoral desire to escape the atomized, socially dissolute city. You could be lonely in a city crowd, but you could find solitude on a mountain-top.

Robert Macfarlane

Gordon and Fran on summit of Black Mountain, NW Peak, Errol, NH

The phrase, *"If you don't like the weather in New England now, just wait a few minutes,"* attributed to Mark Twain, rang true when I rolled out of my sleeping bag to a bright, warming sun. The previous day Fran, Reuben and I were hiking in 20 degree temperatures with snow blowing in our faces. Now the snow was melting around our campsite, puddles were forming in the logging road and the trees were freeing themselves from a coating of white. When we planned this trip to New Hampshire's North Country we assumed we would be hiking in seasonable autumn weather, not winter conditions. As I peeked my head out of the tent a warming breeze blew across my face. A new day arrived, bringing with it changing conditions. I was hopeful we could complete our goal.

Fran, Reuben and I were in the northern wilderness for two days to bushwhack to the summits of four peaks: Crystal Mountain Northwest, Blue Ridge North Peak, Crystal Mountain South Peak and Black Mountain Northwest Peak. These four mountains, north of the notches, along with many others are not well known and rarely climbed. With the exception of North Country natives and hunters, only a handful of hikers or peak baggers are aware that these mountains exist. Both of us have spent several years hiking to remote mountain peaks throughout the state, and now we were about to complete our goal of summiting the last four mountains on the list of the highest 200 in New Hampshire.

When we started our drive to Dixville Notch, we questioned our decision to even begin our journey, facing snow and gusty wind. In addition there was another concern: The only way to access the mountains was from logging roads, built many years ago by the paper companies to provide wood pulp for the paper mills in Berlin and Groveton. There was a good chance that these rutted roads would be choked with snow and covered with ice. Would we even be able to reach the start our planned bushwhacks? Nevertheless, we knew we had a small window of time to complete our goal and we would have to take our chances. Winter was closing in and soon the logging roads would be inaccessible. As we traveled through Franconia Notch, Twin Mountain, Lancaster, Groveton and Colebrook the snow continued to fall, but at least conditions weren't getting worse. When we arrived at Corser Brook Road, a gravel logging road off Route 26, we saw only a few inches of snow cover, and headed into the wilderness.

Fran inched his truck down steep grades and over deep ruts for twelve miles, finally arriving at the start of our bushwhack to Blue Ridge, North Peak (3,009 ft.). The snow continued to fall and the wind picked up as we climbed higher on the mountain. We weren't totally prepared for hiking in winter conditions, but were determined to reach the summit. Within four hours we had summited Blue Ridge North and were beginning our second climb of the day to Crystal Mountain, Northwest (3,230 ft.). With darkness approaching we needed to reach the peak and return to the truck to set up camp for the night. The snow was beginning to lighten, but the wind continued to howl, sending snow off the trees into our faces. It was a long, arduous trek to the summit and back, but we made it just in time to set up our tents under the dimming light of the setting sun. After our meal Reuben, Fran and I hunkered down in our sleeping bags for the evening (Reuben's sleeping bag is his pink blanket). As the skies cleared during the night, the moon appeared, shining through the tent with an eerie light. The weather was changing.

The next day arrived with clearing skies and warming temperatures, a new day at daylight. We quickly tore down our tents, packed up our supplies and equipment and began driving Roaring Brook Road to our next destination, the base of Crystal Mountain, South Peak (2,960 ft.). As with many of our north woods treks we would have to wind our way through a logged out forest, full of slash, briars and hobble bush. Hiking through the maze of stubby growth, we continually looked for open woods. As we climbed

Moose grazing in Dixville Notch, NH

bed higher on the mountain, the logged area gave way to open woods, interspersed with bands of small spruce. These spruce bands stood like ramparts of a castle blocking our track. We had to fight relentlessly through the forest wall, while Reuben always seemed to find a narrow tunnel leading to a small clearing, a moose bed or patch of moss where he could rest. Finally reaching the summit, my legs aching with fatigue, we signed the register located in the canister and said together, "Three down and one to go," Black Mountain, Northwest Peak (2,944 ft.).

We hustled down the mountain (it's much easier pushing through the spruce bands going downhill). My body no longer felt drained as I anticipated our finish. I think the hormones were pumping through my body, making me feel light-headed and joyful. Black Northwest was our final peak of the trip and the last mountain we had to climb to reach our goal of summiting the 200 highest peaks in New Hampshire. When we reached the truck to begin our drive to Black Northwest Reuben looked at me as if to say, "Are we going home now"? I told him, "one more climb". His ears collapsed around his head and he reluctantly climbed into the truck.

The sun was now directly overhead, beaming down its warming rays. Today was a complete turnaround from yesterday's freezing temperatures, snow and biting wind. We struck out through another logged-out area, scrambling through thickets of briars and hobble bush, before we reached a beautiful glade of mature birch and maple. Fran was a wizard with his GPS taking us directly to the peak. When we found the canister, marking the true summit, we celebrated with a "high-five", signed the register and headed back down the mountain. Our mission was successful, despite the weather conditions we encountered on our first day. Like Mark Twain said, *"If you don't like the weather in New England now, just wait a few minutes."* (In our case it was wait a day). Shortly after turning onto Route 26, just east of Dixville Notch, we were greeted by a female moose and her offspring, leisurely grazing along the highway, capping off our two day expedition to the wildness of New Hampshire's North Country.

Afterword

Hike Smart and Stay Safe

Getting to the top is optional, getting down is mandatory.

Ed Viesturs

On one of the coldest days of the year, Fran and I drove to Randolph, NH to climb South Black Crescent Mountain. We planned the trip well in advance of this cold snap and we weren't going to be deterred by below zero temperatures and gusty winds. We were prepared for severe weather and have climbed to summits in similar conditions. We wore several layers of clothing, plus we had extra socks, shirts, hats, gloves and mitts stored in our packs, along with a sleeping bag, bivy sack, hand warmers, balaclava, face mask and other gear necessary for winter hiking.

When we arrived at the trailhead located at the end of Randolph Hill Road, we began our trek on the Cook Path. The temperatures were hovering around -10 F., and the wind was whipping the fresh-fallen snow into our faces as we strapped on our snowshoes. Ensured that we had all our gear, we set off on the trail. At the terminus of the Cook Path, the trail veered right into the deep recesses of Ice Gulch. We knew we didn't want to descend into this deep crevice carved out millennia ago. Fran took out his GPS to set our track to the summit. However, lo and behold, the GPS was frozen. It wasn't functional. The extremely cold temperatures made the electronic device worthless, the batteries were dead. We had depended on his GPS many times before to set our track, but not today. This meant using the "tried and true method" of off-trail, back country hiking: map and compass, which we always carry. With the map of the Crescent Range in hand, we set our course and headed up the mountain. If we didn't have a map or compass we would have had to turn around and abort the mission or continue on with the distinct possibility of losing our way and having to spend the night in sub-zero temperatures. As we progressed through the forest of mixed hardwoods and conifers, we found the hiking fairly easy except for the stands of hobblebush that continually impeded our trek. We reached the north ridge of the mountain and after scrambling through thick stands of spruce, laden with a foot of snow, we found the summit canister.

By this time of the day the temperature had "warmed" to around zero, but the wind was howling at the summit and we wanted to get off the mountain quickly, returning the way we came. We reset our compass bearing and returned to the Cook Path and eventually the parking lot where the truck was waiting. We reached our goal because we hiked safe and smart: extra clothing and gear for extreme winter weather, map and compass, an itinerary left with my wife and a lot of common sense.

There are many people who don't hike smart or safe and are just plain foolish. Some even lose their lives because of poor planning, and bad decision making. I regularly read the Accident Reports in *Appalachia*, a mountaineering journal published by the Appalachian Mountain Club. These reports always have something to teach me about hiking safely. Below are summaries from a few accident reports found in *Appalachia*, as well as some from my own experiences.

Two years ago in the late fall I was hiking with some friends, returning from a summit of Owl's Head Mountain in the Pemigewasset Wilderness. It was late in the afternoon when we noticed a young man walking toward us. We thought it strange that he was hiking into the wilderness at this time of day. Darkness would be on us soon. We also noticed he wore only a t-shirt and a thin jacket. He obviously had no intention of staying overnight as he had no backpack. He then asked us where the parking lot was. We told him, "It's in the opposite direction you're headed". "Oh," he said, "I guess I'm lost". We found out he was on a day hike, but had become disoriented. He had no map, compass, little clothing, food or water. He was totally unprepared for even a day hike, let alone an overnight stay in late November when temperatures dip to well below freezing at night. He followed us out to his car and thanked us for his rescue. If our paths hadn't crossed, his hike may have ended in disaster.

On February 16, 2016 a 31 year old hiker, Mark, began a hike at the AMC's Cardigan Lodge in Alexandria, NH, intending to summit Mount Cardigan and return via Firescrew Mountain. On his descent he fell and injured his leg. He couldn't walk and called 911 for help. If you are familiar with Mount Cardigan, you know that much of the mountain's summit is above tree line. Temperatures that evening were falling through the 20s with winds reaching 30 mph; no night to be spending on the mountain. When the rescue team reached him they found Mark had no extra clothing or gear. Without the rescue, the outcome would have been very different. (*Appalachia, Winter/Spring 2017*).

Another example of a hike gone bad, involves a 25 year old hiker, Andy, who hiked to the summit of Mount Washington and was planning to take the Cog Railway off the mountain. When he reached the summit he learned the Cog wasn't running that day. He was advised to hike the Nelson Crag Trail to Pinkham Notch. He then began to follow some other hikers off the mountain, but lost sight of them. Dusk was approaching and he consulted his map he bought earlier in the day. He then decided to take the Huntington Ravine Trail, which showed a more direct route. Without knowing the difficulty in descending this trail he pushed forward. The Huntington Ravine Trail is one the most challenging trails in the White Mountains and the sign at the trailhead says so. When Andy got part way down Huntington Ravine, which is very steep in sections, he could go no further. His legs began to cramp and he resorted to calling 911 for a rescue. When rescuers arrived, they rigged him with a rope, guided him back to the Huntington Ravine ridgeline and led him down the auto road to safety below. (*Appalachia, Winter/Spring 2017*).

And finally, in June, 2015 a pair of hikers, Jon and Isabelle, were found after losing their way on Mount Washington. N. H. Fish and Game reported they had taken a picture (with their cell phone) of a map of the area and were trying to use it to navigate along with the GPS in his phone. They were attempting to hike off the mountain via the Boot Spur Trail, but ended up on the Davis Path near Mount Isolation. They lost reception with their cell phone, but were eventually rescued by AMC Lake of the Clouds personnel who hiked through the night, meeting up with them at 5:30 a.m. In a statement issued by NH Fish and Game, "*Hikers should not rely on electronic devices in the back country. Batteries fail and there is no replacing a map and compass if you know how to use them.*" (New Hampshire Fish and Game Press Release, June 4, 2015).

The above incidents are only a few examples of people heading into the mountains unprepared for their hike. In the words of Sandy Stott, Editor of the Accidents Section of *Appalachia*, "*(There's) no shortage of stories about people finding ways to use new tech poorly, in place of tangible, old-style tech (Map, Compass, current weather report and common sense.*" Remember to always hike smart and safe and you won't have to rely on rescuers to come and fetch you out of the wilderness. In addition anyone hiking or biking in the New Hampshire woods should obtain a Hike Safe Card. This card can be purchased on line from N. H. Fish and Game. The purchase of the card supports New Hampshire Fish and Game, search and rescue efforts and you may be exempt from liability in repaying search and rescue fees. Remember to always plan properly and hike safe.

For Seniors: Getting and
Staying Fit for the Trail

The old that is strong, does not wither.

J.R.R Tolkien

As we age we need to be ever mindful of maintaining a level of fitness that will get us to our destination and back. I would like to share some insights that have helped me to continue hiking all around the northeast, from Mount Marcy in the Adirondacks of New York, to Mount Katahdin in Baxter State Park, Maine. I've learned a few things over the years and the most important is to remain physically fit. As we age our bodies change: muscle loss, weaker bones, loss of flexibility, joint deterioration (I've had two knee replacements), depressed lung capacity and so on. The trails seem longer and steeper now. It's not the trail that has changed, it's our bodies. We need to recognize what our bodies are telling us and do all we can to ameliorate the conditions of aging, and at the same time accept the fact we are getting old.

The two most important things you can do to continue hiking, whether it's climbing a 4,000 foot mountain or taking a leisurely stroll to your favorite vista, is to eat well and exercise. I have a shirt with the saying, "Food is Medicine." How true this is. What we put into our mouths can do harm or good. The food we eat is literally the gas that makes our engine run. When I plan for a day hike I'm sure to have plenty of carbohydrates to keep the engine running. My favorite is peanut butter and honey on a toasted English muffin. I also carry cashew nuts, dried fruit, candy bars and an orange or apple. Prior to the hike I'll down a bowl of hot oatmeal, granola and a banana. This combination of food provides me with a good balance of carbs, protein and vitamins. There is plenty of good information available in books and on the web to help you to choose a diet that will provide the necessary nutrition for a vigorous day hike or a leisurely amble.

The other part of the equation is fitness. Getting fit and staying fit are essential for a healthy and fruitful life. Many of the aches and pains we experience every day, let alone on the trail, can be reduced if not eliminated by a regular exercise regime. I prescribe to a regular routine of yoga, about an hour a day, 2-3 days per week. Stiff joints or a sore back can be relieved by engaging in exercises to improve flexibility and strengthen core muscles (pelvic, abdominal muscles). Before starting any hike, it's advised that you stretch the muscles of the legs, doing deep knee bends, front body bends, downward dog (yoga term) combined with loosening the muscles of the upper body with full body twists. Begin slowly, walking a mile or less and gradually increase the distance, including hills in your daily regimen. I also strongly advise you to consult with your personal physician before your plan for exercise turns into reality. Your physician should have sound advice and may recommend a specific exercise program.

There are many resources you can turn to for guidance, on the web as well as book stores and libraries. An excellent book that I've referred to in writing this article is *Go Take a Hike, Hiking Tips and Outings for Seniors in Western Maine and the White Mountains*, by Allen Crabtree. Rick Wilcox, owner of International Mountain Equipment in N. Conway writes, *"Go Take a Hike should be required reading for any of us aging hikers."*

Leave No Trace, a Trail Ethic

When we see land as a community to which we belong, we may begin to use it with love and respect.

Aldo Leopold

A pile of refuse on the trail

I have hiked well over 4,000 miles of trails in New Hampshire, in at least 12 other states, as well as parts of Canada. I am continually saddened by the sight of litter, graffiti, garbage and human waste on the trails. Two years ago my daughter and I hiked the John Muir Trail in California. As we reached basecamp on Guitar Lake to begin our climb of Mount Whitney, the highest summit in the continental U.S., I stumbled over human waste that was left on the trail. We were hiking a national treasure and to find it desecrated by human waste made me sick. Similarly when hiking the Squam Mountain Range with friends, we stumbled across cans and clothing thrown to the side of the trail. This is a beautiful trail bordering Squam Lake, or Golden Pond as some say, yet someone didn't have the common sense or respect for the land to pick up their own garbage. I have found graffiti painted on the rock shelter at the summit of Mount Major. The human waste and the garbage can be removed, graffiti will remain on the rocks for many years.

These are just a few examples of the disregard that people have for our hiking trails. Therefore, I feel compelled to remind others that we need to adhere to the practice of "leave no trace." In other words leave the environment, (trails, campsites and streams) as you found them, or better yet, in better condition than when you found them. Leave no trace is a set of ethical principles and practical techniques to protect the environment and the experience of those who enjoy the natural world. These principles and practices are meant to protect our fragile environment, as well as providing enjoyment on the trail while creating minimal impact.

There are several practices than can be followed to minimize human impact in the natural environment. The following Leave No Trace practices have been gleaned from the Appalachian Trail Conservancy, Leave No Trace Program, (*appalachiantrail.org/home/ explore-the-trail/leave-no-trace*).

- **Plan Ahead and Prepare**

Poor advance planning and preparation can cause damage to the environment. So plan ahead and prepare for your hike. For example, use trail maps and guidebooks; camp in recognized campsites; carry a litter bag, a zip lock baggie for used toilet paper, a small garden shovel to bury human waste, a waterproof bag and rope to hang food and personal items away from wildlife while you are camped. I recommend purchasing a food or bear canister for storing not only food, but other items that attract wildlife. Avoid camping in overused campsites and if hiking with others keep group size below ten.

- **Dispose of Waste Properly**

Improper disposal of food, feces and wastewater spreads disease, changes the habits of wildlife and spoils the beauty of the natural surroundings. Therefore, "pack it in and pack it out." Always be aware of the small scraps of packaging that may fall to the ground after opening that candy bar or granola bar. These small bits of waste are often scattered along the trail despoiling the beauty of the woodland floor. When camping, don't burn, bury or leave any extra litter or food, carry it out. Use a privy only for human waste and toilet paper, nothing else. Pack out disposable wipes and feminine hygiene products. If there is no privy, bury feces in a hole, six to eight inches deep and at least 200-feet away from streams, trails, campsites and shelters. Don't hide your waste under a rock; it won't decompose quickly. Pack out your toilet paper in a ziplock bag. Disperse urine, toothpaste and strained dishwater at least 100-feet away from campsites, so wildlife are not attracted by the odors and become pests. Don't throw waste water into rivers or streams.

- **Leave What You Find**

Leave nature's beauty on the trail so others may enjoy the experience. Plants, flowers, stones, cultural artifacts should left where they are. Many hikers alter the environment by removing or destroying natural or historic items. Remember not to carve or mark on shelters, signs, trees, or rocks. Use only dead and downed branches and limbs for campfires. Take with you only pictures and leave the natural gifts for others to enjoy. It is illegal to remove historical or cultural artifacts from national parks, monuments or national forests.

- **Travel and Camp on Durable Surfaces**

Walk only on well-defined tread-ways. Don't take a shortcut when hiking switchbacks. Stay within the marked trail, especially when hiking above tree line. Take breaks on a rock, grass or other durable surfaces. Camp at designated campsites or other defined camping areas. If none are available along the route, find a site that is at least 200-feet from the trail and in a place where soil is firmly packed. Stay on bog bridges, rocks or other trail surfaces that avoid wet areas, and don't create a new pathway by avoiding puddles or mud. Wear waterproof boots and gaiters.

- ### Minimize campfire Impacts

Use stoves for cooking. If you need a fire, build one only where there is an existing fire ring, don't create a new one, and keep the fire small. Don't cut live trees for fire wood. Use dead limbs and branches that are already on the ground and leave saws and hatches at home. Don't attempt to burn trash. This includes foil, plastic, glass, cans, tea bags, food or anything with food on it. Leave fire rings clean.

- ### Be Considerate of Other Visitors

The sounds of nature should prevail, not the cacophony of other hikers. The Baxter State Park Authority recently threatened to re-route the AT to due excessive celebrating and partying on this most sacred mountain. Be respectful of the solitude, speak softly and keep extraneous noise to a minimum. Don't use cell phones or other audio equipment when near others. Limit the stay in a shelter or campsite to two nights and make room for others in the shelter when possible (you don't own it). If you are hiking with your dog, keep it leashed at campsites and shelters and keep it away from water and food sources.

- ### Respect Wildlife

Remember, we are visitors to the forests and mountains. This is home to the creatures of the woods: bear, deer, fox, raccoon, birds and many others. Respect their land by storing your food safely. Food canister are becoming mandatory in many parks and National Forests. Improperly stored food, dropped tidbits and food wrappers all attract wildlife including bears. A clean camp-site is a safe campsite. Store your food and scented article (toothpaste, sunscreen, insect repellent, lip balm, etc.) out of reach of bears and other wildlife by using a waterproof bag or a bear vault. Hang food and garbage 12-feet from the ground and six-feet out on a limb or trunk. Protect wildlife by being respect-ful of their environment. Your dog is also a visitor so keep Fido leashed or under voice control and not chasing after a spruce grouse who maybe sitting on a clutch of eggs.

Some Basic Elements of Winter Hiking

When there's snow on the ground, I like to pretend I'm walking on clouds.

Takayuki Ikkaku

Reuben leading the way on a path less traveled

Clear cold days, rime ice, outstanding views, ice crystals hanging from spruce boughs, solitude on a snow covered trail and no bugs: these are some of the many reasons why I and many others take to the mountains during the winter season. A winter tramp in the woods and mountains of the Lakes Region and beyond can be an experience that some would say is addicting. Others I know cannot fathom the idea of trekking up a mountainside in three-feet of snow, with the wind howling and temperatures hovering around zero. But with careful planning, appropriate skills and knowledge it can be a wonderful, exhilarating experience with incredible intrinsic and physical rewards.

261

However, a winter hike can also end in misery or even disaster if you are not properly prepared. Several years ago I was hiking the Bondcliff Trail in November with my son and as we climbed tothe top of the cliff edge, we were blasted by wind and snow. As we looked up the trail, we saw two figures struggling to find their way. When we approached them we noticed they wore only light-weight clothing, running shoes and small packs hung from their backs. They had lost their way in the changing weather conditions. They had no map, compass or other gear to get them back to safety below the cliff edge. After a brief exchange of words, we led them back down the mountain to the shelter of the woodlands below. Their winter sojourn could have ended in disaster, because of poor planning and being ill-equipped for hiking in winter conditions.

If you are contemplating a winter hike and do not want to end your hike as these two characters did, there are several things you need to consider. First and foremost is planning. Research the route or trail you plan to hike. Write down the trip itinerary (route, day/time start and end the hike) and leave this with a friend or spouse. Check the most recent weather report. As most of us know, weather can change quickly in the mountains, so you need to be prepared for any and all conditions. In addition, the conditions at the base of the mountain or the trailhead are usually much different than at higher elevations, particularly on the summits. It isn't rare to see flatlanders hiking up Mount Lafayette totally ill-equipped for weather at 5,000 ft.

The Quebecois have a saying, "s'habiller comme un oignon", which literally means to dress like an onion, in layers. Proper clothing and layering are the most important part of any winter journey. Layering enables you to easily adjust your clothing to regulate body moisture and temperature. After you begin hiking, your body will start to warm. You do not want to get overheated and sweat. Adjust your layers of clothing to prevent heat buildup and sweating. Three layers are considered normal: a liner layer against your skin, a fleece layer for insulation and a wind/water-proof layer. This applies to both your upper and lower torso. You should also have additional clothing in your pack for further warmth and protection. None of your clothing should be cotton. As the expression goes, "COTTON KILLS". Cotton clothing holds moisture when it gets wet, either from perspiration, snow or rain. Wear only wool or a synthetic material. Over half of your body's heat loss occurs through the head. A balaclava and cap will ensure you stay warm. I was told, "If your feet are cold, put on a hat." Two pair of insulated mittens or gloves with liners are also an important ingredient for a safe and happy hike. As Sir Ranulph "Ran" Fiennes, author, explorer, mountaineer and extreme adventurer said, "There is no such thing as bad weather, only inappropriate clothing". Your footwear should be of well-oiled leather or plastic winter hiking boots, with good insulating qualities. Do not wear summer hiking shoes. There is nothing worse than hiking in cold, wet feet. Snowshoes, trail crampons and mountaineering crampons are also going to be needed depending on the conditions of the trail. Even though there may be green grass around our homes, the higher elevations in the mountains could have three to four feet of snow and ice. Trekking poles are important for balance in snow or going over icy spots. You also may want to consider wearing gaiters. They add extra warmth to your lower legs and keep snow and ice out of your boots.

Bring plenty of food and water. I usually carry two liters of water in insulated bottle jackets. I boil the water before pouring it into my water bottle to ensure it doesn't freeze during the hike. Hot soup in an insulated bottle is also a great addition to your food litany. You could also place your bottles in heavy wool socks. It's very important to include plenty of carbohydrates in your food bag to provide fuel for hiking and for simply keeping your body warm. I like to bring two peanut butter and honey sandwiches made from Nancy's home-made bread and our own home-grown honey.

Other considerations:
  Being in good physical condition.
  Hike with a buddy.
  Carry a headlamp, with extra batteries.
  Bring a first aid kit.
  Pack a map and compass and know how to use them.

One last point: Do not depend on your GPS, cell phone or other electronic devices for trail finding or to call home when you get lost. In the mountains cell phone service is not always available and batteries die in cold conditions. These devices can be helpful, but depending on them is not wise.

If you would like to learn more about winter hiking and backpacking there are several good books and web sites. The Appalachian Mountain Club also offers winter hiking/camping workshops.

Check their website for dates and location at (*www.outdoors.org*). Hike safely and sensibly are key words for any tramp in the woods and take on extra significance in the winter as there is little room for error. Plan your winter hike wisely, so you can return to the trail and enjoy those crystal-clear views that only winter can offer.

Reuben's Words of Wisdom

Dogs are our link to paradise. They don't know evil or jealousy or discontent. To sit with a dog on a hillside on a glorious afternoon is to be back in Eden, where doing nothing was not boring-it was peace.

Milan Kundera

My wife Nancy, Reuben and I were spending a quiet week in Eastport, Maine, where we rented a cabin overlooking Cobscook Bay. Reuben and I were sitting quietly watching the waves roll into the bay and I asked him if he would share his thoughts about hiking. He appeared to be in a contemplative mood, perfect for sharing his innermost thoughts. He looked at me inquisitively, thought deeply for a few moments and with a glow in his eyes began.

"Gordo (he calls me this name), when you get your pack ready the night before a hike, I worry that I won't be going along and I'll be left behind. I sleep next to your pack all night, so when you get ready to leave the next day you won't forget me. There have been times when you have done that, and my feelings get hurt. I wonder why I can't go along. I mope around the house all day, depressed, wanting to be on the trail with you.

"When we do hit the trail I worry that you won't have enough water and snacks for me, as you know how I get hungry and love to eat dog treats while we hike. I like it when we hike with your friends, because they always have treats for me, better than the kibble you usually bring. Plus you sometimes forget, but they don't. I especially like Dick. He brings me a specially made steak sandwich. Also, I have a way of looking at your friends and if I stare long enough they'll break down and give me part of their lunch. It's much better when you hike with your friends. Another thing Gordo, is water. I drink lots of water when we hike and when water is scarce, like above tree line, it's really essential that you carry enough water for me.

"What's important for me when we hike is to be in the lead, staying ahead of you on the trail. When we bushwhack (hiking where there are no trails) I can find herd paths and openings in the woods you can't see. I think my calling is to lead the way and run ahead of you, out of sight with my ears back, flapping in the wind. I know you get annoyed with me, but I always come back to see you and check in. I want to make sure you're okay. I think this is my role as a dog. I do wish you were a bit faster though, because you are really slow at times. When you call my name I'll always come back to you. I know it's important for you to keep me in close sight and under control. At times I just can't help myself. My animal instincts take over. I can understand when you need to put me on a leash, especially when we approach other hikers, as I get really excited. Just don't get mad at me. I'm just a dog, doing what comes naturally.

"The most important thing about hiking is the freedom to choose my own path. When I'm at home I have to stay close to the house. You don't want me running off to the neighbors. Life gets pretty boring laying around all day. But when I'm on the trail I can run through the woods to my heart's content. When I see a big, muddy pool of water I can jump in, roll around and come out looking like I have changed colors. I also love those ponds and streams of crystal clear water to drink, bathe and cool off on a hot day. When we're in the woods I can smell and hear things you can't, like moose tracks, coyote scat, the sound of a porcupine, a deer running through the brush, a bird call, even the smell of an apple core buried under the snow. It's all very magical and I revel in the opportunities to be free, to take the path less trodden.

"So many dogs are cooped up at home, never given the opportunity to run free through the woods and find their own path. But when I hike with you and your friends I can be myself, a dog, doing what comes naturally to all canines. After all, we evolved from wild dogs, wolves to be exact. We hunted for our own food, mated freely and had a home in the wilderness called a den. When I hike with you it's like I'm returning to my roots. Stepping off the path of the known into the unknown, like we do when we hike off-trail. This is what I like the most, going from the familiar and safe to that of the mysterious and mystical. The solitude I find in hiking brings me into a deeper unity with myself. So many dogs just bark and bark, like people, talk, talk, talk. When I get to a mountaintop or a rock ledge, I just like to sit down, think about life and contemplate the future. People are sometimes in a rush to move on, to push ahead up the mountain and they miss the beauty that is all around them. When we stop for a break, I like digging around in the soft turf, find a nice soft spot to lay down and listen to the silence. So don't be in a hurry, celebrate the moment of the hike. Remember, it's my hike too.

"That's all I have to say for now. I'm tired from all this talking. It's time for my nap and to rest up for tomorrow's hike. If your pack is on the floor you know where to find me."

In 2015 Reuben completed his quest to summit the forty-eight, 4,000 foot peaks in New Hampshire. This is a goal you may want to pursue with your dog. It can be an extremely rewarding accomplishment for you and your dog. However, your dog must be prepared for the challenge. The Appalachian Mountain Club recognizes this achievement with a certificate and a canine patch which is awarded in the spring of each year at the AMC Four Thousand Footer Awards Ceremony. Go to (www.amc4000footer.org) for more information. The process requires your dog to submit an application letter. Below is Reuben's letter.

"I began my quest on October 10, 2012 by hiking Mounts Lincoln and Lafayette when I was four years old. I have hiked all 48-4,000 ft. mountains, along with most of the hundred highest mountains in New Hampshire. I have also hiked much of the Long Trail and the Appalachian Trail in VT, NH and ME. I can't say which climb was the most memorable, as all were outstanding, especially since I could explore new places, sights and smells while everyone else trudged up the mountain. My friends were very supportive of my hiking and were always willing to join Gordo and me when we wanted company. But for many of our adventures I just wanted to hike with Gordon. Some people would say to Gordon, "Reuben doesn't care about hiking the 4,000 footers, it's just Gordon's goal." That statement is the furthest from the truth, as I truly looked forward to our mountain adventures together."

Not every dog or individual is interested in summiting the highest mountains in New Hampshire, but for those of you who like to hike with your dog or who are considering it, here are some helpful points to keep in mind: Tick season is almost always with us now and according to most authorities their territory and numbers are increasing. Ticks are a dreaded enemy of many animals including dogs, cats and humans. Whenever you walk or hike with your dog, the threat of tick infestation is always present, especially in woods, grassy or brushy areas. Ticks are lurking around waiting for a prospective host (you and your dog). It will attach itself to soft tissue (skin, mouth parts, eyes, ears) and begin to feast on the victim's blood. A tick bite can be a serious issue, given they can be a vector for disease, so the sooner a tick is located and carefully removed, the lower the risk of infection. Symptoms of infection include fever, joint swelling and lethargy. If you think your dog may be infected, contact your veterinarian immediately. During tick season (which is almost year-round, thanks to climate change) you should take preventative measures to reduce the changes of a tick-born disease. There are several prevention products available to choose from. Consult with your vet for the safest and most effective product. Remember to ALWAYS check your dog for ticks when you return from your hike. If you do find a tick on your dog: Use a pair of tweezers to grasp the head of the tick where it's attached to the skin; pull on the tick gently and steadily; put disinfectant on the bitten area; kill the tick by placing it in a jar of alcohol.

Plan your hike carefully, with your dog in mind, so you and your buddy know what to expect. Some parks, particularly state parks, national parks and conservation areas don't allow dogs or you must keep them leashed. It may be wise to keep your dog leashed at all times if they are on an active trail with mountain bikers, families and small children. At the very least you must keep your dog under voice control to avoid unpleasant situations. Reuben always has a bear bell on his collar. This gives bear, moose and other wildlife an advanced warning that Reuben is on the trail. Bears especially don't like to be surprised and neither would you or your dog. You may also want to carry a rope to tie your dog to a tree when resting or eating lunch.

If you are in an area where you can let your dog run freely (which I usually am) be diligent about your dog's whereabouts. When I hike in winter I am very concerned about Reuben getting stuck off-trail in a spruce trap, wandering too close to an icy drop-off or jumping into a fast running river or steam. My daughter lost her dog on Mount Pisgah in Vermont when Friskie ran off chasing a rabbit and tumbled over the cliffs, never to be seen again. Remember, your best friend is depending on you to lead them safely down the trail.

I once hiked with a friend who brought his dog along. The most exercise the dog ever got before this hike was plodding from the couch to his food dish. The dog was terribly over weight and not conditioned to hike in mountainous terrain. It took us eight hours to hike four miles. The dog's owner had to keep prodding his dog to follow along. This was not only an unpleasant experience for the dog, but also for me. Be sure your dog has the appropriate level of fitness for the trail. Some dogs just don't have the stamina to do a ten-mile hike and you don't want to end up carrying your pooch five miles to the finish. Ease your dog into the routine of hiking. If you have a puppy, wait until they are at least one year old before you begin hiking with them. Begin by walking one or two miles. Gradually increase the distance and build their endurance, just as you build your own. Older dogs may not be able to hike long distance, so pick your hikes carefully if you have an older dog. Your vet is also a great resource for advice on the exercise level that is right for your dog.

Hydration is crucial for an active dog. Research your hike in advance to learn of water sources along the trail. Remember that during dry periods, many small streams and ponds may be dry. Always carry at least one liter of water for Fido, along with a collapsible water dish to drink from. Carry enough kibble or treats to ensure your dog will be getting the right amount of calories for the estimated energy that will be expended for the entire hike.

Clean up after your dog, just as you should do, following Leave No Trace practices. Dogs are not wild animals, and their refuse is not part of nature. Bring along a plastic bag to carry out the poop or bury the waste in a hole that's at least six to eight inches deep.

You need to always be in control of your dog. Be respectful of other hikers and dogs on the trail. When you know other hikers are coming your way, leash your dog to avoid any unpleasant confrontations. Not all people are dog lovers and some, especially children, may be afraid of dogs. You and your pooch may be great friends, but that doesn't mean other hikers love your dog as you do. Also, do not allow your dog to dig up plants, especially when hiking in the alpine zone where plants are fragile and shouldn't be trampled on.

You may want to consider purchasing dog booties when hiking in rough, rocky terrain, especially above tree line. Dog's pads are not made of leather and can easily be cut open by sharp rocks found in higher elevations. Booties may be helpful in winter to keep snow from clumping in your dog's paws. Reuben didn't take to them and chewed them off his feet, but it's worth a try if the snow clumping hinders your dog's gait. Another winter option when hiking in snow is using a salve. I've used Musher's Magic and had some success. However, it must be applied periodically as it wears off. Reuben licks it off his paws. Maybe it tastes good.

During fall hunting season it's extremely important that your dog wear a hunter-orange vest or coat, just as it is for you. You don't want them to be mistaken for a deer as they run through the forest. You also may want to consider purchasing a coat or vest for increased warmth during very cold conditions, as well as keeping ticks at bay during the spring and summer months.

Reuben and I were hiking Vose Spur, heading up a rock slide which leads to the summit. I noticed blood on the rocks where Reuben had plodded. He had torn one of his pads on the sharp rocks. I opened my first aid kit and swabbed first aid cream on his pad. We rested a while to let the pad heal. On that day I learned dogs can injure themselves just as we can. Always carry a first aid kit not only for yourself, but for your canine companion. There are other risks that your dog may encounter such as ticks, porcupine quills, or strained ligament or tendon. A good resource for first aid is *Field Guide to Dog First Aid, Emergency Care for the Outdoor Dog,* by Randy Acker, DVM.

Hiking with your dog, as it is for me, is a wonderful way to foster the relationship with your pooch. Like Reuben, your dog may always be waiting to go on your next adventure. Most importantly, you want it to be a positive experience for both you and your beloved hiking companion.

Jana Christy

Thanks

Thanks to all the readers of my column and those who attended my slide-lectures. It was you who first suggested I write this book.

Thanks to Adam Draphco, journalist at the Laconia Daily Sun, for giving me the opportunity to write a weekly hiking column and thanks to Ginger Kozlowski, former Managing Editor, and current Managing Editor Roger Carroll. Without their guidance and support this book would never have happened.

Thanks to the leaders and members of the Cardigan Writers Group. In the fall of 2016 I attended a creative writing workshop, *Writing From the Mountains*. The workshop, held at the Appalachian Mountain Club's Cardigan Mountain Lodge, was led by

Christine Woodside, Editor of the AMC's quarterly mountaineering journal, *Appalachia*. Christine, along with co-leaders and authors Sandy and Lucille Stott, as well as members of the Cardigan writer's group provided the encouragement and inspiration to actually begin the process of writing this book.
A special thanks to Sandy Stott for his encouragement and initial critique of the manuscript.

Thanks to Susan DiPietro, copy editor, who unselfishly gave many hours to reading the manuscript, suggesting changes, correcting my spelling and grammar, and providing encouragement all along the way to publication.

Thanks to Dick Widhu, graphic artist, for his editing of the original drafts of each column before they went to print in the Laconia Daily Sun and for his many hours spent in the arrangement of the manuscript before it went to the publisher.

Thanks to Steven D. Smith for his edits of factual information, proofing the manuscript and providing critical feedback.

Thanks also to the small, close-knit group of hikers and friends who accompanied me on many of my treks described I this book: Fran and Karen Maineri, Tom and Karen Barker, Steve, Beth and Skipper Zimmer, Karen and Ken Robichaud, Dick Widhu, Susan DiPietro, Sandy Price, Mike LaRoss, Dave Unger, and others.

Thanks to my neice and artist Jana Christy for her illustration of page 273.

Thanks to my nephew and artist Mike DuBois for his illustration on page iv.

Thanks to Peter Crane of the Mount Washington Observatory Discovery Center in North Conway NH for his contributions on the history of the Village of Livermore.

Thanks to Kirsty Walker, President of Hobblebush Books, for her editorial advice.

Thanks to my daughters Annemarie and Meghan for their encouragement and companionship on the trail.

Thank you to writers John Muir, Donald Hall, Mary Oliver and Robert Frost for their inspirational poetry and prose.

I also owe a great deal of gratitude to my most loyal hiking partner Reuben who is always ready for a hike.

Most of all I am deeply indebted to my wife Nancy for the support and encouragement to hike and write.

References

Belcher, C. Francis, *Logging Railroads of the White Mountains, Revised Edition,* Appalachian Mountain Club, Boston, Massachusetts, 1980

— *Complete Poems of Robert Frost,* Holt, Rinehart and Winston, 1967

Crabtree, Allen, *Go Take a Hike, Hiking Tips and Outings for Seniors in Western Maine and the White Mountains,* Self-Published, 2017

Crane, Peter, Ph. D., *Glimpses of Livermore: Life and Lore of an Abandoned White Mountains Woods Community,* Peter Crane, Ph.D., unpublished dissertation, 1993

Gove, Bill, *Logging Railroads of New Hampshire's North Country, Logging Railroads Along the Pemigewasset River, and Logging Railroads of the Saco Valley,* Bondcliff Books, Littleton, New Hampshire

Julyan, Robert and Mary, *Place Names of the White Mountains, Revised Edition,* University Press of New England, Hanover, New Hampshire, 1973

Lauzier, Peter, edited by, *A Small Gore of Land, A History of the Town of New Hampton, NH,* New Hampton Bicentennial Committee, 1976

Long, Jay and Roberts, Dave, *Stepping Stones Across New Hampshire, A Geological Story of the Belknap Mountains,* Peter E. Randall Publishing, Portsmouth, New Hampshire, 2005

Nilsen, K. R., *The Cohos Trail: 170-Miles of Hiking Trail from the Whites to Canada, Fourth Edition,* The Cohos Trail Association

O'Connor, Marianne, *Haunted Hikes of New Hampshire*, Publishing Works, Inc., Exeter, New Hampshire, 2008

Parsons, Greg and Watson, Kate, *New England Waterfalls: A Guide to More Than 400 Cascades and Waterfalls, Second Edition*, Countryman Press, Woodstock, Vermont, 2010

Ramsey, Floyd W., *The Night the Bomber Crashed, The Story of North Woodstock's Famous World War II Bomber Crash*, Bondcliff Books, Littleton, New Hampshire, 1994

Roberts, Elizabeth and Amidon, Elias, edited by, *Earth Prayers From Around the World, 365 Prayers, Poems and Invocations for Honoring The Earth*, Harper Collins, New York, NY

Smith, Steven D. and Dickerman, Mike, compiled and edited by, *Appalachian Mountain Club, White Mountain Guide, 29th Edition*, Appalachian Mountain Club Books, Boston, MA, 2012

Smith, Steven D. and Daniell, Gene, *Southern New Hampshire Trail Guide, Third Edition*, Appalachian Mountain Club Books, Boston, Massachusetts, 2010

Waterman Laura and Guy, *Forest and Crag, A History of Hiking, Trail Blazing and Adventure in the Northeast Mountains*, Appalachian Mountain Club, Boston, Massachusetts, 1989

Waterman Laura and Guy, *Wilderness Ethics, Preserving the Spirit of Wilderness, First Edition*, The Countryman Press, Woodstock, Vermont, 1993

Internet Websites

— *A Cold War Relic, The East Haven Radar Station, Closed 50 Years Ago*, The Caledonian Record, August 8, 2013, (www.vtdigger.org)

— *Beebe River Railroad, Campton*, (www.whitemountainhistory.org)

— *Belknaps Range Trails, Trails and Features in the Belknap Mountains, New Hampshire*, (www.belknaprangetrails.org)

— *Forest Reservation Guide*, Society for the Protection of New Hampshire Forests, (www. forestsociety.org/reservation-guide)

— *Historic Lime Kilns of Haverhill, NH*, (www.haverhill-nh.com)

— *Lakes Region Conservation Trust Maps*, (www.lrct.org)

— *Meredith Conservation Commission Maps*, (www. meredithnh.org/conservation-commission)

McGarry, MaryAnn, *Volcanos in New Hampshire*, (www.plymouth.edu)

— *Mt. Whittier Ski Area, West Ossipee, NH*, (www.nelsap.org/nh)

Russack, Rick, *Bretton Woods 1884, A Changing Landscape*, (www.whitemountainhistory.org)

Smith, Steve, *Exploring the Bowl*, 5/30/13,(www.mountainwandering.blogspot.com)

Swenson, Steve and Russasck, Rick, *The Redstone Granite Quarries, The Town of Redstone and Its Granite Quarries,* (www.whitemountainhistory.org)

— *The Cohos Trail website,* (www.cohostrail.org)

— *The History of Old Hill Village,* (www.hillhistoricalsociety.-com/our-story)

— *The People, Places and Events That Made New Hampshire History,* (www.whitemountainhistory.org)

— *The Silent People of Finland,* (www.atlasobscura.com/places/the-silent-people)

Gordon is a columnist for the Laconia Daily Sun, Laconia NH, a daily newspaper covering the Lakes Region of New Hampshire.

He has lectured throughout New Hampshire on his hiking exploits.

In 2011 he completed hiking the Appalachian Trail (2,285 miles). He has also hiked the Long Trail in Vermont, the International Appalachian Trail in Quebec, Canada, the Cohos Trail in northern NH and the John Muir Trail in CA.

Gordon has summited New Hampshire's 200 hundred highest peaks, the Northeast 111 highest peaks, the Trailwright's 72, 4,000 footers, the Adirondack 46 highest peaks and the New England hundred highest in winter.

Gordon worked for forty years as a recreation therapist, special educator and human services administrator in the disability field. He taught at the University of Southern Maine, the University of New Hampshire and the Community College System of New Hampshire. In 2011 he co-directed and wrote the documentary film *Lost in Laconia*, that traces the history of Laconia State School, NH, an institution that once warehoused over 1,200 people with intellectual disabilities. The institution closed in 1991

Gordon is a member of the New Hampton Conservation Commission and past President of the New Hampton Historical Society. He spends much of his time hiking in the White Mountain National Forest with his dog Reuben and especially enjoys hiking in the Lakes Region due to the proximity to his home in New Hampton. He can often be found exploring the many hiking trails in the Lakes Region of New Hampshire.

(back cover)

Many a fascinating tale is told in this outstanding collection of hiking columns penned by avid tramper Gordon DuBois. *Paths Less Traveled* takes the reader along trails – and sometimes off-trail - far and wide across the Lakes Region, the White Mountains, and the lonesome North Country. Within these pages you'll find vivid narratives of treks to peaks, ponds, waterfalls, old logging railroad grades, abandoned villages, big trees, little-known conservation lands, and many other interesting destinations. The trips range from family-friendly strolls to epic bushwhacks and daunting rock scrambles. Along the way the author provides a generous helping of local historical lore. Also included are useful tips on safe hiking in summer and winter, leave no trace principles, senior fitness, and a canine perspective from Reuben, the author's faithful trail companion. *Paths Less Traveled* will be a treasured addition to any New Hampshire hiker's bookshelf.

Steven D. Smith, Co-Editor of the *AMC White Mountain Guide*

Paths Less Traveled describes several trails in Meredith complete with details on how to find them and what to expect when I get there. I am a novice hiker with a young dog and Gordon's book has helped us to get started on adventures without feeling overwhelmed by trails that are too challenging or too crowded for us.

Erin Apostolos, Director Meredith Public Library

If you are an explorer who likes to seek out destinations that are a bit different or are off the radar away from the crowds, *Paths Less Traveled* is for you. Author Gordon DuBois draws upon his extensive experience hiking throughout New England to bring the reader to some locations that are more well-known and many that are not, some by trail and others by bushwhack. Peppered with personal anecdotes and interesting historical narratives, *Paths Less Traveled* is a captivating read and will appeal to both the experienced and novice hiker.

Ken MacGray, Co-Editor of the *AMC Southern New Hampshire Trail Guide, 5th Edition*

All mountains have stories to tell. It is good to be guided in those mountains by someone with a clear eye, a gentle voice and an appreciation for history. Those attributes combined can bring you to a ledge or a glen or a pond where you are fully present. No superhero or uber-climber delivered you there. Really, you think, I got here on my own...with a little help. Gordon DuBois is such a guide. He knows where he goes; he will show you the way. But the journey and all its arrival-stories will be yours. DuBois' *Paths Less Traveled* is true to its title and just the book to set you on your way.

Sandy Stott, author of Critical Hours -- *Search and Rescue in the White Mountains*; Accidents Editor, *Appalachia Journal*.

Whether enjoying a short and easy walk to a beaver pond in the Lakes Region on a stroll suitable for the entire family, or toiling on a trailless near-epic ascent, bushwhacking to an obscure, viewless, but in its own way satisfying North Country summit, DuBois' writing is infectious with his affection for the out of doors. Many a hiker or walker will find the tales of his adventures to be inspirational. By the time the reader is halfway through the book, he or she may be faced with a dilemma – do I keep reading, or do I put this book down, lace up my boots, and hit the trail?

Peter Crane, Curator, Mount Washington Observatory